I0094019

Urban gardening and the struggle for social and spatial justice

Manchester University Press

Urban gardening and the struggle for social and spatial justice

Edited by Chiara Certomà, Susan Noori and
Martin Sondermann

Manchester University Press

Published by Manchester University Press
Oxford Road, Manchester M13 9PL
www.manchesteruniversitypress.co.uk

British Library Cataloguing- in- Publication Data
A catalogue record for this book is available from the British Library

ISBN 978 1 5261 2609 2 hardback
ISBN 978 1 5261 9134 2 paperback

First published 2019
Paperback published 2025

The publisher has no responsibility for the persistence or accuracy of URLs for any external
or third- party internet websites referred to in this book, and does not guarantee that
any content on such websites is, or will remain, accurate or appropriate.

EU authorised representative for GPSR:
Easy Access System Europe – Mustamäe tee 50, 10621 Tallinn, Estonia
gpsr.requests@easproject.com

Typeset by Newgen Publishing UK

Contents

Figures

Tables

Contributors

Mags Adams, PhD, is a senior research co-ordinator in the interdisciplinary Institute of Citizenship, Society and Change at the University of Central Lancashire. She has led recent projects exploring urban food landscapes and ways of tackling urban food poverty. She is the chair of the Food Geographies Working Group of the RGS-IBG and chairs a sub-group of the Greater Manchester Food Poverty Alliance on the underlying causes of food poverty.

Giuseppe Aliperti, PhD, has ten years of international working experience in the tourism industry with a special focus on marketing and MICE. Former visiting scientist at the Disaster Prevention Research Institute, Kyoto University, and at the United Nations University (UNU-EHS), his research interest focuses on the relationship between the tourism industry and disaster risk management. After completing the International PhD in Change and Complexity Management at Scuola Superiore Sant'Anna, Pisa (Italy), he has been awarded the JSPS Fellowship and since 2018 he is Post-Doc Researcher at Kyoto University, focusing on risk communication to tourists.

Melissa Barker is a teacher in geography at a secondary school but was previously a research assistant on the Incredible Edible project. Melissa's work mainly revolved around qualitative research and grassroots sustainability. She has resided in Todmorden for most of her life and thus explored her town as both a resident and researcher.

Luke Beesley, PhD, is a research fellow at the James Hutton Institute, Aberdeen. He has a broad interest in soils, specifically improving degraded urban and contaminated soils using organic amendments. In this respect he is particularly interested in how degraded brownfield sites may be reclaimed by the addition of recycled wastes, and how stabilisation using vegetation can be promoted on these sites. More recently, Luke has been involved in several projects exploring urban agriculture and contaminated soils.

Chiara Certomà is Marie Skłodowska-Curie Fellow at the Centre for Sustainable Development (CDO), Ghent University. Chiara's research interest lies at the junction of the two macro areas of science, society and technology studies and space, society and the environment. Her work focuses on innovative modes of geographical production, planning and governance performed by heterogeneous, multilayered and multiscalar networks.

Alma Clavin, PhD, has a background in geography, planning and design. She has published research on wellbeing in urban environments and wellbeing impacts of urban food growing. Her current post as Lecturer in Urban Geography reflects her additional research interest in critical pedagogy and critical participative enquiry in urban areas.

Efrat Eizenberg is an environmental psychologist and an assistant professor at the Faculty of Architecture and Town Planning, The Technion. Her research topics include urban nature and landscape perception, planning with communities, urban regeneration, urban struggles and the politics of space. She is the author of *From the Ground Up: Community Gardens in New York City and the Politics of Spatial Transformation* (Routledge, 2016).

Runrid Fox-Kämper is Head of Research Group Built Environment at the ILS Research Institute for Regional and Urban Development in Aachen, Germany. Her research interests include adapting residential areas to social change and the role of green infrastructure in urban development. She was chair of COST Action TU1201 Urban Allotment Gardens in European Cities.

Beata J. Gawryszewska, PhD, is a landscape architect and associate professor in the Department of Landscape Art at Warsaw University of Life Sciences WULS – SGGW, Poland, and alumnus of WULS – SGGW. She specialises in the theory of garden and the inhabited space, e.g. home garden, allotment garden, neighbourhood yard and community space. She is the author of a number of projects and realisations of social, community and family gardens as well as numerous publications on the art of gardening, social space analysis, urban inhabiting space revitalisation, home and social space design theory and management.

Michael Hardman, PhD, is Lecturer in Geography at the University of Salford. He is the author of *Informal Urban Agriculture: The Secret Lives of Guerrilla Gardeners*, the first book in the Springer international urban agricultural series. Mike's research is interdisciplinary which crosses planning, ecology, geography, sociology and other disciplinary boundaries: he has several book chapters, a variety of journal articles and has keynoted at major international events on urban agriculture.

Maciej Łepkowski, MSc, is a PhD student in the Department of Landscape Art in Warsaw University of Life Sciences (WULS), Poland. With a Master in Philosophy, he was a participant of postgraduate studies in 'Public space, art and democracy: Relations and possibilities' at the University of Social Psychology. He is a member of the art collective Parque-no and Lab of Commons Foundation and co-creator of events and projects in the border of art, culture animation and activism.

Sofia Nikolaidou, PhD, is an urban and regional planner. She received her PhD in 2012 from the School of Architecture, Department of Urban and Regional Planning, National Technical University of Athens, Greece. She is currently a teaching fellow at Panteion University of Social and Political Sciences, Athens. Her research and teaching topics cover spatial planning and new approaches to sustainable urban development, with particular focus on urban sprawl, urban–rural relationships, local development and green space governance.

Susan Noori, PhD, is a sociologist and a social research consultant. Her PhD topic was investigating the social-cultural aspects of housing with a focus on compatibility of traditional lifestyles with modern environments. She is an affiliated researcher with the Birmingham School of Architecture, where she was also a visiting lecturer on the subject of multicultural cities. She was a chair of Sociology Working Group COST Action TU1201. Susan's research interests are environment–behaviour interaction, place, culture and gender.

Hannah Pitt, PhD, is a researcher at the Sustainable Places Research Institute, Cardiff University. She is a cultural geographer whose research focuses on the nature of place and community as experienced in everyday environments, and is delivered in partnership with third sector organisations. This has included considering community gardens as more-than-human spaces of care and investigating the effectiveness of social initiatives for food sustainability. Current work focuses on blue-green spaces as sites of wellbeing, and how environmental management organisations can foster inclusive public use of shared sites.

Parama Roy is an urban-environmental geographer with a PhD from the University of Wisconsin-Milwaukee. She is presently working as a lead researcher for Okapi Research & Advisory and an adjunct faculty at the Indian Institute of Technology-Madras. In the past she has worked as an assistant professor of geography at Georgia State University in the United States and at the University of Copenhagen in Denmark. Her work on community gardening and urban greening has been published in peer-reviewed journals such as *Urban Affairs Review*, *Geoforum* and *Space and Polity*.

Silvia Sarti, PhD, currently works as postdoctoral researcher at the Institute of Management of Sant'Anna School of Advanced Study in Pisa, Italy, working on sustainability management. She a former visiting scholar at the School of Public Affairs at Arizona State University, Phoenix. She holds a PhD in Management from Sant'Anna School of Advanced Study, an MSc in Economics and Management and a BA in Business Economics from the University of Perugia, Italy.

Martin Sondermann, PhD, is a cultural geographer and researcher in spatial planning. After his studies at Humboldt-Universität zu Berlin he did his PhD at Leibniz Universität Hannover on 'Planning cultures of cooperative urban greening'. He was member of COST Action TU1201 and is currently Head of Department I 'Society and Culture' at the Academy for Spatial Research and Planning (ARL) in Hannover, Germany. His research interests are on planning cultures, democratic urban development and spatial conflicts.

Anna Wilczyńska, MSc, is a landscape architect, PhD student of Warsaw University of Life Sciences, and member of Miastodwa culture-making Association in Warsaw, Poland. She studied in Poland and Estonia, and gained experience while working in Paris and Warsaw and taking part in international projects and workshops. Her research interests are landscape design theory in the context of intangible values of social space and its material expression in the process of urban change, community and temporary gardening in revitalisation processes, public participation and interdisciplinary designing methods.

Lucy Rose Wright is a PhD researcher in human geography in the School of Environmental Sciences at the University of Hull. Her research focuses on the narratives of the organisers involved in initiating and running urban agriculture projects. She has recently completed her thesis titled 'Urban agriculture: established and emerging projects in Kingston upon Hull, UK and Copenhagen, Denmark'. Prior to this, she attained a MSc in Corporate Social Responsibility and Environmental Management from the University of York and a BSc in Sustainable Product Design from the University of Brighton. Her passion for the subject comes from a long-standing interest in understanding behaviour change and what motivates people to initiate and persist in developing community-based projects. She is also particularly interested in opportunities for food and project knowledge facilitation across cities.

Ross Fraser Young is a PhD researcher in human geography in the College of Physical Sciences at the University of Aberdeen. His research involves understanding the different forms of urban agriculture, their conceptualisations and effects on practitioners. His thesis title is 'Urban agriculture: concepts and practice'. Ross obtained a first class honours in food, nutrition and health at Abertay University and spent the subsequent year as a teaching fellow in physiology and food science before taking up his current role as a PhD researcher. His passion for the subject comes from a desire to know how food systems can be integrated into urban areas and the effects they have on people who interact with these spaces.

Acknowledgements

The editors would like to thank Manchester University Press for their kind invitation to work on the exciting project of this book and for their constant support and suggestions.

The COST Action TU1201 'Urban Allotments Gardens in Europe', led by Runrid Fox-Kämper, provided the scientific networks and a vibrant research context for the collective reflections proposed in this book.

The work on this book was made possible by the Marie Sklodowska-Curie grant agreement No 740191.

Moreover, the editors are grateful for the support of the Academy for Spatial Research and Planning (ARL).

Foreword

Runrid Fox-Kämper

Worldwide cities have to meet challenges arising from growing societal, economic and environmental inequalities that affect the urban system as a whole and threaten common practices in urban development, urban planning and everyday life. Urban gardening as a new or re-invented form of green infrastructure is increasingly recognised for offering opportunities to meet these challenges. The growing of crops and ornamental plants for food and other uses in (semi-)public spaces within and around cities has received increasing attention over the last decades as a practice with multiple benefits (Van Veenhuizen, 2006). Ecological functions of urban gardening in general and in particular for improving biodiversity are acknowledged (Andersson et al., 2007); however, its potential to contribute to broader food security is a subject of debate, e.g. major challenges for growing food within cities seem to derive from the exposure to pollutants (Hursthouse and Leitão, 2016). From an economic perspective urban gardening supports local identity- and place-making (Been and Voicu, 2006), although its contributions to saving household income or reducing public maintenance costs seem to be limited (CoDyre et al., 2015). Despite these constraints, urban gardening and – on a larger scale – urban agriculture remains one of the few alternatives to the predominant, resource-intensive agro-food system, which relies on long supply chains and large-scale distribution and retail companies. The benefits of urban gardening for social cohesion, interaction and community-building are highly valued (Guitart et al., 2012). Participating in an urban gardening project is supposed to contribute to an active, healthy lifestyle, especially for older people (Van den Berg et al., 2010); however, it can be questioned who benefits from these initiatives in the long term and who is excluded.

Urban gardening and the struggle for social and spatial justice offers a well-balanced overview of the correlation between urban gardening practices and spatial justice, questioning the effectiveness of urban gardening in addressing the current social and spatial injustices in cities. Can urban gardens be a remedy against inequality in society? Or can they – at a smaller scale – counteract inequalities in urban development? Are they manifestations of the cultural turn in planning and of the right to the city movement in neoliberal cities (Purcell and Tyman, 2015) or do they create new inequalities by excluding the public from space that was public before? As elaborated in the introduction, these questions have not been explored sufficiently up to now, and this book will contribute to closing a gap in research on spatial justice and the meaning of urban gardening.

From a personal perspective, this book is strongly linked to the research and network activities conducted in COST Action Urban Allotment Gardens in European Cities, which I had the honour to chair from 2012 to 2016, and in which the editors of this book actively participated. The Action brought together around 170 researchers and practitioners from thirty-one countries all over Europe (and New Zealand), who for the first time ever examined urban gardening in great detail and across a continent, looking at policy and planning aspects, social and ecological benefits and design aspects. This included a comprehensive review of research and academic and other literature as well as a collection of case studies around Europe through which it was possible to look at the wide range of different traditions and practices of urban gardening and their challenges and opportunities across Europe. In this COST Action it was possible to bring together the most recent research, to discuss the latest evolution of practices and to raise awareness and fill knowledge gaps about the subject. Some of the chapters of this book are based on presentations held during the final conference of the Action, 'Growing in Cities', in Basel in 2016.

One of the central findings of the Action is that there is a linkage between crises and the emergence of urban gardening, not only in a historic perspective: 'Whenever there is crisis, there is urban gardening', stated Elke Krasny (2014) in her keynote in one the Action's plenary sessions in Riga, in 2014. Economic crises such as depressions or food shortages during wars have been strong drivers for growing food within cities ever since. While we think of these crises as a phenomenon of the past in some European regions – e.g. around the Mediterranean Sea – crisis is taking place, and it is no coincidence that new forms of urban gardening have spontaneously emerged there. In addition, growing imbalances between and within cities worldwide are affecting the urban environment, questioning common practices in urban planning. They have opened a stage for urban gardening initiatives, partly – in growing cities – in niches that are not in the focus of urban developers, partly – in shrinking cities – as tool for urban regeneration, place-making and local identity. Finally, in some European cities, urban gardening is used as a remedy to meet social polarisation, fragmentation and segregation as well as to cope with the effects of demographic change.

In all these forms of economic, spatial and social upheaval urban gardening is praised for its role to supply healthy food to low-income groups, to create identity or to support social cohesion. Many of these assumptions could be confirmed by researchers within the COST Action, e.g. that there is some evidence that motivations for taking part in urban garden initiatives derive from the wish for a meaningful engagement, the desire to overcome isolation in times of unemployment, while at least in the study projects examined, the contribution to household income by self-grown food seems to have been of minor importance. However, in this emerging topic many questions had to be left unanswered during the course of the Action; e.g. how do urban garden initiatives contribute to gentrification processes in cities, where in the last decades urban gardens were welcomed as part of an urban regeneration strategy on underused or abandoned land resulting in times of increasing real estate values now? Can garden initiatives contribute to social cohesion in the long term and what is needed to assure that different social groups have a chance to take part in urban gardening initiatives in particular and planning processes in general?

I am very glad and proud to see that the COST Action managed to create a fruitful network of scientists and stakeholders that did not exist as such before and in which members go on exploring open questions in research proposals and compilations such as in this *Urban gardening and the struggle for social and spatial justice* book. This book will be a useful and significant source of information for those who want to explore the socio-political role of urban gardening, its options to overcome spatial disparities in urban regions and to connect citizens to natural resources.

References

Andersson, E., Barthel, S. and Ahrné, K. (2007): Measuring social-ecological dynamics behind the generation of ecosystem services. *Ecological Applications* 17 (5): 1267–1278. www.stockholmresilience.org/download/18.6b38234911d6cedb12580009510/barthelphd.pdf (accessed 5 April 2018).

Been, V. and Voicu, I. (2006): The effect of community gardens on neighbouring property values. *New York University Law and Economics Working Papers* 46. http://lsr.nellco.org/nyu/lewp/papers/46 (accessed 5 April 2018).

CoDyre, M., Fraser, E. D. and Landman, K. (2015): How does your garden grow? An empirical evaluation of the costs and potential of urban gardening. *Urban Forestry & Urban Greening* 14 (1): 72–79.

Guitart, D., Pickering, C. and Byrne, J. (2012): Past results and future directions in urban community gardens research. *Urban Forestry & Urban Greening* 11 (4): 364–373.

Hursthouse, A. S. and Leitão, TE. (2016): Environmental pressures on and the status of urban allotments. In: Bell, S., Fox-Kämper, R., Keshavarz, N., Benson, M., Caputo, S., Noori, S. and Voigt, A. (Eds): *Urban Allotment Gardens in Europe*. New York: Routledge, 142–164.

Krasny, E. (2014): Growing the seeds of change: crisis sows urban gardens. In: Keshavarz, N. and Fox-Kämper, R. (Eds): *Urban Allotment Gardens in European Cities: Future, Challenges and Lessons Learned*. Event Report. Riga, 9. www.urbanallotments.eu/fileadmin/uag/media/D_Meetngs/Riga/Riga_Report_Final_NK.pdf (accessed 5 April 2018).

Purcell, M. and Tyman, S. K. (2015): Cultivating food as a right to the city. *Local Environment* 20 (10): 1132–1147.

Van den Berg, A., Van Winsum-Westra, M., De Vries, S. and Van Dillen, S. (2010): Allotment gardening and health: a comparative survey among allotment gardeners and their

neighbours without an allotment. *Environmental Health* 9 (74) doi: 10.1186/
1476–069X-9-74

Van Veenhuizen, R. (Ed.) (2006): Cities farming for the future: urban agriculture for
green and productive cities. Ottawa: IDRC and IIRR Publishing. RUAF Foundation.
www.ruaf.org/publications/cities-farming-future-urban-agriculture-green-and-
productive-cities (accessed 5 April 2018).

Abbreviations

CA	Capability Approach
COST	European Cooperation in Science and Technology
IE	Incredible Edible
IET	Incredible Edible Todmorden
IUR	integrated urban renewal
UA	urban agriculture
UG	urban gardening

1

Urban gardening and the quest for just uses of space in Europe

Chiara Certomà, Martin Sondermann and Susan Noori

Every bit of land you see around you, from the lawn across the street to the street itself to the schoolyard at the end, is used according to a decision made by someone. The decision may not have involved you at the time, but you're involved now because it makes a difference in the kind of world you live in and react to every day. If land matters, so too do all the things that may or may not grow on it … You're a player, which means you help determine how those spaces get used. (Tracey, 2007: 32)

Introduction

It seems that there are plenty of reasons to separate the humble, simple, minimal act of planting tomatoes from the noble and ambitious act of contesting the multiple manifestations of injustice. Consequently, urban gardening practices have been considered a trivial object of research for a long time, far from serious societal and political studies. Nevertheless, by seeing everyday practices as a form of political resistance (de Certeau, 1984), cultural geographers, urban planners and social scientists have been able to detect the highly revolutionary impact of gardening (in) the city for both transforming the urban environment and the constitution of society. This involves recognising the relevance of a myriad of supposedly non-significant acts – which support particular forms of life (Wittgenstein, 1953) while eradicating others – on the growth of the social and political imaginary. Planting tomatoes – under specific conditions and in specific contexts – has thus been broadly appreciated as a political gesture, and seeding wildflowers has acquired the status of a dignified social protest (see Certomà and Tornaghi, 2015). Very few scholars would today affirm that a bunch of people silently, even obstinately, caring for a piece of brownfield in the void left over by urban sprawl, are not advancing their claims about the character of place they want to live in and the society they want to be a part of (Tracey, 2007). The political nature of gardening, despite not immediately evident, has now been amply demonstrated by recent grassroots (e.g. the international Guerrilla Gardening organisation or the Incredible Edible Network) and institutional initiatives in Europe (see for instance the European networks supported by the COST Action TU1201 *Urban Allotment Gardens in European Cities* and the COST Action TD1106 *Urban Agriculture Europe*; the urbact project Agri-Urban; and Urban Green Labs), and documented by scholarly research (Eizenberg, 2012; McKay, 2011; Reynolds 2008).

In this book, however, we want to take a step beyond the simple claiming and legitimising political aspects of urban gardening, as we aim to investigate whether and how urban gardening practices are able and suitable to address social and spatial (in)justice in the urban context. The relationship between urban gardening practices and socio-spatial justice has been rarely investigated (see for instance McClintock, 2014; Milbourne, 2012; Miller, 2005; and Reynolds, 2014). This book aims to fill this gap through presenting scholarly analyses and reflections that unveil the consequences, potentialities and contradictions of urban gardening practices in the constitution of urban spaces and urbanity and examine their ability to address issues of social and spatial justice. Therefore, the contributions collected in our book principally explore the social and political aspects of urban gardening.

The focus on European cases is motivated by two primary reasons. First, the book builds upon the intense research conducted by European scholars collaborating on the COST Action *Urban Allotment Gardens in European Cities*, which devoted special attention to the analysis of land-use regimes in Europe and their historical development (Keshavarz and Bell, 2016). This means that although the chapters included report on examples from a set of European countries (notably the UK,[1] Italy, Denmark, Poland, Switzerland, Greece and Ireland), they are nonetheless 'imprinted' by a broader competence in the European context as a whole, acquired in the course of three years of joint research with COST Action colleagues. Second, the European understanding of social justice, together with the long-lasting commitment to the development and support of public welfare systems and the more recent focus on the constitution of an 'enabling welfare state' (BEPA, 2011), has always devoted particular attention to the proactive role of citizens (Davies and Simon, 2013). This makes Europe a perfect location for investigating urban gardening as a form of political agency combating social injustice and enabling democracies. Moreover, emerging interest in innovative forms of participatory urban planning and spatial governance has given rise to a new experiment in managing the commons (Bauwens and Niaros, 2018; Fox-Kämper et al., 2018) in the crowded European cities, largely inspired and supported by the

[1] The slight prevalence of UK cases is justified by the ongoing academic research tradition on urban agriculture and gardening in Anglo-Saxon academia that has produced a greater amount of research on the topic than other countries.

social innovation mantra of European spatial policies (Caulier-Grice et al., 2012). With the aim of providing a comprehensive framework, the following pages discuss the nature of social and spatial justice, describe our understanding of urban gardening initiatives and explain how the latter are connected with the multiple manifestations of (in)justice in the city.

From social justice to spatial justice

Justice is a term we use in everyday language, but we are especially aware of justice in moments in which we are confronted with its negative manifestation – injustice. The meanings of justice range from individual virtues to ideals of societal order in which material and immaterial goods are fairly distributed, everyone has equal opportunities, and no one is privileged. Accordingly, *social justice* is considered as a guiding principle for individual action and societal coexistence in democratic and egalitarian societies (Özmen, 2014). The idea of 'social justice as equality' became largely popular during the 1970s, most notably after the publication of John Rawls' work *The Theory of Justice* (Rawls, 1971). Since then justice has been variously conceptualised in the field of political theory with competing views entering the debate over time. The most impactful perspectives include the aforementioned John Rawls' liberal approach of justice as (procedural) fairness in (structural) equal contexts of decision-making (Rawls, 1971); Jürgen Habermas' deliberative approach pursuing a democratic consensus through rational arguments (Habermas, 1995); and more radical or agonistic approaches (especially Mouffe, 1993) which focus on (or, at least, positively acknowledge) the power of dissent.

Despite their differences, all these approaches revolve around the classic dispute of the alternative overall goals of liberty and equality (Bond, 2011; Mouffe, 2000; Özmen, 2014). In Rawls' perspective on political liberalism, justice is a concept that works entirely in the political realm (Rawls, 1995). This includes the formal principle stating that everyone should be treated as equal in the absence of relevant reasons to discriminate, and the substantial principles that everybody is entitled to an equal distribution of benefits and burdens on the basis of needs. A broader societal view is advanced in Habermas' theory of communicative action (Habermas, 1984; 1987), stressing the importance of communicative processes (under ideal theoretical conditions) as a pathway to more just practices in democratic societies. This theory has been widely reproduced in the field of spatial planning and development as a procedural ideal of communicative, cooperative or collaborative planning, especially in the urban context (e.g. Healey 1996; 2011). However, despite its enormous success in inspiring academics and practitioners, this democratic ideal of spatial planning is hardly fulfilled in spatial planning practices (Bond, 2011; Dyer et al., 2017) and it is questionable whether finding a consensus leads to just decisions at all (Cooke and Kothari, 2011).

Consensus-oriented approaches have attracted, in fact, a number of critical reactions, most notably Chantal Mouffe's radical and agonistic pluralism theory, which argues that a consensus orientation encourages less active participation in democratic decision-making. It is rather the 'power of dissent' that vivifies democracy by 'allowing for passions to be mobilised politically within the spectrum of the democratic process' (Mouffe, 2005: 24). Hence the existence of alternative perspectives on the substantive meaning of social justice (and ways of achieving it) is one of the most important matters of dissent in modern democracies. Whatever definition of justice one might prefer, however, there are some points that need to be addressed. These include: the general/theoretical understanding of what justice is (substantive dimension); how decision-making processes are just and lead to more justice (procedural dimension); and to what extent the adopted form of resource allocation determines just and fair outcomes. Space is both a condition for the allocation process to occur – and thus represents one of the structural conditions for the exercise of justice – and a resource to be allocated. The chapters in this book make evident how spatial conditions and the use and distribution of spaces impact on many other aspects of life, including access to goods and services, education, and healthcare. To address the relationship between society and space, we need to shed some light on the substantive, procedural and spatial dimensions of justice – and their interdependencies. According to the societal concept of space proposed by Läpple (1992), physical spaces are products of societal practice, regulated through normative and institutionalised regulatory systems (Figure 1.1).

Physical spaces refer to patterns of functions and uses of space and therefore to their just (or unjust) distribution of spatial goods and functions (e.g. proximity to green spaces and social infrastructures, exposure to noise, quality of built environment, etc.), which are artefacts of societal practice. Societal practice encompasses all human actions (such as political decision-making over land use and spatial planning) and can vary considerably in terms of procedural justice (e.g. inclusive versus exclusive decision-making). In general, societal practice is always based on the systems of meaning which are shared by a society or societal groups, respectively. These systems of meaning encompass values, beliefs, attitudes and orientations of actors – here justice is addressed in its *substantive* (or ethical) dimension. Among

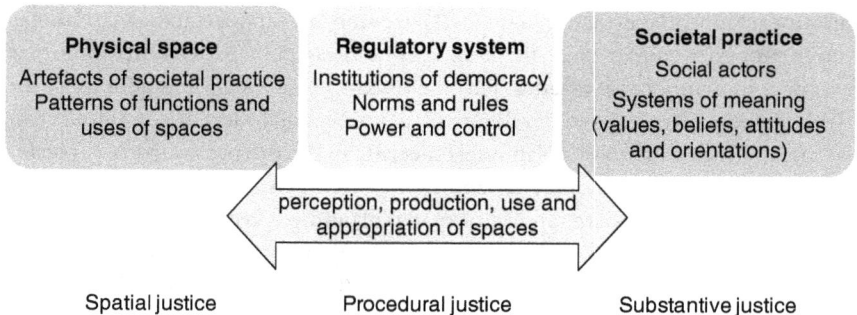

Physical space	Regulatory system	Societal practice
Artefacts of societal practice	Institutions of democracy	Social actors
Patterns of functions and	Norms and rules	Systems of meaning
uses of spaces	Power and control	(values, beliefs, attitudes and orientations)

perception, production, use and appropriation of spaces

| Spatial justice | Procedural justice | Substantive justice |

Figure 1.1   Relational understanding of space and justice (own elaboration)

these interdependencies, *procedural justice* plays a key role. Justice is inherent in the specific ways in which spaces are perceived, produced, used and appropriated by social actors. These processes are influenced or framed by regulatory systems including the institutions of democracy, and written and unwritten norms and rules, which encompass the various interpretations of (substantive) justice. These regulatory systems (see Figure 1.1) include substantive justice as a normative key principle in the (political, communicative, rational and emotional) struggles about the making of spaces, which should be – in the best manner possible – just to all individuals in pluralistic societies regarding the fair distribution of spatial goods, functions and living conditions (Läpple, 1992; Mouffe, 2005; Özmen, 2014; Soja, 2010). Particularly, with regard to the regulation of land use, procedural issues of social justice target the questions of whether and how diverging interests are considered and decisions are made.

Such an understanding of both space and planning is in line with contemporary work in social and cultural sciences, human geography and spatial studies (see Massey, 1994; Othengrafen and Reimer, 2013; Peer and Sondermann, 2016; Soja, 1996). Approaches from critical geography provide especially useful theoretical tools for linking political theory with physically constrained and place-based practices of gardening in the city, most notably the theory of spatial justice (see below), here understood as an indispensable complement to social justice theory. Soja reminds us that 'spatial (in)justice can be seen as both outcome and process, as geographies or distributional patterns that are in themselves just/unjust and as the processes that produce these outcomes' (Soja, 2010: 62).

Spatial considerations of justice emerged with the 'spatial turn' in social sciences (Warf and Arias, 2009), which promotes more explicit reflection about socio-spatial differences. From the early 1970s, social scholars demonstrated their interest in how the living conditions of different social groups play a major role in determining their wealth, opportunities, health outcomes and educational attainment, and influence virtually all aspects of quality of life (Harvey, 1973; 1996; Lefebvre, 1991; Young, 1990). While the first accounts of injustice underscored economic factors and the unequal distribution of resources (Harvey, 1973), gender and post-colonial scholars highlighted how injustice needs to be understood as based on domination and oppression. Furthermore, they showed that the spatially unequal distribution of economic and social resources overlaps with an unequal distribution of power through the social body (Haughton, 1999; Young, 1990). Moreover, from the 1990s onward, closer attention has been paid to environmental issues, leading to the elaboration of an environmental justice approach. The focus thereby is on how social groups are unequally affected by the distribution of environmental burdens (human natural hazards, environmental risks, degradation and pollution, marginalisation, etc.) and poor living conditions (unhealthy, unsafe, precarious environmental balance) on the basis of their spatial location (Agyeman, 2005; Haughton, 1999; Sachs, 1993). The injustice aspect of the phenomenon arises from interaction between the distribution of population characteristics (such as being a disadvantaged group because of economic, ethical, health and social reasons) and the *location* of environmental burdens and conditions, leading to the multiple deprivation of these groups. Such research makes clear that the normative ideal of justice as a one-size-fits-all recipe does not necessarily serve everyone equally, because it is important to understand the 'geographies of injustice' – i.e. how spaces are socially produced and, in turn, impact social groups and their opportunities (Harvey, 1996).

The city context provides an adequate terrain for investigating existing forms of injustice (Dorling, 2010; Fainstein, 2010; Marcuse, 2009; Merrifield and Swyngedouw, 1996), especially when globalisation and neoliberalisation (Williams, 2017) forces shape urban life according to privatisation and commodification principles. Documenting urban injustice in spatial processes (Marston, 2010; Smith, 1997), the concept has been influenced by the 'grassroots urban uprisings of the late 1960s and earlier and contemporary meditations on our urban worlds' (Heynen et al., 2018: 301). This was of concern in the research of many critical geographers (Massey and Catalano 1978; Sandercock, 1977) and particularly of urban geographers (Iveson, 2011). These works also gave rise to a debate on whether spatial injustice is a derivative (Marcuse, 2009) or causal effect of social injustice. Soja, representing the latter position, claims that 'a new emphasis on specifically urban spatial causality has emerged to explore the generative effects of urban agglomerations not just on everyday behavior but on such processes as technological innovation, artistic creativity, economic development, social change as well as environmental degradation, social polarization, widening income gaps, international politics, and, more specifically, the production of justice and injustice' (Soja, 2009: 2). Contemporary works (e.g. Fainstein, 2010) 'seek to re-enliven the tradition established in those earlier works of not being content to describe and analyse cities as they are, but to prescribe (or at least explore!) the kinds of policies and plans that might make them better' (Fincher and Iveson 2012: 232). Building upon the 'geographically uneven nature of development in cities' (Williams, 2017: 2221), several scholars suggest that urban relations and politics can be valuable means for addressing material, political and social exclusion (Mitchell, 2003; Purcell, 2002; Sandercock, 2006; Yiftachel, 2009).

Urban planning can be a vector to articulate different forms of power, domination, resistance and alternatives to the current state of unequal distribution of benefits and burdens in space, as public institutions, private and civil societal actors interact and negotiate spatial needs and courses of action. In this context, questions of justice might be easy to ask, but they are difficult to answer: who benefits from a planning project or actual use of space – and who does not? Who can legitimately take decisions about land use? To what extent are processes of spatial planning just to everyone involved and especially to those who are not involved?

In the search for an actual just city, Williams (2017) suggests paying attention to everyday forms of activism in situated contexts – alongside the spectacular forms of justice activism. This requires downtoning the connotation of resistance as always being a radical or progressive force (Staeheli, 2008), and recognising the role of 'creating other ways of being/doing/thinking urban life, [as] important parts of the urban and important moments of social change' (Williams 2017: 2222). Such a perspective has been adopted in our book. Inspired by the performative ontological politics approach (Cameron, 2012; Gibson-Graham, 2006; 2008; Law and Urry, 2004) and the enactment practices of environmental justice (Hobson, 2006), Williams proposes 'a conception of justice as a relational and situated ethic practiced as responses to particular injustices … that are always in a state of becoming' (Williams, 2017: 2222). The production of transformative trajectories and alternative realities (Law and Urry, 2004), starting from the here and now (Gibson-Graham, 2008), characterises performative politics of possibility (Williams, 2017). This is also inherent to gardeners' everyday processes of experiential learning and in-becoming responses to space politics (Hobson, 2006). Empirical observations in the field of urban gardening illustrate that both understandings and practices of spatial planning can change over time based on learning processes, positive experiences and the overcoming of conflicts (Sondermann, 2017). A number of implications in terms of justice are explored in the contributions presented in this book.

Urban gardening as socio-political agency

Urban gardening initiatives are blossoming cities worldwide, climbing skyscraper walls, invading brownfields and interstitial spaces in the density of built urban environments, restoring derelict traffic islands in the middle of nowhere and bringing back unexpected forms of life to the city. While the phenomenon does not need further presentation as it has been largely popularised by the media worldwide, its forms and meanings are still the object of discussion and subject to different interpretations.

In this book, we define urban gardening as a set of socio-political actions directed towards design, organisation, realisation and cultivation of crops and ornamental plants in (semi-)public spaces. This includes caring for existing gardens or the establishment of new ones through a broad array of practices ranging from the spontaneous or loosely formalised (Hou, 2010) to the sophisticated and professional. As a consequence, here urban gardening is adopted as an inclusive label, encompassing community gardens (McKay, 2011), guerrilla gardening spots (Tracey, 2007), urban allotments (Ferris et al., 2001) and initiatives of urban agriculture or food-growing activities in the city (Hodgson et al., 2011).[2] Still largely

---

[2] While aware of the relevance of the food production issue in urban gardens, we intentionally decided not to focus on the subject of food justice. This is because while food justice is the subject of considerable debate in the Anglo-Saxon literature (Reynolds and Cohen, 2016; Tornaghi, 2014), this is not equally true in the rest of Europe.

context-dependent (particularly concerning the distinction between the global North and South) and internally diversified, these practices can be interpreted as part of a social movement engaging people in actively shaping their urban environments (Hou, 2010; Ioannou et al., 2016; Reynolds, 2008). Urban gardeners generally network with other social actors (i.e. civil society organisations, political and administrative institutions and private organisations) and establish new relations with non-human actors (such as living beings and non-living matter), which contribute to the making of urban ecologies (Certomà, 2011).

Today, it is almost impossible to provide a full panorama of all existing initiatives, as different societies and cultural traditions produce different manifestations of planning and land use, which correspond with a myriad of gardening traditions, approaches and practices, and extend to differences in naming. For instance, the focus on urban agriculture is stronger in the Anglo-Saxon world, as a claim to alternative quality food production and distribution chains or to combat the diffusion of 'food deserts'; while in the global South, urban gardening is often a subsistence practice, closely related to peri-urban agricultural practices.

With reference to the different purposes and degrees of socio-political commitment, we tentatively classify urban gardening activities into the following categories:

- urban agriculture, including in some cases urban farming on private property for food production and animal breeding in urban and peri-urban areas;
- urban allotments, provided by the local administration in public areas for the private cultivation of food and recreation;
- community gardens and other forms of gardens as a social activity;
- guerrilla gardening, which involves extemporaneous green interventions for greening the city.

From a historical perspective, traditional allotment gardens in the nineteenth century were established by administrations almost everywhere in Europe as self-help tools for poor and disadvantaged people (Loggins and Christy, 2013), a development fuelled by the needs of the burgeoning lower-class population (Hou, 2017) and by the poverty of wartime and economic depression (Lawson, 2004). While in their historical form allotments were intended for helping the needy (Crouch and Ward, 1988), in the contemporary form they are often also used by retired or middle-class people for growing quality fresh vegetables and enjoying some outdoor activity.

It was only with the rise of the social justice movement and the urban counterculture in the 1960s and 1970s that allotments were complemented with a different form of urban garden, community gardens, reflecting a politics of dignity and self-help in the context of urban divestment (Hou, 2017). Recalling Hancock (2001), Hou explains the difference between allotments and community gardens in the fact that the community gardens build social capital '"because, unlike an allotment garden, they are created and managed by the community itself and depend upon a cohesive social network to organize and manage the gardens" (Hancock, 2001: 279). Indeed, the collective labour needed to maintain the garden as well as the informal social interactions occurring regularly in a garden all contribute significantly to the making of urban community gardens as an important and unique urban social space' (Hancock, 2001, in Hou, 2017: 117). Community gardens often supported the 'right to the city' claims and called for the re-appropriation of public urban space by following Lefebvre's seminal work (1968). Progressively, urban gardening practices became characterised as 'political gardening' (Certomà and Tornaghi, 2015), whose major roots are in the famous Liz Christy's and the Green Guerrilla group's intervention in New York, in the 1970s, aimed at recovering abandoned areas of the city used as dumps and granting local inhabitants enjoyable green space (McKay, 2011). Since then, collective or community gardens have been created thanks to the stronger socio–political commitment of citizens towards public or abandoned private land, e.g. former parks and brownfields, where they have taken opportunities to plan and run gardening projects aimed at community-building and at advancing socio-environmental values, such as decreasing delinquency, marginalisation and poverty, and recovering polluted or derelict areas. These may include self-managed areas for horticulture, sports, eating, the performing arts and small allotments. While in some cases straightforward agreements with local administrations are reached, collective gardens can also emerge in the absence of any agreement, or even in open contradiction to institutional plans, leading to initiatives to occupy land. Even stronger is the socio–political agenda of guerrilla gardening or street gardening initiatives, which spontaneously and illicitly adopt

Figure 1.2 A 'crowded' flowerbed in Rome, via dei Noci, performed by the guerrilla gardening group *Giardinieri Sovversivi Romani*

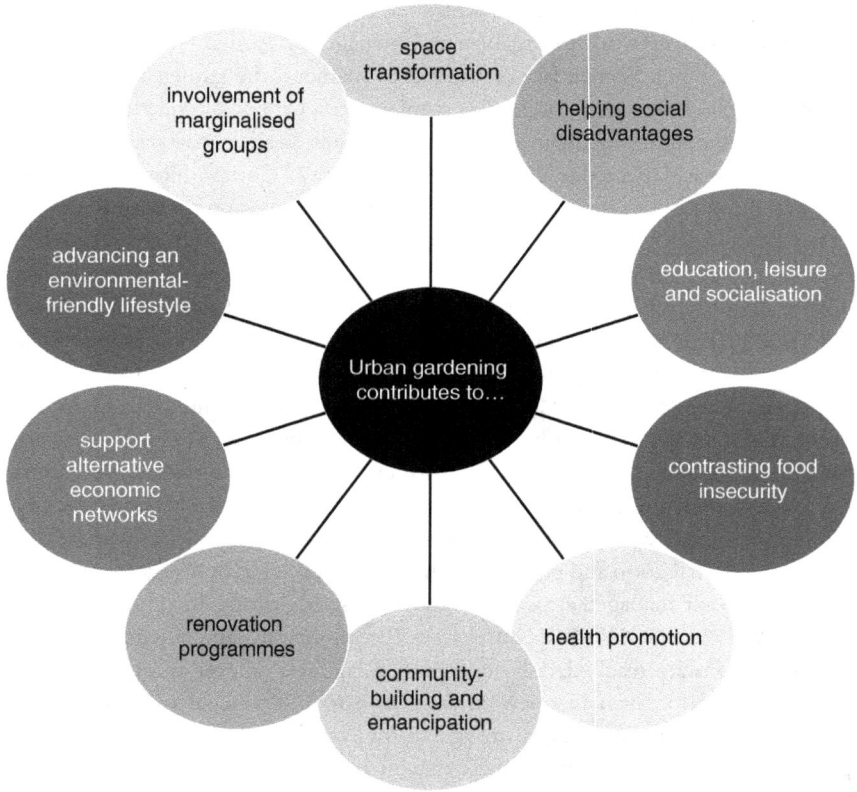

Figure 1.3   Functions of urban gardening (own elaboration)

a public space in need of care and cultivate it. These actions, in general, do not envisage a real planning activity, and are rather aimed at attracting the attention of other citizens and the administration to the need to care for the city, and providing it with more green and accessible areas.

The socio-political character of urban gardening has only been recently openly recognised as a distinctive feature of gardening initiatives (Certomà and Tornaghi, 2015), when a more extended interpretation of the political based on the substantive micropolitics of life was adopted (Dean, 1999; Foucault, 2007). Accordingly, a wide number of functions of gardening (Figure 1.3) aside from the mere purpose of 'greening' the city are acknowledged, including:

- social cohesion and community-building (Beckie and Bogdan, 2010; Bin and Voicu, 2006; Hinchliffe and Whatmore, 2006; Purcell, 2002);
- the contestation of existing food production and trading regimes, and the combating of food insecurity (McClintock, 2008; Milbourne, 2012; Pinkerton and Hopkins, 2009);

- countering social disadvantages (Emmett, 2011);
- the provision of marginalised social groups with dedicated spaces for self-improvement and rights protection (Flachs, 2010);
- the re-creation of urban ecosystems and life-cycles (Barton, 2000; Bendt et al., 2013; Miller, 2005); and
- advancing alternative uses of public space (Schmelzkopf, 1995).

Focusing on the social dimension of gardening, we can define urban gardens as multimodal spaces, i.e. a convivial space (Hou, 2014; Hou et al., 2009) where 'social events and activities make the gardens function more than a place to grow food and facilitate social interactions and building of social bonds between gardeners and non-gardeners' (Hou, 2017: 121). This condition leads to the enhancement of cultural experiences (Eizenberg, 2012) because 'the diversity of gardens ... enables gardeners to express and experience their culture collectively, rather than privately' (Hou, 2017: 122), providing opportunities for different people, plants and traditions to integrate (Krasny and Tidball, 2009). Most importantly for our investigation, collective gardens are experiments of democracy because 'through collective decision-making and sharing of responsibilities, gardens can serve as a space for democratic practices ... In all of these instances, regardless of conflicts or collaboration, community gardens serve as important sites for social mobilization and political engagement – a critical component of active democracy' (Hou, 2017: 124–125).

As a matter of fact, while advancing their socio-environmental plans, urban gardeners point out the less visible and sometimes ignored sides of urban governance, planning and management. They are able to both determine and perpetuate (socio-spatial) injustices through the physical disposition of living beings and non-living things in everyday space. Consequently, urban gardening may question the inequality-biased structuring and functioning of social formations (most notably urban deprivation, lack of public decisions/engagement, marginalisation, etc.) and to conversely create (or allow the creation of) spaces of justice in contemporary cities.

Urban gardening projects can be seen as good examples of democratic actions in urban development as they are based on civil societal engagement and the inclination to collectiveness. Equality and fairness thereby serve as principles for activists whose grassroots movements can successively contribute to achieving socio-spatial justice in the planning and active use of urban spaces (Ioannou et al., 2016).

The intersection of gardening and justice was explored by Paul Milbourne in a seminal work in 2012. Drawing on Lefebvre's writings on everyday life, he highlighted the complexity of relations between socio-ecological justice and everyday urban spaces, suggesting that an everyday perspective provides a 'new way of beginning to imagine ordinary forms of [socio-ecological] justice and of contemplating frameworks of action to mitigate against banal forms of disadvantage'

(Milbourne, 2012: 669). Many contributors showed how different gardening projects potentially reduce inequalities – at least in determined economic and social conditions (Miller, 2015; Purcell and Tyman, 2014). At the same time, they stressed the apolitical character of many of these initiatives (Miller, 2015), particularly in the age of the post-political (Swyngedouw, 2009; Tornaghi and Certomà, 2018) where several projects are co-opted by institutions and neoliberalised practices (Allen and Guthman, 2006; Pudup, 2008). In some cases such gardening can be a neoliberal manifestation of individual and quasi-autarkic citizen action (Pudup, 2008) potentially generating enclosures and gentrification (Rosol, 2012); or a strategic tool adopted by administrations asking people to care for neglected areas of no interest for private investors (Smith and Kurtz, 2003). When urban gardening is not able to challenge the neoliberal agenda (McClintock, 2014), gardening projects can also be non-just in their making and cause new spatial injustices to emerge as people might be excluded from formerly publicly accessible land, or the gardens themselves can turn into quasi-enclosed areas for the benefits of the few. Here gardening turns into a form of 'progressive urbanism largely disconnected from broader left struggles for spatial justice' (Stehlin and Tarr, 2016: 1329) and thus unable to address the dynamics of accumulation and exclusion in the city.

Despite having some degree of truth, these critiques are yet to recognise the transformative power of people's engagement in public life (Schmelzkopf, 1995), which may require time, and perhaps fails, but nonetheless might plant the seeds of democracy that are growing worldwide over time. The discourse of justice is ostensibly part of a struggle over the kind of city one wants to live in (Staeheli et al., 2002). We are interested here in those political gardening experiments that are able to produce alternative processes of social reproduction in the capitalist society (Gibson-Graham, 2006) that generates a performative form of politics in the garden (Hobson, 2006). These provide contested urban green spaces and brownfields with new meanings, while experimenting with forms of 'performative justice' that contest social and environmental injustices in everyday life and in the urban development agenda (Jamal and Hales, 2016).

Making justice through gardening

In line with Mouffe's perspective on social justice, urban gardening can be interpreted as a political gesture of dissent and depicted as a legacy of the right to the city movement (Eizenberg, 2013; Purcell and Tyman, 2014; Tornaghi, 2012), by referring to its spontaneous character and its power to challenge institutional planning (Schmelzkopf, 2002). From this perspective, urban gardening activists question political decisions on land use and spatial planning (Adams et al., 2014) while practically addressing the consequences of neoliberal governmentality, e.g. the erasure of public spaces or the decrease of social cohesion and solidarity links (Hou, 2010). As a matter of fact, referring to defining urban gardening as an act of resistance against rigid social doctrines (McKay, 2011), critical scholars have understood it as a form of democratic and participatory urban development to tackle spatial justice, social cohesion, inclusiveness and equity (Certomà and Notteboom, 2017).

An insightful analysis of the socio-political meanings and effects of urban gardening is provided in this book's chapters, which investigate whether and how gardeners are actually willing and able to change urban spatial arrangements that produce peculiar inequalities in the access to natural resources and services, as well as considerable disparities in living conditions.

By building upon the political gardening perspective outlined above, the first three chapters focus on the ambivalent relationships between *gardening and socio-spatial justice*. Through rich and insightful descriptions of real case studies, the chapters reveal the motivations of gardeners in engaging with the struggle for space and opportunities redistribution. They present an overview of the different trajectories and forms political gardening may take in dealing with justice (Wright and Young), and the alternative vernacular models of democracy for creating green infrastructure (Gawryszewska et al.) and enhancing community cohesion in marginalised areas (Nikolaidou).

Lucy Rose Wright and Ross Fraser Young's contribution proposes an understanding of the *process* of formation of political gardening by groups of people in response to local social and spatial injustices, and its important implication in creating engaged citizens. On the other hand, the *agency* of hybrid networks of human and non-human actors for creating inclusive and open city places, most notably community gardens and common parks as part of urban ecosystem services, is investigated by Beata J. Gawryszewska, Maciej Łepkowski and Anna Wilczyńska. The authors draw on contemporary theories of vernacular democracy and common goods to describe urban wastelands as spaces of opportunities. Finally, with the aim of exploring the daily practices of different social agents in transforming neglected spaces into vibrant and inclusive spaces of justice in the city, Sofia Nikolaidou's chapter explores the right to use and re-appropriate land in various temporary urban gardens in two radically diverse contexts: Greece and Switzerland.

The following chapters critically scrutinise the *consequences of urban gardening initiatives* in terms of their ability and real impact on injustice mitigation. They assess their potentials for place revitalisation and community engagement (Aliperti and Sarti; Roy) and for advancing wellbeing and freedom (Clavin), question the taken-for-granted assumptions on the positive role of local food initiatives (Hardman et al.), and examine the inclusiveness of communities actually generated by gardening initiatives (Pitt). Giuseppe Aliperti and Silvia Sarti analyse a particular urban community garden case study in a mid-size Italian city, in order to evaluate its contribution to spatial justice while examining the notions of the right to the city, democratic control and social inclusion by developing a dedicated assessment process. Parama Roy's chapter discusses the issue of homeless people and ethnic minorities' right to the city within the context of Copenhagen, another traditionally welfare-driven setting – although increasingly neoliberalised. This addresses the multifaceted phenomenon of neoliberalism and its diverse manifestations in shaping socio-environmental and spatial justice through everyday environmentalism. Alma Clavin adopts an alternative evaluation process based on Amartya Sen's Capability Approach to consider the potential of community gardens for advancing human wellbeing, linking the sustainable and just use of urban resources. Michael Hardman, Mags Adams, Melissa Barker and Luke Beesley's chapter provides an interdisciplinary evaluation of the role of local food initiatives, such as the *Incredible Edible* movement, in meeting food sovereignty agendas. They critically examine and question the extent to which such initiatives can be said to be inclusive and what this means in terms of such small-scale urban agriculture being viewed as contributing to food justice and its value to inner-city communities. Hannah Pitt develops a further analytical tool for understanding the kinds of communities that are made through collective urban gardening and whether they can be considered as inclusive and as a basis for tackling inequality. Starting from theorised links between place and community, her chapter asks what relational place contributes to the conceptualisation of community as social relations formed through place-based practice. Second, it interrogates the potential for gardens – place-based initiatives – to effect social change.

Any future for gardening justice?

By investigating whether and how gardeners are actually willing and able to challenge urban spatial arrangements that produce peculiar inequalities in the access to natural resources and services, this book aims at leading the reader to question and reconsider the socio-political meanings and effects of urban gardening. The aim is to understand urban gardening in its relations to socio-spatial (in)justices through different voices and research styles; to unveil the *nature* of political gardening, its impact on city politics and planning, and its potential to tackle spatially distributed disparities in living conditions. This approach critically reflects on the meaning of urban gardening as a micropolitics of everyday life impacting on the capability of re-reading urban spaces in local politics and thus affecting citizens' lives.

Considering urban gardening in its social, political, economic and spatial contexts reveals various interdependencies as urban gardening is dependent on such contexts and – in turn – changes these (see Nikolaidou; Wright and Young). Concerning political contexts, the impact of neoliberal approaches in spatial policies and planning is highlighted in this book (Pitt; Wright and Young). Although urban gardening is considered to counter neoliberal logics and practices, it 'sometimes reinforces neoliberal forces and relations that enhance existing inequalities' (Roy). However, urban gardening is not only influenced by the political landscapes in which it takes place, it also actively changes them by tackling localised societal injustices (see Wright and Young) and questioning common practices in urban planning (Fox-Kämper).

As the chapters of this book illustrate, the question of how justice can be defined and hence what form of spatial development and land use is just or unjust, and for whom, is always ambivalent. Is, for instance, justice defined through the public use of a space for the majority or for the least privileged (e.g. homeless people; see Roy)? Are other people like non-gardening neighbours included in the making of the garden and to what extent do gardens provide benefits to the local community (see Aliperti and Sarti), wellbeing (see Clavin) and food justice (see Hardman et al.)? It can be argued that new forms of collective actions transform not just spaces but also the perception of spatial (in)justice and inclusiveness (see Gawryszewska et al.; Nikolaidou; Wright and Young). On the other hand, the capacities to foster social justice through community gardening are limited and can be 'unintentionally exclusive' (see Pitt). This stresses the ambivalent character of community gardening and spatial justice and hence underlines the importance of negotiations and decision-making processes.

In reaction to inequity in the distribution of green public spaces, gardeners advance self-designing and co-managing (Hou and Rios, 2003; Jiménez, 2014) processes that influence the urban agenda from below (Certomà, 2016; Groth and Corijn, 2005) and overcome the classic public/private dichotomy – in spatial terms as well as in terms of ownership, management and planning practices. While for a long time most people had little comprehension of how planning actually influences their lives, and institutional planners themselves provided few opportunities for the involvement of people, with the acknowledgement of the political character of planning (Nawratek, 2011) it became imperative to consider the role of citizens. Gardening initiatives exemplify the potentiality of grassroots forms of spontaneous planning to positively challenge and engage authorities in detecting spatial and social needs, and in experimenting with innovative solutions by taking ordinary people-led initiatives on board.

Urban gardening practices can be considered as pieces of a puzzle of various (bottom-up) socio-political actions, which can contribute to wider cultural change moving towards more just spatial development by bringing (in)justice onto the agenda of public, political and scientific debates and raising awareness of social and spatial (in)justices, especially on the local level; and by taking practical deliberative action in urban development, increasing the plurality of actors involved and of the uses of space.

At the same time, however, all processes towards a more just spatial development have to be subjected to constant critical reflection, as they have evident limitations, contradictions and ambivalence with regard to justice. Understood as an ongoing and iterative process, urban gardening provides an excellent field to learn about the various foundations and manifestations of (in)justice and to empower oneself and others. Thereby it seems mandatory to constantly consider questions of justice – what is just, what is not, for whom and why? Who is included in negotiations and who is not? Who benefits from a certain use of space and who not?

The in-depth theoretically grounded analyses of urban gardening presented here explore forms of socio-political action that question governance paradigms ranging from neoliberal to community-oriented, antagonist or collaborative, materiality-focused or ideology-inspired. By complementing scholarly perspectives with real cases, the self-contained chapters focus on how these practices are able to address not only environmental and planning questions, but also the most fundamental issues of spatial justice, social cohesion, inclusiveness, social innovations and equality in cities. Particularly, they all revolve around the complex issue of whether, how and to what extent urban gardening practices are able to significantly influence the physical arrangement of urban space, which makes evident (and often determines) social inequalities, particularly where environmental problems are pervasive and severely affect the structures and functioning processes of urban spaces.

References

Adams, D., Scott, A. J. and Hardman, M. (2014): Guerrilla warfare in the planning system: revolutionary progress towards sustainability? *Geografiska Annaler B: Human Geography* 95 (4): 375–387.

Agyeman, J. (2005): *Sustainable Communities and the Challenge of Environmental Justice.* New York: New York University Press.

Allen, P. and Guthman, J. (2006): From 'old school' to 'farm-to-school': neoliberalization from the ground up. *Agriculture and Human Values* 23 (4): 417–421.

Barton, H. (Ed.) (2000): *Sustainable Communities: The Potential for Eco-Neighbourhoods.* London: Earthscan.

Bauwens, M. and Niaros, V. (2018): Changing societies through urban commons transitions P2P foundation. http://commonstransition.org/changing-societies-through-urban-commons-transitions (accessed 20 April 2018).

Beckie, M. and Bogdan, E. (2010): Planting roots: urban agriculture for senior immigrants. *Food Systems, and Community Development* 1 (2): 77–89. doi:10.5304/jafscd.2010.012.004

Bendt, P., Barthel, S. and Colding, J. (2013): Civic greening and environmental learning in public-access community gardens in Berlin. *Landscape and Urban Planning* 109: 18–30.

BEPA (2011): *Empowering People, Driving Change.* Luxembourg: Publications Office of the European Union.

Bin, V. and Voicu, I. (2006): The effect of community gardens on neighboring property values. *New York University Law and Economics Working Papers* 46.

Bond, S. (2011): Negotiating a 'democratic ethos': moving beyond the agonistic – communicative divide. *Planning Theory* 10 (2): 161–186.

Cameron, E. (2012): New geographies of story and storytelling. *Progress in Human Geography* 36: 573–592.

Caulier-Grice, J., Davies, A., Patrick, R. and Norman, W. (2012): Social innovation practices and trends. A deliverable of the project: 'The theoretical, empirical and policy foundations for building social innovation in Europe' (TEPSIE), European Commission – 7 Framework Programme. Brussels: European Commission, DG Research.

Certomà, C. (2011): Critical urban gardening as post-environmentalist practice. *Local Environment* 16 (10): 977–987.

Certomà, C. (2016): A new season for planning: urban gardening as informal planning in Rome. *Geografiska Annaler: Series B, Human Geography* 98 (2): 109–126.

Certomà, C. and Notteboom, B. (2017): Informal planning in a transactive governmentality: re-reading planning practices through Ghent's community gardens. *Planning Theory* 16 (1): 51–73.

Certomà, C. and Tornaghi, C. (2015): Political gardening: transforming cities and political agency. *Local Environment* 20 (10): 1123–1131.

Cooke, B. and Kothari, U. (2011): *Participation as Tyranny*. London: Zed Books.

Crouch, D. and Ward, C. (1988): *The Allotment: Its Landscape and Culture*. London: Faber & Faber.

Davies, A. and Simon, J. (2013): Engaging citizens in social innovation: a short guide to the research for policy makers and practitioners. A deliverable of the project: 'The theoretical, empirical and policy foundations for building social innovation in Europe' (TEPSIE), European Commission – 7th Framework Programme. Brussels: European Commission, DG Research.

de Certeau, Michel (1984): *The Practice of Everyday Life*. Berkeley: University of California Press.

Dean, M. (1999): *Governmentality: Power and Rule in Modern Society*. London: Sage.

Dorling, D. (2010): *Injustice: Why Social Inequality Persists*. Bristol: Policy Press.

Dyer, M., Corsini, F. and Certomà, C. (2017): Making urban governance, planning and design a participatory goal: a collaborative urbanism agenda. *Proceedings of the Institution of Civil Engineers – Urban Design and Planning* 170 (3): 173–186.

Eizenberg, E. (2012): Actually existing commons: three moments of space of community gardens in New York City. *Antipode* 44 (3): 764–782.

Eizenberg, E. (2013): *From the Ground Up: Community Gardens in New York City and the Politics of Spatial Transformation*. Farnham and Burlington: Ashgate.

Emmett, R. (2011): Community gardens, ghetto pastoral, and environmental justice. *Interdisciplinary Studies in Literature and Environment* 18 (11): 67–86.

Fainstein, S. S. (2010): *The Just City*. Ithaca, NY: Cornell University Press.

Ferris, J., Norman, C. and Sempik, J. (2001): People, land and sustainability: community gardens and the social dimension of sustainable development. *Social Policy Administration* 35 (5): 559–568.

Fincher, R. and Iveson, K. (2012): Justice and injustice in the city. *Geographical Research* 50 (3): 231–241.

Flachs, A. (2010): Food for thought: the social impact of community gardens in the greater Cleveland area. *Electronic Green Journal* 1 (30): 1–9.

Foucault, M. (2007): *Security, Territory, Population: Lectures at the Collège de France 1977–1978*. Basingstoke: Palgrave Macmillan.

Fox-Kämper, R., Wesener, A., Münderlein, D., Sondermann, M., McWilliam, W. and Kirk, N. (2018): Urban community gardens: an evaluation of governance approaches and related enablers and barriers at different development stages. *Landscape and Urban Planning* 170: 59–68. doi:10.1016/j.landurbplan.2017.06.023

Gibson-Graham, J. K. (2006): *A Postcapitalist Politics*. Minneapolis: University of Minnesota Press.

Gibson-Graham, J. K. (2008): Diverse economies: performative practices for 'other worlds'. *Progress in Human Geography* 32: 613–632.

Groth, J. and Corijn, E. (2005): Reclaiming urbanity: indeterminate spaces, informal actors and urban agenda setting. *Urban Studies* 42 (3): 503–526.

Habermas, J. (1984): *The Theory of Communicative Action. Vol. 1: Reason and the Rationalization of Society*. Boston: Beacon.

Habermas, J. (1987): *The Theory of Communicative Action. Vol. 2: Lifeworld and System: A Critique of Functionalist Reason.* Boston: Beacon.

Habermas, J. (1995): Reconciliation through the public use of reason: remarks on John Rawls's political liberalism. *The Journal of Philosophy* 92 (3): 109–131.

Hancock, T. (2001): People, partnerships and human progress: building community capital. *Health Promotion International* 16 (3): 275–280.

Harvey, D. (1973): *Social Justice and the City.* Baltimore: Johns Hopkins University Press.

Harvey, D. (1996): *Justice, Nature and the Geography of Difference.* Oxford: Basil Blackwell.

Haughton, G. (1999): Environmental justice and the sustainable city. *Journal of Planning Education and Research* 18: 233–243.

Healey, P. (1996): The communicative turn in planning theory and its implications for spatial strategy formations. *Environment and Planning B* 23 (2): 217–234.

Healey, P. (2011): Performing place governance collaboratively: planning as a communicative process. In: Gottweis, H. and Frank, F. (Eds): *The Argumentative Turn Revisited: Public Policy as Communicative Practice.* Durham, NC and London: Duke University Press, 58–82.

Heynen, N, Aiello, D., Keegan, C. and Luke, N. (2018): The enduring struggle for social justice and the city. *Annals of the American Association of Geographers* 108 (2): 301–316.

Hinchliffe, S. and Whatmore, S. (2006): Living cities: towards a politics of conviviality. *Science as Culture* 15 (3): 123–138.

Hobson, K. (2006): Enacting environmental justice in Singapore: performative justice and the Green Volunteer Network. *Geoforum* 37: 671–681.

Hodgson, K., Caton Campbell, M. and Bailkey, M. (2011): *Urban Agriculture: Growing Healthy, Sustainable Places.* Washington, DC: American Planning Association.

Hou, J. (2010): *Insurgent Public Space: Guerrilla Urbanism and the Remaking of Contemporary Cities.* New York: Taylor & Francis.

Hou, J. (2014): Making and supporting community gardens as informal urban landscapes. In: Mukhijia, V. and Loukaitou-Sideris, A. (Eds): *The Informal American City: Beyond Taco Trucks and Day Labor.* Cambridge, MA: MIT Press, 79–96.

Hou, J. (2017): Urban community gardens as multimodal social spaces. In: Tan, P. Y. and Jim, C. Y. (Eds): *Greening Cities: Advances in 21st Century Human Settlements.* Singapore: Springer Nature Singapore, 113–130.

Hou, J. and Rios, M. (2003). Community-driven place making. *Journal of Architectural Education* 57 (1): 19–27.

Hou, J., Johnson, J. M. and Lawson, J. L. (2009): *Greening Cities, Growing Communities: Learning from Seattle's Urban Community Gardens.* Seattle: University of Washington Press.

Ioannou, B., Moran, N., Sondermann, M., Certoma, C. and Hardman, M. (2016): Grassroots gardening movements: towards cooperative forms of green urban development? In: Bell, S., Fox-Kämper, R., Keshavarz, N., Benson, M., Caputo, S., Noori, S. and Voigt, A. (Eds): *Urban Allotment Gardens in Europe.* Abingdon: Routledge, 62–90.

Iveson, K. (2011): Social or spatial justice? Marcuse and Soja on the right to the city. *City* 15 (2): 251–259.

Jamal, T. and Hales, R. (2016): Performative justice: new directions in environmental and social justice. *Geoforum* 76: 176–180.

Jiménez, A. C. (2014). The right to infrastructure: a prototype for open source urbanism. *Environment and Planning D: Society and Space* 32 (2): 342–362.

Keshavarz, N. and Bell, S. (2016): A hisotry of urban gardens in Europe. In: Bell, S., Fox-Kämper, R., Keshavarz, N., Benson, M., Caputo, S., Noori, S. and Voigt, A. (Eds): *Urban Allotment Gardens in Europe.* Abingdon: Routledge, 8–32.

Krasny, M. E. and Tidball, K. G. (2009): Community gardens as contexts for science, stewardship, and civic action learning. *Cities Environ* 2 (1): 1–18.

Läpple, D. (1992): Essay über den Raum: für ein gesellschaftswissenschaftliches Raumkonzept [Essay concerning space: towards a societal concept of space]. In: Häußermann, H., Ibsen, D., Krämer-Badoni, T., Läpple, D., Rodenstein, M. and Siebel, W. (Eds): *Stadt und Raum: soziologische Analysen* [*City and Space: Sociological Analyses*]. Pfaffenweile: Centaurus. *Stadt, Raum und Gesellschaft* 1, 157–207.

Law, J. and Urry, J. (2004): Enacting the social. *Economy and Society* 33: 390–410.

Lawson, L. (2004): The planner in the garden: a historical view into the relationship between planning and community gardens. *Journal of Planning History* 3 (2): 151–176.

Lefebvre, H. (1968): *Le droit à la ville*. Paris: Anthropos.

Lefebvre, H. (1991): *The Production of Space*. Oxford: Basil Blackwell. Originally published in 1974.

Loggins, D. and Christy, L. (2013): History of New York City open space. *Community Greening Review* 18: 14–19.

Marcuse, P. (2009): From critical urban theory to the right to the city. *City* 13: 185–197.

Marston, S. (2010): Introduction: geographies of social justice. In: Smith, S., Pain, R., Marston, S. and Jones, J. (Eds): *The Sage Handbook of Social Geographies*. Los Angeles and London: Sage, 411–418.

Massey, D. (1994): *Space, Place and Gender*. Cambridge: Polity Press.

Massey, D. and Catalano, A. (1978): *Capital and Land: Landownership by Capital in Great Britain*. London: Edward Arnold.

McClintock, N. (2008): From industrial garden to food desert: unearthing the root structure of urban agriculture in Oakland, California. *Institute for Study of Societal Issues Working Papers*. http://escholarship.org/uc/item/1wh3v1sj (accessed 20 April 2018).

McClintock, N. (2014): Radical, reformist, and garden-variety neoliberal: coming to terms with urban agriculture's contradictions. *Local Environment*, 19 (2): 147–171.

McKay, G. (2011): *Radical Gardening*. London: Frances Lincoln Limited.

Merrifield, A. and Swyngedouw, E. (1996): *The Urbanization of Injustice*. London: Lawrence & Wishart.

Milbourne, P. (2012): Everyday (in)justices and ordinary environmentalisms: community gardening in disadvantaged urban neighbourhoods. *Local Environment* 17 (9): 943–957.

Miller, J. (2005): Biodiversity conservation and the extinction of experience. *Trends in Ecology and Evolution* 20 (8): 261–268.

Miller, W. (2015): UK allotments and urban food initiatives: (limited?) potential for reducing inequalities. *Local Environment* 20(10): 1194–1214.

Mitchell, D. (2003): *The Right to the City Social Justice and the Fight for Public Space*. New York and London: The Guilford Press.

Mouffe, C. (1993): *The Return of the Political*. London and New York: Verso.

Mouffe, C. (2000): *The Democratic Paradox*. London: Verso.

Mouffe, C. (2005): *On the Political*. London: Routledge.

Nawratek, K. (2011): *City as a Political Idea*. Exeter: Short Run Press.

Othengrafen, F. and Reimer, M. (2013): The embeddedness of planning in cultural contexts: theoretical foundations for the analysis of dynamic planning cultures. *Environment and Planning A* 45: 1269–1284.

Othengrafen, F. and Sondermann, M. (2015): Konflikte, Proteste, Initiativen und die Kultur der Planung – Stadtentwicklung unter demokratischen Vorzeichen? In: Othengrafen, F. and Sondermann, M. (Eds): Städtische Planungskulturen im Spiegel von Konflikten, Protesten und Initiativen. *Planungsrundschau* 23. Berlin: Verlag Uwe Altrock, 7–30.

Özmen, E. (2014): Zwischen Konsens und Dissens. Zeitgenössische politikphilosophische Perspektiven auf die Demokratie [Between consensus and dissent: contemporary political-philosophical perspectives on democracy]. In: Reder, M and Cojocaru, M.-D.

(Eds): *Zukunft der Demokratie. Ende einer Illusion oder Aufbruch zu neuen Formen?* [*Future of Democracy: End of an Illusion or Awakening of New Forms?*] Stuttgart: Kohlhammer Verlag, 125–137.

Peer, C. and Sondermann, M. (2016): Planungskultur als neues Paradigma in der Planungswissenschaft [Planning culture as a new paradigm in planning science]. *disP – The Planning Review* 52 (4): 30–42.

Pinkerton, T. and Hopkins, R. (2009): *Local Food: How to Make It Happen in Uour Community.* Devon: Green Books.

Pudup, M. B. (2008): It takes a garden: cultivating citizen-subjects in organized garden projects. *Geoforum* 39 (3): 1228–1240.

Purcell, M. (2002): Excavating Lefebvre: the right to the city and its urban politics of the inhabitant. *GeoJournal* 58 (2–3): 99–108.

Purcell, M. and Tyman, S. K. (2014): Cultivating food as a right to the city. *Local Environment* 20 (10): 1132–1147. doi: 10.1080/13549839.2014.903236

Rawls, J. (1971): *The Theory of Justice.* Cambridge, MA: Belknap.

Rawls, J. (1995): Political liberalism: reply to Habermas. *The Journal of Philosophy* 92 (3): 132–180.

Reynolds, K. (2014): Disparity despite diversity: social injustice in New York City's urban agriculture system. *Antipode* 47 (1): 240–259.

Reynolds, K. and Nevin Cohen, N. (2016): *Beyond the Kale: Urban Agriculture and Social Justice Activism in New York City.* Athens: The University of Georgia Press.

Reynolds, R. (2008): *On Guerilla Gardening: A Handbook for Gardening without Boundaries.* London: Bloomsbury.

Rosol, M. (2012): Community volunteering as neoliberal strategy? Green space production in Berlin. *Antipode* 44 (1): 239–257.

Sachs, W. (1993): Global ecology and the shadow of 'development'. In: Sachs, W. (Ed.): *Global Ecology: A New Arena of Political Conflict.* Halifax, Nova Scotia: Fernwood Books, 3–21.

Sandercock, L. (1977 [1975]): *Cities for Sale.* Carlton: Melbourne University Press.

Sandercock, L. (2006): Cosmopolitan urbanism: a love song to our mongrel cities. In: Binnie, J., Holloway, J., Millington, S. and Young, C. (Eds): *Cosmopolitan Urbanism.* London and New York: Routledge, 37–52.

Schmelzkopf, K. (1995): Urban community gardens as contested space. *Geographical Review* 85: 364–381.

Schmelzkopf, K. (2002): Incommensurability, land use, and the right to space: community gardens in New York City. *Urban Geography* 23 (4): 323–343.

Smith, C. and Kurtz, H. (2003): Community gardens and politics of scale in New York City. *Geographical Review* 93 (2): 193–212.

Smith, N. (1997): Social justice and the new American urbanism: the revanchist city. In: Merrifield, A. and Swyngedouw, E. (Eds): *The Urbanization of Injustice.* New York: New York University Press, 117–136.

Soja, E. (1996): *Thirdspace: Journey to Los Angeles and Other Real-and-Imagined Places.* Cambridge: Blackwell.

Soja, E. (2009): The city and spatial justice [La ville et la justice spatiale]. *Justice spatiale / spatial justice* 1. www.jssj.org/article/la-ville-et-la-justice-spatiale (accessed 29 August 2018).

Soja, E. (2010): *Seeking Spatial Justice.* Minneapolis: University of Minnesota Press.

Sondermann, M. (2017): Planungskultur als Sinnsystem. Eine Untersuchung am Beispiel kooperativer Stadtgrünentwicklung in Düsseldorf. *Raumforschung und Raumordnung* 75 (1): 45–56. doi: 10.1007/s13147–016–0460–1

Staeheli, L. A. (2008): Citizenship and the problem of community. *Political Geography* 27: 5–21.

Staeheli, L. A., Mitchell, D. and Gibson, K. (2002): Conflicting rights to the city in New York's community gardens. *GeoJournal* 58 (2–3): 197–205.

Stehlin, J. G. and Tarr, A. R. (2016): Think regionally, act locally? Gardening, cycling, and the horizon of urban spatial politics. *Urban Geography* 38 (9): 1329–1351. doi: 10.1080/ 02723638.2016.1232464

Swyngedouw, E. (2009): The zero-ground of politics: musings on the post-political city. *NewGeographies* 1: 52–61.

Tornaghi, C. (2012): Public space, urban agriculture and the grassroots creation of new commons: lessons and challenges for policy makers. In: Viljoen, A. M. and Wiskerke, J. S. C. (Eds): *Sustainable Food Planning*. Wageningen: Wageningen Academic Publisher, 349–364.

Tornaghi, C. (2014): Critical geography of urban agriculture. *Progress in Human Geography* 38: 551–567.

Tornaghi, C. and Certomà, C. (Eds) (2018): *Urban Gardening as Politics*. London: Routledge.

Tracey, D. (2007): *Guerrilla Gardening: A Manualfesto*. Gabriola Island: New Society Publishers.

Warf, B. and Arias, F. (2009): *The Spatial Turn: Interdisciplinary Perspectives*. New York: Routledge.

Williams, M. (2017): Searching for actually existing justice in the city. *Urban Studies* 54 (10): 2217–2232. doi: 10.1177/0042098016647336

Wittgenstein, L. (1953): *Philosophical Investigations*. Trans. G. E. M. Anscombe. Oxford: Blackwell.

Yiftachel, O. (2009): Critical theory and 'gray space': mobilisation of the colonised. *City* 16 (2–3): 240–256.

Young, I. M. (1990): *Justice and the Politics of Difference*. Princeton: Princeton University Press.

2

Conflation in political gardening: concepts and practice

Lucy Rose Wright and Ross Fraser Young

Introduction

This chapter introduces the re-emerging political characteristic of urban gardening (UG) (Certomà and Tornaghi, 2015). Our contribution presents an understanding of the importance *process* has for a group seeking spatial justice through engagement in UG. The garden's local political environment shapes the *process* by which a group seeks to tackle localised spatial injustice. Spatial justice refers to 'an intentional and focused emphasis on the spatial or geographical aspects of justice and injustice' (Soja, 2009: 2). To understand this 'political characteristic', the chapter will explore the influence of and relationship between neoliberalisation and UG. There is a general acceptance of 'new' urban-based social movements as a result of neoliberalisation (Castells, 2015). Political UG has emerged as one form, which includes allotments, urban farms, 'guerrilla' and community gardens (Cone and Myhre, 2000; Hermann et al., 2006; Hoffman and Doody, 2014; Lawson, 2005; Orsini et al., 2013; Ousset et al., 1998). This chapter will provide a reading of political gardening literature, outlining rationales for 'public' engagement with UG. This informs a framework that maps the trajectories groups take in pursuit of spatial justice. We illustrated with UK case studies. The conclusion speculates a definition for political UG that reflects the *process* by which gardens 'turn' political. The implication of this political 'turn' through *process* is the creation of active 'democratised' citizens who recognise injustice and hold a heightened awareness of rights.

Neoliberal processes and political urban gardening

Context is critical for understanding the conditions which have led the public to re-evaluate 'everyday space' in the urban realm (Hou, 2010; Milbourne,

2012: 944), for example, parks, markets, streets and verges (Certoma, 2015; Hou, 2010). Neoliberalism has been and continues to be a dominant mode of political economic restructuring and form of governmentality. It is underpinned by appropriate relationships between the State, capital, private enterprise and the public (Ong, 2006). Characteristics include belief in the free market, corporate power and financial globalisation (Olssen, 2004). Its trajectory has intensified as a result of the 2008 global economic crisis and subsequent European debt crisis (Overbeek, 2012). The State's response has been expansionary policies, austerity measures and structural reforms. Austerity measures relate to decisions by the State to reduce deficits through spending cuts or tax rises, i.e. spending cuts through withdrawal of State support for public services and welfare. Structural reform includes *entrepreneurialism* through increasing competition and encouraging partnership between the State and private sectors. Additionally, the State encourages the involvement of the voluntary and private sector in services typically provided by the State such as green space, health with social care, and transport. This is commonly considered *privatisation* of state assets and services. *Devolution* occurs when the responsibility for decision-making is regionalised; from national to lower governmental levels. Many argue that the neoliberal hegemony has exacerbated urban socio-economic polarisation (Musterd and Ostendorf, 2013; Skopek et al., 2011). This has led to rising inequality and social injustice (Hedin et al., 2012; Marois and Pradella, 2014; Randolph and Tice, 2014).

'Neoliberalism' is contentious, labelled an 'academic catchphrase' (Boas and Gans-Morse, 2009: 138) and a 'rascal concept' (Brenner et al., 2010). Conflicts arise in discrepancies of what it is responsible for, its role and application. However, it provides a lens to conceptualise the relationship between the changing urban realm and UG. We draw upon Barron's compartmentalisation into *privatisation*, *entrepreneurialism* and *devolution* (Barron, 2017). Exploring each process provides rationale for the re-emergence of political action from 'localised' UG spaces (Rawls, 1971).

Privatisation has led to cuts in spending on public services, with efficiency and profit the dominant force. Where this has occurred the State is subject to increased accountability. This has been evident in the State's re-evaluation of land appropriation, how and what should urban land be used for? Through *devolution* the power for these decisions has been regionalised. Many urban regions hold historical beliefs that the quality of urban produce is inferior to rural produce due to contamination risk (Armar-Klemesu, 2000; Finster et al., 2004; von Hoffen and Säumel, 2014). This may have contributed to the selling off of unused land to the highest bidder with the remainder as parks or 'at risk'. These reforms coincided with a downward trend in allotment popularity during the late 1990s – in the UK – conflating loss of urban green space (Crouch and Ward, 1997). Contracts were put out to tender for remaining spaces with maintenance going to the cheapest contractor. This transitions into *entrepreneurialism* with

increased competition which has resulted in fewer and lower skilled employment opportunities. Reduced maintenance has encouraged anti-social behaviour. This has disproportionately occurred in poorer areas (see the literature on
environmental justice, e.g. McClintock, 2012; Scott and Mooney, 2009; Wolch
et al., 2014). City-dwellers question existing spatial injustice and the disparity in
land access and purpose. They form groups and plan to re-appropriate the land.
They then encounter the State, private and/or third sector. While UG tackles the
group's injustice of not having equal access to green space, it brings awareness of
wider spatial injustice in their area.

We have followed this as a causational relationship whereby political UG
has started as a result of opposition to neoliberalism. Increased privatisation
has led UG groups to mobilise having identified injustice. We recognise a shift
occurring in the relationship between neoliberalism and UG (McClintock,
2014; McIvor and Hale, 2015; Wekerle and Classens, 2015). The relationship is
moving from causational to contributory. Not only are UG groups mobilising
in opposition to Barron's three processes – privitisation, devolution and entrepreneurialism (Barron, 2017), they also embody some of the characteristics of
these processes.

The causational relationship between entrepreneurialism and UG has
seen a push towards making State-owned assets profitable. State land has
investment potential, thus, land assets are reviewed for 'value' and 'useful-
ness' (Schmelzkopf, 2002). Entrepreneurialism has changed how services are
provided with partnerships between the private sector, the third sector and
the public. UG groups have contributed by competing for land with wider
sectors to provide services. This neoliberal process fostered opportunities to
gain power. UG groups also find themselves competing against each other for
funding. To survive, gardens adopt an entrepreneurial approach when applying
for funding. This exacerbates injustices as a result of different internal skills or
social capital. Social capital 'encompasses the social resources on which people
rely when pursuing their livelihoods, including social networks, membership
in groups, relationships of trust and reciprocity, and access to wider institutions
of society' (Gallaher et al., 2013: 390). Some UG groups pull on their social
capital ties to gain more funding than other groups (bonding, bridging and
linking) (Firth et al., 2011). Reynolds, in her work on New York City, found
that spatial injustices were exacerbated as a result of funding distribution. She
observed how some groups were able to access services, funds and land whilst
others encountered barriers, which she terms 'structural racism' (Reynolds,
2015: 249).

Devolution and the shift of authority from national to lower governmental
levels has increased the latter's power to make decisions about land use and ownership. The public have taken advantage and created opportunities to grow. The
transference of authority through devolution has helped gardeners gain access
to decisions regarding green spaces through devolution. UG provides a service

to regional government by giving land 'value' and filling gaps in social provision through shared governance (Mathers et al., 2015).

The relationship between UG processes and neoliberalism is complex. The relationship is complex because it has influenced how political UG has formed, how UG groups engage in and themselves become part of the neoliberal agenda. UG groups engage with the State, using newfound opportunities to increase their potential for political action. They do this seeking to address injustice in the urban realm.

The rise of political UG: understanding resistance

Academic interest in political UG has risen in response to its popularity. This section gives the reader a flavour of the research that has been conducted. In its briefest summation, there is an established history of conflating politics with gardening through a political ecology lens (Hovorka, 2006; Jarosz, 2011; Schroeder, 1993; Walker, 2005). The literature focuses on the rights of marginalised women who take advantage of the social opportunities presented by UG. Recently, there has been a shift in discourse towards conflation of UG and spatial injustice. This shift has seen the development of the term 'political gardening' to describe gardening which is influenced by neoliberalisation and the result of the 'local squeeze' post-2008 (Peck, 2012: 627). An important but lesser known work by Kato on Hurricane Katrina in New Orleans introduced the term in its most recognisable form and identified different political aspects. Kato explored 'difference' in how 'political gardens' seek to address social issues (Kato et al., 2014: 2) and sought to understand the role of political gardens. Kato distinguished the political aspects of gardening by what happened and who caused it (Kato et al., 2014: 4). She found that while some sites may not be initiated with a political agenda, through barriers, people may adopt an explicitly political stance (Kato et al., 2014).

Shortly after, 'a special issue' was published in 2015, titled *Political Gardening*, and as expected, this has been influential (Certomà and Tornaghi, 2015). 'The issue' proliferated the identification of political characteristics in the UA movement. To summarise this and related works, three themes have been identified, as shown in Figure 2.1. The figure shows the degree of the 'political characteristic', from practicality, injustices to deep injustices.

Practicality

The first theme identified relates to the 'vital human need' of access to space to grow food for self-sufficiency and sustenance. The practicality and its effect on household nutrition (Ober Allen et al., 2008), food access (Crush et al., 2011; Zezza and Tasciotti, 2010) and self-sufficiency (Mok et al., 2014) cannot be ignored. A participant from Chan et al. highlights the importance of this after Hurricane Sandy (2015):

Practicality	Injustices	Deep injustices
Feeding families 'sustenance' through self-sufficiency.	Food systems injustice, food access.	Instead of being subjects, becoming agents of change.
Gathering place in times of emergency.	Testing/political experiments. Producing alternatives.	Engaging in more structural justice.
More/better access to public space.	Neoliberal planning and spatial injustice.	UG moving from causational to contributory neoliberal planning.

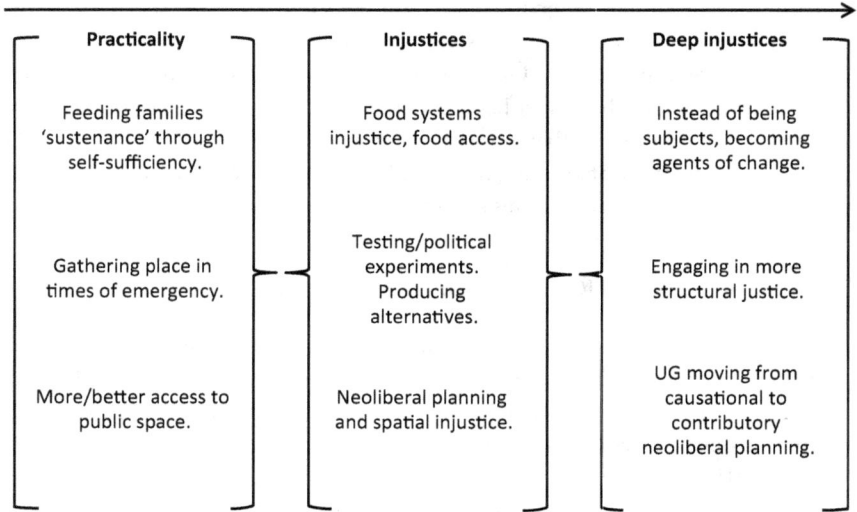

Figure 2.1   Categorisation of the 'political characteristic' in existing political gardening works

> [Talking about a Puerto Rican woman] when [Sandy] happened, she cried so much because she doesn't have documents, she is not legal here, she has many kids, and this was to her everything. After Sandy she said to me, 'You know everyone got help from [the] city. We lost everything because she lived in a basement. We lost everything and nobody help us.' ... She fed her family with the garden.

Although not the most complex concept of spatial injustice, the practical productive aspect of UG is important for community-building and in times of need.

Injustices

This second theme moves to the specific spatial injustices conducive to UG. The themes were challenging neoliberal planning (Wekerle, 2004), 'alterity' of the food system (Feagan, 2007; Kirwan, 2004) and political experimentation (Certomà, 2015). Lyons et al. describe how UA groups are re-imagining urban spaces 'by resisting the continued enclosure of public urban ecologies', 'opening up private spaces' and 'pioneering an alternative agricultural movement' that subverts entrenched social and political boundaries about acceptable uses of public space (Lyons et al., 2013: 160).

This allows people to take advantage of power vacuums left by neoliberal processes through the involvement of those often excluded due to spatial injustice. They engage in decision-making. Purcell and Tyman relate this new power to Lefebvre's 'right to the city' that UG sites are places that 'encourage (and force) people not only to gather, but also to become aware of and negotiate differences and govern their shared space' (Purcell and Tyman, 2015: 1144).

Deep injustices

The third theme is the role of UG in creating engaged 'democratised' citizens. McIvor and Hale's work developed a theoretical framework for 'deep democracy', attempting to bridge the gap from focused democratic actions within food movements to wider applications of democratic practice (McIvor and Hale, 2015: 729). This requires three conditions; the first is to move beyond civic skills (practicality) focusing on long-lasting civic relationships. The second is to progress from superficial relationships (specific injustices) between the public and private/State organisations through the mapping of power dynamics. The third is a move towards 'the commons', which is defined as a recurrent coordinated space of action, full of tension and ambiguity (McIvor and Hale, 2015: 729). These draw on existing works on food democracy (Hassanein, 2003; 2008; McClintock, 2010) and highlight the limitation that 'practical' and 'short-term' UG has limited aims with set deliverables. This improves an area for a time. However, due to funding constraints and opportunities, these projects begin to feed into the neoliberal environment by adopting entrepreneurialism and privatisation. The distribution of social and financial capital can be considered an example. Both can be unevenly distributed, reinforcing spatial injustices across an area. McClintock demonstrates this by mapping non-profit UG in East and West Oakland (California). The areas share similar socio-economic conditions. However, West Oakland had a greater number of non-profit gardens due to their structural inequalities being more 'visible' and having more 'vacant' land (McClintock, 2014: 164). These sites encompass a dualism; they are radical – by temporarily filling gaps in services – and neoliberal, by becoming aware of their surroundings and adopting the same processes. This accepts that the relationship between UG and neoliberalism is more than remedying neoliberal rollbacks. A growing consensus prevails that the relationship is contributory, with UG groups adopting specific neoliberal processes to survive.

Process in practice

The following case studies are from Kingston upon Hull, UK. Case study one shows the process linearly and case study two shows the process as iterative. Hull lies on the Humber estuary, close to the north-east coast of England. Hull is known for being a university city, a city of poets and the home of William Wilberforce, a leader of the slavery abolition movement. Industry has shifted from sea-fishing, whaling and trading to manufacturing, healthcare and renewable energy. Hull consistently ranks near the bottom of measures of social deprivation. In 2017 Hull was the UK City of Culture which has brought renewed interest in the City.

The UG case studies were selected from a study of thirty-three. Semi-structured interviews were conducted individually with the organisers involved in UG projects and initiators were identified using snowball sampling. Six of the projects, representative of different 'types' of UG, were observed over a three-year period.

Case study one: therapeutic community garden

Wendy started the garden (**infancy**) in 1997. She had been working in social housing in North Hull, dealing with land between residential housing and garages that was attracting anti-social behaviour. The land was left over from the shortening of social housing gardens. Concurrently people approached the organisation looking for space to grow food having been unable to get an allotment. Wendy described, 'when I walked in and I stood just near that second bed, bearing in mind there was nothing here, I got a lovely feeling. I don't mean that I saw it like this but I knew it was right; this was going to be a community garden' (Wendy, interview, 2015). A group formed to **negotiate** the transformation of the land and aimed to change its reputation: 'I was that fed up with North Hull having such a bad name. It was constantly in the newspapers … North Hull yobs … The way I have been treated, you would go somewhere and the professional there, even if they were nice, you were treated different … I sometimes could be cut out of meetings' (Wendy, interview, 2015). The group felt injustice because the community was disadvantaged with limited opportunities for local people. The housing organisation had leftover funds and Wendy was determined that 'they were going to leave something on the [local authority] estate' (Wendy, interview, 2015). The **outcome** was the pioneering UG in North Hull. They developed a main aim to facilitate community engagement with an emphasis on individuals using the garden however they wished. The group began **reaping rewards** by fulfilling their aim. They developed raised beds. Having established the site, the group described the space as 'looking nice' but having 'nobody to go and ask for advice because it was unheard of, that was the thing, so we made mistakes … we did a lot of things right and we learnt by our mistakes' (Wendy, interview, 2015). The garden now aims to be an example of what others can do in their own communities.

In the beginning there was a temporal injustice with land security a **barrier**. The initial lease was twenty-five years. Wendy felt this was inadequate: 'I was in my fifties, I was offered a lease and I thought really … 25 years I could be dead by then and other people are going to have to fight to carry on the lease so I did fight for it' (Wendy, interview, 2015). Having personally invested and developed social capital through the site, the group pushed back against the State, securing a ninety-nine-year lease and providing the opportunity to undo deeper spatial injustice in the area. The popularity of UG in the area impacted the garden by creating more competition, 'it became the "in" thing to grow food. So all these food projects set up and we're all fighting for the same pot of money. I think it should go to more established projects with a track record, it should go to them first. And also if you've got a couple of growing groups in one area, don't let another group in, we're all fighting for residents to come to our projects' (Wendy, interview, 2015). This shows the territorial nature of UG and directly correlates to the neoliberal agenda, which promotes increased competition. The group has managed to employ two paid staff members by playing on the project's longevity. The project had been close to **dissolving**.

'There was one time … because it had been vandalised every volunteer had walked out. A week went by, then another … I've cried, I've sat at home and I've cried about stuff like that but you always get more back. There's been more marvellous things than there has been bad things' (Wendy, interview, 2015).

Case study two: urban community orchard

Numerous groups and factors influenced the start of the orchard in 2004. The city council sold part of the allotment for a housing development and a plot holder wanted to ensure the remaining plots were not privatised. Concurrently the National Health Service (State-owned) needed land to promote a 'five a day – fruit and vegetables' initiative. It perceived a need to increase healthy food consumption, access and education. The NHS gained access to two acres of unused land. Volunteers and residents – helped by the State – planted trees. Subsequently, the NHS lacked financial resources and withdrew support. Julie describes **flux** as 'sink or swim' (Julie, interview, 2016). The State recommitted until the group 'became self-sufficient' (Julie, interview, 2016). The State maintained financial and practical help after thefts and vandalism. A State employee identified a skill deficiency in the group and asked Julie 'to write the minutes of the meetings'; Julie obliged (Julie, interview, 2016). The orchard began **reaping rewards** with 350 trees producing twenty-six varieties of apple. The group of mostly retired people visits the site every day and runs sessions at harvest time. The remit expanded beyond food provision, hosting wider community events. The group faced **barriers** in seeking non-State funding due to the gated access to the site. The group developed internal strategies, becoming financially independent by asking for donations. Allotment rules meant they were not able to sell it. There was a period of **re-negotiation**, during which differences became evident. The group disagreed about 'who the orchard is for' (Julie, interview, 2016). Some wanted to invite people experiencing 'depression, anxiety, ex-drug offenders, ex-alcohol offenders' (Julie, interview, 2016). Julie described involving these people in order to aid their mental health. Others thought this would create vulnerability with the potential for anti-social behaviour. Julie argued that 'they might fall in love with the place like we have' (Julie, interview, 2016). Paperwork proved challenging in encouraging school visits. Land ownership was problematic with group members 'treating it like they own it but it's for everyone' (Julie, interview, 2016). The **outcome** was that the group 'couldn't get any agreement' with Julie describing how

'I just exploded because I had seriously had enough … I was absolutely beyond livid and I said that's it … I'm resigning, completely resigning' (Julie, interview, 2016). With a smaller group the orchard struggled and it looked likely that land management would return to the State. Julie, having left, heard about this and returned to ensure this did not happen. The result has been a period of **flux**, with members returning and initial group members conceding (opening access to more communities), which is resulting in **restructuring** to secure its future. Julie called this a 'transition', having 'a new set of people around the table' (Julie, interview, 2016). With renewed enthusiasm, they hope to 'persuade the council [State] to let us take over another strip of land' (Julie, interview, 2016). The group aims to rebrand to reflect the new direction of increased accessibility. They are now **renegotiating**, coming together to work out how to promote localised food production, healthy eating and exercise through outdoor activity.

Identifying the *process* in political urban gardening

Urban gardens are used as a place for people to gather, a form of political agora for discussing injustice as well as being a space to 'test' and implement alternatives. Evident in the literature is a garden-centric approach, participants are acknowledged and given agency but usually the garden takes priority when it comes to spatial injustice. The neoliberal emphasis is on the provision of space, how profitable it is, what 'use' it has and what can be measured as a tangible output. The case studies show our shift of focus back onto the individuals newly operating these spaces and the process they experience, as shown in Figure 2.2.

The process described above is iterative, however, to create the basis of understanding across political UG it is necessary to present them in the most commonly observed linear means. Throughout we will draw on specific examples from the case studies injustice(s) and highlight how the political nature of UG is a result of the *process*.

Infancy

The first phase marks the inception of an idea. An individual has experienced a specific injustice(s) (case study one – reputation of the area, 'fed up of North Hull having a bad name'). They experience Rawls' first principle, observing inequality as a result of unjust resource distribution and access. These could include a lack of food freedom, food poverty, a lack of community cohesion and inadequate access to green space. In case study one this was due to inadequate allotment provision and in case study two it was poor diet and food education. Ideas and opportunities for change begin to form, which challenge this. They mobilise, forming groups around common interests and mutual concerns. An urban garden manifests as the solution to resolve injustice. Injustice(s) is the glue holding the group together but it remains unorganised.

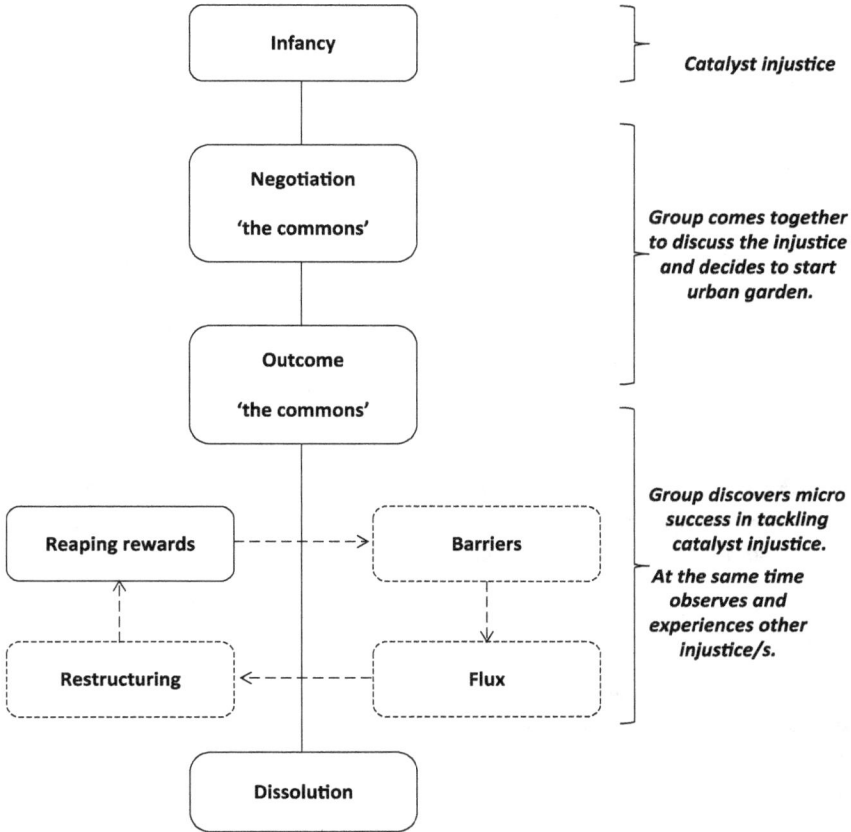

Figure 2.2   Framework of the process of UG, highlighting how 'justice' changes and broadens as a result of engagement

Negotiation: 'the commons'

In mobilising, ideas percolate. There is *internal negotiation* with groups debating identity. Formalised plans (aims) shape relating to what they are trying to do or change. In case study one, the aim was to facilitate community engagement using the garden. The aims draw on the group's expertise and local knowledge. In case study two, the group on the site lived locally and they had knowledge about growing because they had their own allotment plots in addition to the orchard. Two attributes *impact* negotiation. The first is that they are navigating their roles. Resources and power are distributed across the group. Individuals are given responsibilities related to their skill-set. This can be split both equally and unequally within the group. They put aside 'difference' for the betterment of the group or the community at large (Rawls' second principle). The second is the susceptibility of the group. Influences include the characteristics of specific pieces of land or community resources, which are at 'risk'. In case study two – while stated as a barrier – an example of this is that the group did not anticipate their gated site being a challenge in qualifying for funding.

Outcome: 'the commons'

The group has agreed aims and roles. They gain confidence and begin to co-manage through collaboration, cooperation and communication (Hardt and Negri, 2004). Negotiation moves from internal to external. As internal negotiation generates knowledge and understanding of the processes necessary to form an urban garden, the group begins to engage with *external negotiation*. This includes securing land access and applying for funding. The group engages (beyond the local) with the 'State' governing the space, which it seeks to access and control. In case study one we observed Wendy engage with the 'State' to fight for an increase in the land lease from twenty-five years to ninety-nine years. Through engagement the group gains new knowledge, learning political language. The group compromises and changes aims to reflect its external engagement and new-found 'deep democracy'.

Reaping rewards

The group has a site and begins to grow. They experience the cycle of progress and reward through food production. They see progress in tackling injustice, which they initially set out to change. On a micro-scale the group is improving the area and addressing food access. In case study two the orchard comprised of 350 trees producing twenty-six varieties of apple. The retired group was visiting the site every day and ran sessions during harvest. The remit expanded beyond healthy food provision and the group hosted wider community events. In turn they create 'value' through social capital, which could be social, cultural, environmental and economic. The group begins to understand the injustices experienced by its volunteers. They look for ways to expand the 'reach' and beneficiaries of their work. Case study one was the first community garden in Hull and changed its aims to be an example for what other communities could do. Through engagement in internal processes (communication and collaboration) and external processes (applying for funding), the group observes other injustices. The group develops a taste for tackling more issues and re-enters negotiations to widen their aims.

Barriers, flux and restructuring

After a period of 'good times' the group begins to face *barriers* in tackling other injustices. The group experiences a period of *flux*. An example could be financial insecurity with initial infrastructure funding ending. The group may use its own resources to keep the space active. They may be experiencing a skill deficiency, unable to write funding bids or manage resources. There may be a group breakdown with members leaving to pursue employment or as the result of opinion 'difference'. In case study two there was a period of flux, members left and others joined. Julie identified the group as going through a *transition*.

Internal barriers lead the group to look outwards for support, typically from local and national governmental organisations and the third sector. In the group's attempts to access support they face external barriers, which manifest as feelings of injustice. Without support they re-evaluate. The group begins to understand their 'relative position', realising they have limited social capital and are unable to create change. This was evident in case study one. The group felt that the popularity of UG meant that they were competing for funding with other groups they had supported. They identified having a 'limited position' despite being a pioneering UG group in the city. They feel marginalised by their restricted access. The aims of the garden are unfulfilled and the group feels injustice in their ability to access and practice democracy in line with expectations.

Flux and the group's experience have repercussions for UG. The positive is that the group is able to *restructure*, it learns from destructive patterns and realises that success is based on collaboration. At this point the group is engaging in deep democracy in trying to change its area through local action. They put aside 'difference' and come together for the sake of the garden and return to a return to a negotiation of aims. They moves beyond the initial interest or concern that brought them together and realises that the garden can be used to address other social injustice(s). Their aims are broadened to improve systemic societal issues. Gardening at this point is no longer the primary function with the experience of process resulting in a political 'turn' of the garden. The group feels (re-)empowered and attempts to become a source of resistance. Case study two demonstrated the re-empowerment the group felt as a result of restructuring and hoped to 'persuade the council [State] to let us take over another strip of land' (Julie, interview, 2016). The negative repercussion is that groups that remain in a state of flux, unable to move past barriers and restructure to remediate injustice, dissolve.

Dissolution

Case study one demonstrated when a UG group is at risk of dissolution. Vandalism caused every volunteer to walk out and Wendy doubted her ability to continue the project. If the UG group is unable to restructure it may dissolve back into individuals or smaller groups. This does not necessarily mark the end of the UG group but often the creation of more specific issue-focused projects.

Conclusion and working definition for political gardening

This chapter has introduced the reader to the importance of *process* when investigating the political character of UG groups. It began with context, exploring the effects of neoliberal processes (*entrepreneurialism*, *privatisation* and *devolution*).

It highlighted how UG spaces can emerge as both a response to neoliberalism and as producers of neoliberal processes. The chapter then presented three thematic layered rationalisations of participation from current scholarship (*practicality*, *injustice* and *deep injustice*). We used a framework to take a human-centric approach to UG, personified through two case studies. From the themes, we presented a multi-phase linear framework, which accounts for the important implication of process. We propose to bring forward the following conclusions. The process of political gardening can be both linear and iterative with groups revisiting stages of the process depending on their circumstances. Groups are more likely to engage with the political process when they reach 'the commons – outcome' and face 'barriers and flux'. This allowed us to acknowledge the individuality of political UG groups and observe commonalities in how a group experiences process. To conclude we provide a working definition for 'political gardening', which accounts for the important implication of process:

> Political gardening; the product of people brought together by shared interest and/or mutual concern for spatial injustice(s). The political gardening process, which these people undergo through engagement is both influenced by (causational) and changes (contributory) the political landscape in which gardeners operate. The process is iterative; with gardeners mobilising to tackle localised injustice(s), (re-)negotiating and catalysing awareness of broader systemic societal injustice(s).

References

Armar-Klemesu, M. (2000): *Urban Agriculture and Food Security, Nutrition and Health*. Feldafing: Deutsche Stiftung für internationale Entwicklung (DSE).

Barron, J. (2017): Community gardening: cultivating subjectivities, space and justice. *Local Environment* 22 (9): 1142–1158. https://doi.org/10.1080/13549839.2016.1169518

Boas, T. C. and Gans-Morse, J. (2009): Neoliberalism: from new liberal philosophy to antiliberal slogan. *Studies in Comparative International Development* 44 (2): 137–161. https://doi.org/10.1007/s12116–009–9040–5

Brenner, N., Peck, J. and Theodore, N. (2010): After neoliberalization? *Globalizations* 7 (3): 327–345.

Castells, M. (2015): *Networks of Outrage and Hope: Social Movements in the Internet Age*. Cambridge: John Wiley & Sons.

Certomà, C. (2015): Critical urban gardening. *Think Global, Eat Local: Exploring Foodways* 1: 13–17.

Certomà, C. and Tornaghi, C. (2015): Political gardening: transforming cities and political agency. *Local Environment* 20 (10): 1123–1131. http://doi.org/10.1080/13549839.2015.1053724

Chan, J., DuBois, B. and Tidball, K. (2015): Refuges of local resilience: community gardens in post-Sandy New York City. *Urban Forestry & Urban Greening* 14 (3): 625–635. https://doi.org/10.1016/j.ufug.2015.06.005

Cone, C. and Myhre, A. (2000): Community-supported agriculture: a sustainable alternative to industrial agriculture? *Human Organization* 59 (2): 187–197. http://doi.org/10.17730/humo.59.2.715203t206g2j153

Crouch, D. and Ward, C. (1997): *The Allotment: Its Landscape and Culture*. Nottingham: Five Leaves.

Crush, J., Hovorka, A. and Tevera, D. (2011): Food security in Southern African cities. *Progress in Development Studies* 11 (4): 285–305. http://doi.org/10.1177/1464993 41001100402

Feagan, R. (2007): The place of food: mapping out the 'local' in local food systems. *Progress in Human Geography* 31 (1): 23–42. http://doi.org/10.1177/0309132507073527

Finster, M. E., Gray, K. A. and Binns, H. J. (2004): Lead levels of edibles grown in contaminated residential soils: a field survey. *Science of the Total Environment* 320 (2–3): 245–257. http://doi.org/10.1016/j.scitotenv.2003.08.009

Firth, C., Maye, D. and Pearson, D. (2011): Developing 'community' in community gardens. *Local Environment* 16 (6): 555–568. http://doi.org/10.1080/13549839.2011.586025

Gallaher, C. M., Kerr, J. M., Njenga, M., Karanja, N. K. and WinklerPrins, A. M. G. A. (2013): Urban agriculture, social capital, and food security in the Kibera slums of Nairobi, Kenya. *Agriculture and Human Values* 30 (3): 389–404. http://doi.org/10.1007/s10460-013-9425-y

Hardt, M. and Negri, A. (2004): *Multitude: War and Democracy in the Age of Empire*. New York: Penguin.

Hassanein, N. (2003): Practicing food democracy: a pragmatic politics of transformation. *Journal of Rural Studies* 19 (1): 77–86. http://doi.org/10.1016/S0743-0167(02)00041-4

Hassanein, N. (2008): Locating food democracy: theoretical and practical ingredients. *Journal of Hunger & Environmental Nutrition* 3 (2–3): 286–308. http://doi.org/10.1080/19320240802244215

Hedin, K., Clark, E., Lundholm, E. and Malmberg, G. (2012): Neoliberalization of housing in Sweden: gentrification, filtering, and social polarization. *Annals of the Association of American Geographers* 102 (2): 443–463. http://doi.org/10.1080/00045608.2011.620508

Hermann, J. R., Parker, S. P., Brown, B. J., Youmasu, S. J., Denney, B. A. and Walker, S. J. (2006): After-school gardening improves children's reported vegetable intake and physical activity. *Journal of Nutrition Education and Behavior* 38 (3): 201–202. https://doi.org/10.1016/j.jneb.2006.02.002

Hoffman, A. J. and Doody, S. (2014): Build a fruit tree orchard and they will come: creating an eco-identity via community gardening activities. *Community Development Journal* 50 (1): 104–120. https://doi.org/10.1093/cdj/bsu023

Hou, J. (Ed.) (2010): *Insurgent Public Space: Guerrilla Urbanism and the Remaking of Contemporary Cities*. London: Routledge.

Hovorka, A. J. (2006): The No. 1 Ladies' Poultry Farm: a feminist political ecology of urban agriculture in Botswana. *Gender, Place & Culture* 13 (3): 207–225. http://doi.org/10.1080/09663690600700956

Jarosz, L. (2011): Nourishing women: toward a feminist political ecology of community supported agriculture in the United States. *Gender, Place & Culture* 18 (3): 307–326. http://doi.org/10.1080/0966369X.2011.565871

Julie Interview (2016): In Wright, R. L. (2018): Urban Agriculture: Established and Emerging Projects in Hull and Copenhagen. Doctor of Philosophy in Human Geography. University of Hull, Kingston Upon Hull, UK. Cameo 19 Urban Community Orchard 237.

Kato, Y., Passidomo, C. and Harvey, D. (2014): Political gardening in a post disaster city: lessons from New Orleans. *Urban Studies* 51 (9): 1–17. https://doi.org/10.1177/0042098013504143

Kirwan, J. (2004): Alternative strategies in the UK agro-food system: Interrogating the alterity of farmers' markets. *Sociologia Ruralis* 44 (4): 395–415. http://doi.org/10.1111/j.1467-9523.2004.00283.x

Lawson, L. J. (2005): *City Bountiful: A Century of Community Gardening in America.* London: University of California Press Ltd.

Lyons, K., Richards, C., Desfours, L. and Amati, M. (2013): Food in the city: urban food movements and (re)- imagining of urban spaces. *Australian Planner* 50 (2): 157–163. https://doi.org/10.1080/07293682.2013.776983

Marois, T. and Pradella, L. (2014): Polarising development: introducing alternatives to neoliberalism and the crisis. In: Pradella, L. and Marois, T. (Eds): *Polarizing Development: Alternatives to Neoliberalism and the Crisis.* London: Pluto Press, 1–12.

Mathers, A., Dempsey, N. and Frøik Molin, J. (2015): Place-keeping in action: evaluating the capacity of green space partnerships in England. *Landscape and Urban Planning* 139: 126–136. http://doi.org/10.1016/J.LANDURBPLAN.2015.03.004

McClintock, N. (2010): Why farm the city? Theorizing urban agriculture through a lens of metabolic rift. *Cambridge Journal of Regions, Economy and Society* 3 (2): 191–207. http://doi.org/10.1093/cjres/rsq005

McClintock, N. (2012): Assessing soil lead contamination at multiple scales in Oakland, California: implications for urban agriculture and environmental justice. *Applied Geography* 35 (1–2): 460–473. http://doi.org/10.1016/j.apgeog.2012.10.001

McClintock, N. (2014): Radical, reformist, and garden-variety neoliberal: coming to terms with urban agriculture's contradictions. *Local Environment* 19 (2): 147–171. http://doi.org/10.1080/13549839.2012.752797

McIvor, D. W. and Hale, J. (2015): Urban agriculture and the prospects for deep democracy. *Agriculture and Human Values* 32 (4): 727–741. http://doi.org/10.1007/s10460–015–9588–9

Milbourne, P. (2012): Everyday (in)justices and ordinary environmentalisms: community gardening in disadvantaged urban neighbourhoods. *Local Environment* 17 (9): 943–957. http://doi.org/10.1080/13549839.2011.607158

Mok, H.-F., Williamson, V. G., Grove, J. R., Burry, K., Barker, S. F. and Hamilton, A. J. (2014): Strawberry fields forever? Urban agriculture in developed countries: a review. *Agronomy for Sustainable Development* 34 (1): 21–43. http://doi.org/10.1007/s13593–013–0156–7

Musterd, S. and Ostendorf, W. (Eds) (2013): *Urban Segregation and the Welfare State: Inequality and Exclusion in Western Cities.* Abingdon: Routledge.

Ober Allen, J., Alaimo, K., Elam, D. and Perry, E. (2008): Growing vegetables and values: benefits of neighborhood-based community gardens for youth development and nutrition. *Journal of Hunger & Environmental Nutrition* 3 (4): 418–439. http://doi.org/10.1080/19320240802529169

Olssen, M. (2004): Neoliberalism, globalisation, democracy: challenges for education. *Globalisation, Societies and Education* 2 (2): 231–275. http://doi.org/10.1080/14767720410001733665

Ong, A. (2006): *Neoliberalism as Exception: Mutations in Citizenship and Sovereignty.* Durham, NC: Duke University Press.

Orsini, F., Kahane, R., Nono-Womdim, R. and Gianquinto, G. (2013): Urban agriculture in the developing world: a review. *Agronomy for Sustainable Development* 33 (4): 695–720. http://doi.org/10.1007/s13593–013–0143–z

Ousset, P. J., Nourhashemi, F., Albarede, J. L. and Vellas, P. M. (1998): Therapeutic gardens. *Archives of Gerontology and Geriatrics* 26: 369–372. http://doi.org/10.1016/S0167–4943(98)80053–8

Overbeek, H. (2012): Sovereign debt crisis in Euroland: root causes and implications for European integration. *The International Spectator* 47 (1): 30–48. http://doi.org/10.1080/03932729.2012.655006

Peck, J. (2012): Austerity urbanism: American cities under extreme economy. *City* 16 (6): 626–655. https://doi.org/10.1080/13604813.2012.734071

Purcell, M. and Tyman, S. K. (2015). Cultivating food as a right to the city. *Local Environment* 20 (10): 1132–1147. http://doi.org/10.1080/13549839.2014.903236

Randolph, B. and Tice, A. (2014): Suburbanising disadvantage in Australian cities: sociospatial change in an era of neoliberalism. *Journal of Urban Affairs* 36 (s1): 384–399. http://doi.org/10.1111/juaf.12108

Rawls, J. (1971): *A Theory of Justice.* Cambridge, MA: Harvard University Press. https://philpapers.org/rec/RAWATO-4

Reynolds, K. (2015): Disparity despite diversity: injustice in New York City's urban agriculture system. *Antipode* 47: 240–259. https://doi.org/10.1111/anti.12098

Schmelzkopf, K. (2002): Incommensurability, land use, and the right to space: community gardens in New York City. *Urban Geography* 23 (4): 323–343. http://doi.org/10.2747/0272-3638.23.4.323

Schroeder, R. A. (1993): Shady practice: gender and the political ecology of resource stabilization in Gambian garden/orchards. *Economic Geography* 69 (4): 349. http://doi.org/10.2307/143594

Scott, G. and Mooney, G. (2009): Poverty and social justice in the devolved Scotland: neoliberalism meets social democracy? *Social Policy and Society* 8 (3): 379. http://doi.org/10.1017/S1474746409004916

Skopek, N., Buchholz, S. and Blossfeld, H. P. (2011): *Wealth Inequality in Europe and the Delusive Egalitarianism of Scandinavian Countries.* Munich: Munich Personal RePEc Archive.

Soja, E. W. (2009): *The City and Spatial Justice.* Minneapolis: University of Minnesota Press.

von Hoffen, L. P. and Säumel, I. (2014): Orchards for edible cities: cadmium and lead content in nuts, berries, pome and stone fruits harvested within the inner city neighbourhoods in Berlin, Germany. *Ecotoxicology and Environmental Safety* 101: 233–239. http://doi.org/10.1016/j.ecoenv.2013.11.023

Walker, P. A. (2005): Political ecology: where is the ecology? *Progress in Human Geography* 29 (1): 73–82. http://doi.org/10.1191/0309132505ph530pr

Wekerle, G. R. (2004): Food justice movements. *Journal of Planning Education and Research* 23 (4): 378–386. http://doi.org/10.1177/0739456X04264886

Wekerle, G. R. and Classens, M. (2015): Food production in the city: (re)negotiating land, food and property. *Local Environment* 20 (10): 1175–1193. http://doi.org/10.1080/13549839.2015.1007121

Wendy Interview (2015): In: Wright, R. L. (2018): Urban Agriculture: Established and Emerging Projects in Hull and Copenhagen. Doctor of Philosophy in Human Geography. University of Hull, Kingston Upon Hull, UK. Cameo 16 Therapeutic Community Garden 218, 147.

Wolch, J. R., Byrne, J. and Newell, J. P. (2014): Urban green space, public health, and environmental justice: the challenge of making cities 'just green enough'. *Landscape and Urban Planning* 125: 234–244. http://doi.org/10.1016/j.landurbplan.2014.01.017

Zezza, A. and Tasciotti, L. (2010): Urban agriculture, poverty, and food security: empirical evidence from a sample of developing countries. *Food Policy* 35 (4): 265–273. http://doi.org/10.1016/j.foodpol.2010.04.007

3

City wastelands: creating places of vernacular democracy

Beata J. Gawryszewska, Maciej Łepkowski
and Anna Wilczyńska

Introduction

When considering the issue of social justice in relation to space and landscape, questions regarding human rights (Mitchell, 2016), green spaces distribution and accessibility and space preferences (Rigolon, 2016) need to be asked. Egoz et al. (2016) classified human rights into two groups, namely the right to means to sustain life, meaning resources supporting human biological existence, as well as the right to dignity, comprising the right of unrestrained exploitation and shaping of the surroundings.

The European Landscape Convention (Council of Europe, 2000) specifies landscape as an area, as viewed by individuals, whose character is the outcome of the action and communication of natural and human elements. This definition may be applied to every kind of space, especially to urban landscape. The continuing depletion of the natural resources of our planet, which could include the constantly shrinking urban greenery available to inhabitants, make it necessary to look for new landscapes which so far have been neglected in considerations on the subject of social justice. Urban wastelands are undoubtedly one of those landscapes.

There have been many studies devoted to the issue of wastelands, mainly in the context of their ecological values (Kowarik, 2011; Tredici, 2014) and the resulting tendency to transform such areas into places of ecological education (Jakubowski, 2015; Stöcker et al., 2014). Many cities can already boast vast achievements in this field among which there are parks designed and maintained with an aim to protect their natural resources, making them available at the same time. These include Schöneberger Südgelände, Park am Gleisdreieck in Berlin, Port Sunlight

Figure 3.1   Map of Warsaw

in Liverpool or the Warsaw Praska Ścieżka Rowerowa [Praga Cycling Route] through the Vistula marshy meadows.

Warsaw still has a relatively great number of wastelands as a result of its uneven development following the destruction of the Second World War, industrial collapse, absorption of agricultural lands as well as changes connected with railway infrastructure, etc. Many of these areas have taken over the function of developed urban green areas as an alternative and a complement to them (Łepkowski et al., 2016; Trzaskowska, 2008). In land-use plans and local development plans, an overwhelming number of these areas are intended for housing development (see Figure 3.1). This hunger for new residential premises does not decrease while there is a growing pressure for sensible State policy and undertaking real actions aimed at the reduction of this uncontrolled development. The Polish government states that in the near future development investments are going to be joined by a gigantic state housing scheme, 'Mieszkanie Plus', which means that both the capital city and other big cities in Poland await another wave of investments.

As a result, the majority of today's wastelands will be developed and new residential quarters will entail building new infrastructure and services, such as roads, schools, shops and churches, as well as parks and other green areas. In the future they will become green islands in the density of newly developed residential quarters and housing estates (see Figure 3.2). Today, they can be only distinguished from among hundreds of hectares of Warsaw's wastelands by their recording in planning documents, i.e. ZP (public greenery). However, these areas have their users who treat them as their everyday landscape. Regarding Ray Oldenburg's theory of third places (Oldenburg, 1989), wastelands are important element of the public spaces structure (Łepkowski et al., 2016).

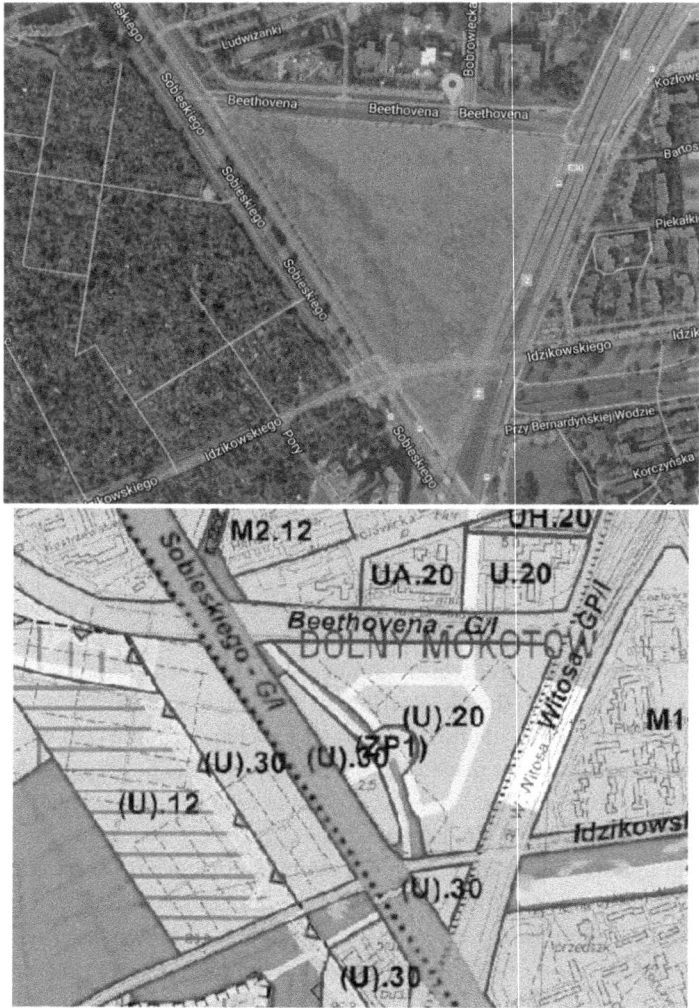

Figure 3.2   Example of Warsaw's wasteland transformations

Materials and methods

The first part of the research is based on the comparative assessment of ten selected case studies from Warsaw, conducted in the period of 2015–17. These case studies were selected according to the following criteria:

- free access, open areas;
- lack of municipal control;
- existence of free vegetated and uncultivated plants;
- located within the administrative borders of Warsaw, in different districts.

The Warsaw area was chosen to ensure the accessibility of the case studies for extended, in situ research across different seasons. Additionally, out of the ten case studies, five focus on lands intended for urban greenery within the framework of the research project *Inwentaryzacja i waloryzacja wybranych terenów zdegradowanych i zanieczyszczonych w Warszawie – potencjał przyrodniczy i społeczny nieużytków* [*Inventory and valorisation of selected degraded and polluted lands in Warsaw – natural and social potential of wastelands*], which since 2017 has been carried out by scientists from Warsaw University of Life Sciences at the request of the Department of Green Areas of the Capital City of Warsaw, while the remaining five cases, although being outside the interest of the Department of Green Areas and having no prospects for becoming green areas in the future, are a good example of bottom-up space development and vernacular land use.

The goal of the first part was to answer the questions:

- Who is the beneficiary of the wastelands' transformation?
- What is the function of the wastelands?
- Can wastelands, according their characteristic, be recognised within the concept of ecosystem services?

The second part of the research was the comparison of results from the first part with eight examples of transformation of urban wastelands in Poland, Lithuania, Switzerland, Germany, Spain and Portugal (Gawryszewska et al., 2016). The goal was to see whether and how the values and functions of informal space may be expressed in the design and whether and how should wastelands be transformed.

The principal methods of analysis within the framework of the case studies in question included:

- Inventory of territoriality markers – to establish the function of wastelands and the model of use.
- Inventory of plant groups types – to show free vegetation and manners of users' interference – interaction with plants (mowing, fruit picking, planting additional plants) as well as the connection between types of vegetation, the manner of use and the target group.
- Observation of the users' activities – to study a model of spatial use, main activities.
- Qualitative interviews – in order to determine users' profile, their needs fulfilled by the wastelands and places of recreation selected by the users. Interviews were focused on the topic of functions and motivations to visit the wastelands, as well as activities.

Case studies, examples and chosen methods are shown in Table 3.1.

Table 3.1 Specification of case studies, examples and data collection methodologies

Country	Town	Case study no.	Place name and characteristics	Methods
First part: comparative assessment of ten case studies from Warsaw				
Poland	Warsaw	1	Fort Służew: *c.* 1ha wasteland accompanying the former military fort, behind a residential area of semi-detached and terraced buildings.	Inventory, qualitative interviews, observations
		2	Siarczana: *c.* 1.8ha former private garden of nineteenth-century manufacturer's villa, near housing area of multi-family and semi-detached buildings and nineteenth-century tenements.	
		3	Bartycka: *c.* 6ha former allotment garden complex and wasteland, today a community garden by Reclaim the Fields Poland occupies half of the area.	
		4	Lektykarska: *c.* 1ha former wasteland, a multi-family building construction area, near detached housing estate.	
		5	Fort Bema: *c.* 12ha urban wasteland surrounding the old fort in the immediate vicinity of the new multi-family housing development.	
		6	Huta: *c.* 10ha land located between a large housing estate and a falling ironworks near the last subway station.	
		7	Railroad in Nowy Żoliborz: *c.* 0.5ha old railway siding in new residential area of multi-family block of flats, activists try to convert it into community line-park.	
		8	Górka Kazurka: *c.* 4ha urban wasteland with a high hill in the biggest Warsaw multi-family block-of-flats residential area – Ursynów.	

Table 3.1 (Cont.)

Country	Town	Case study no.	Place name and characteristics	Methods
		9	Sielecki Canal: *c.* 2ha urban wasteland near multi-family housing area and a big communication node near Siekierkowski Bridge.	
		10	Jazdów: *c.* 3ha social activity centre, NGO and community garden area built in former private family garden settlement of Finnish wooden houses in the centre of Warsaw.	

Secondpart: eight examples of transformation

Country	Town	Case study no.	Place name and characteristics	Methods
Switzerland	Basel	11	Holzpark Klybeck: *c.* 4.5ha, an open air cultural centre, created in the former port area under the long-term transformation process.	Ex-situ observations
Lithuania	Vilnius	12	Naujoji Vilnia, Linksmoji gatvė: *c.* 6.5ha wild meadow between two parts of a big multi-family block-of-flats settlement.	Qualitative interviews, ex-situ observations
Germany	Berlin	13	Prinzessinnengarten: 0.7ha community garden and social activity centre created on abandoned square.	Qualitative interviews, ex-situ observations
Spain	Barcelona	14	L'espai Germanetes: 0.5ha former wasteland in the highly populated district of Barcelona.	Ex-situ observations
Portugal	Portimao	15	Avenida das Olimpiadas garden: *c.* 0.2ha former wasteland with a small (*c.* 50m²) informal allotment garden.	Ex-situ observations
Germany	Berlin	16	Park am Gleisdreieck: 36ha park established at railway wasteland abandoned since Second World War.	Ex-situ observations
Poland	Warsaw	17	Park Kozłowskiego: *c.* 11ha park built at former informal allotment garden complex.	Qualitative interviews, ex-situ observations

(*continued*)

Table 3.1 (Cont.)

Country	Town	Case study no.	Place name and characteristics	Methods
Poland	Warsaw	18	Praska Ścieżka Rowerowa: *c.* 8.5km linear park built over the right side of the Vistula river, among a semi-natural marshy meadow.	Ex-situ observations

Who are the beneficiaries of the wastelands and how?

The problem of a lack of public services accompanying the residential function (including accessible green areas) is not so much evident in Polish cities as their uneven and chaotic distribution. The main reason for this state of affairs is the fact that for twenty-five years the shape and direction of urban development have been conditional upon private capital acting in the economic interest but not for public benefit (Buczek, 2014).

In this context, the role of wastelands may be perceived in two different ways: as a specific substitute of the deficit of the designed green areas and as their necessary complement. Both perspectives refer to the idea of spatial justice and even distribution of goods (Soja, 2009).

Wastelands as substitutes of parks

Deficiency of public green spaces constitutes one of the many evident negative results thereof. The inhabitants of such deficient areas are much less active, and the clear health consequences of it are emphasised by researchers and scientists (McCurdy et al., 2010). Whereas the lack of contact with nature leads to psychocultural disturbances popularised by means of the term Nature Deficit Disorder (Louv, 2005). What is more, the report of the World Health Organization, *Preventing Disease through Healthy Environments*, specifies that those most affected by the deficient urban environment are children, which means that the consequences of the present spatial dysfunctions will be suffered for many years, determining the lives of present and future families (Prüss-Üstün et al., 2016).

The lack of green areas in Warsaw is partially compensated by the neighbouring undeveloped lands (Trzaskowska, 2008) which may make up until 30 per cent of the entire city area (Zagospodarowanie przestrzenne, 2016). These are an extremely significant factor in the real estate market, since they influence individual decisions pertaining to the purchase of an apartment, where the neighbourhood of open spaces in the form of fields, shrubland, woods and other so-called wastelands is a big plus. However, due to their informal character in the first place, such lands cannot guarantee all the values of the park. They are not illuminated or cleaned. They lack hard surfaced paths and are not guarded by security services, etc. Therefore, the accessibility threshold is much higher for some groups of people such as the elderly – it is uncrossable, and the number of persons who actively use such lands is usually small. Furthermore, these lands are subject to successive disappearance. The situation in question took place in Warsaw district Bielany (case study four) where the residents of the premises neighbouring the wasteland protested when construction of a new housing estate started. Although the land was already inaccessible for a long time, they wanted to see trees from their windows and not multi-family estates.

Sometimes in response to such a state of affairs desperate residents get together to protect the remaining undeveloped space. The case of Warsaw district Nowy Żoliborz (case study seven), where there was no green public space provided for in land-use plans and development projects, may be an example. For several years, the residents have been fighting for the establishment of a linear park located along the unused railway siding – the last 'free' area in the neighbourhood going through almost the entire housing estate. Their attempts were finally recognised by a large number of inhabitants and the district authorities, which, supported by two cycles of the participatory budget, led to the area being cleaned, partially hard-surfaced and new architectural and sporting elements erected (see Figure 3.3). The corridor, a popular place for alcohol consumption (which is illegal in public areas in Poland), which used to be covered with bushes and litter, slowly became space that is popular and willingly visited by the new inhabitants of the area – the young middle class.

In Naujoji Vilnia, Linksmoji Gatvė (case study twelve), people go for walks with their dogs on 'a meadow'. This is a place for a walk, but also a place where medicinal herbs deemed as 'natural' may be obtained. Users said that this is a place where one can often meet hedgehogs, lizards, colourful butterflies or dragonflies. 'A two-minute walk from my home and I am "outside the city".'

Wastelands as gardens

According to the theory of the garden as a place in the inhabited landscape (Gawryszewska, 2013), the bottom-up creativity in wasteland landscape shows the natural human need to create gardens, territorialise space thereby adapting and appropriating it (Hennecke, 2016), to assign values and meanings, as well as to establish connections and attachment (Lewicka, 2011). In the model structure of the inhabited space there is continuity of developed (front garden and proper garden) and undeveloped space observed, which may be both within the territory of a real estate behind its fence, as well as outside it (being partially or totally undeveloped). The garden situated within the area of a real estate or in the front yard of a housing estate is therefore accompanied by the vicinity of lands that may be called wastelands (Gawryszewska, 2013).

Figure 3.3   Railroad wasteland in Nowy Żoliborz

The spatial structure of Fort Służew (case study one), a housing estate of terraced houses in Warsaw, is typical. There are small back gardens behind the buildings (approx. 300m²), which are followed by a wasteland located partially on the crown and partially on the escarpment of the historical fort's moat. The land is planted with half-natural plants which are similar in species composition to the oak-hornbeam forests. On the flat area of the fort's crown, between the residents' own gardens and the escarpment, an informal park was built (see Figure 3.4). The inhabitants of the estate planted ornamental trees and shrubs there, adding benches and picnic tables as well as setting up firepits. When asked for the reason for developing this part of the wasteland, they said that they wished to make this space more attractive as well as to develop it since 'there used to be nothing here'. What is more, they said that such a partially developed area is 'natural' on one hand and safer on the other. It is interesting that the

Figure 3.4   Fort Służew residential area

inhabitants felt responsible for the space located near their homes, which constituted a natural continuation of the gardens. The further area remained undeveloped, and the residents' attitude towards it is communicated by the sign saying 'Do not enter! There is only an animal path further. Do not scare animals. There is no way down here'.

A slightly different situation can be observed in Targówek, at Siarczana Street (case study two), where, because of not having a single park available for a walk, the residents of the old terraced houses and substandard multi-family buildings visit the old garden located at the nineteenth-century factory owner's residence to walk their dogs, to meet others for a beer or go jogging in the morning. They claim that 'there are no places to go to' in their neighbourhood and indicate 'the need for some green space' near their houses. Moreover, they say that they have no gardens and the nearest park is located too far away, and everyday access to greenery is indispensable, especially for children.

In Warsaw Ursynów between the Kabacki urban forest and the buildings of a large housing estate, there is a large wasteland with a hill commonly referred to as Górka Kazurka [Mount Kazurka] (case study eight). The residents of the buildings, constituting a multi-family housing estate, set up their own windowsill gardens. What is more, they mow the grass and keep order in the area of the wasteland, thus treating it as continuation of their inhabited space. They claim that 'order is indispensable', 'it is safer this way since one cannot see what is going on in the area if the grass is too high', as well as that 'it is necessary to look after the land so that it is not overgrown with grass'. The last response is typical for home garden owners when asked for the reason for mowing lawns frequently, especially if they do not use them for recreational purposes. What is even more interesting is the fact that grass with a height of fifteen centimetres is deemed 'too high' as 'one cannot see what is in there'. On the other hand, high shrubs on wastelands that are located further away do not bother the people, and are even regarded as a feature of the 'natural' land.

Urban wasteland spaces also include abandoned gardens such as Rodzinne Ogrody Działkowe (allotment gardens in Poland). For example, the garden at Bartycka St. (case study three) is a place where anarchists from the Reclaim the Fields group set up a social garden where they grow fruit and vegetables and meet almost every day to share their opinions and tighten bonds (see Figure 3.5). Apart from vegetable beds, fruit trees 'inherited' from the old allotment garden and temporary houses, the members of the group created meeting spots with seats, firepits, a clay bread oven and a 'shop' aimed at the free exchange of goods. However, community gardens are not only created on abandoned gardens. There are plenty examples of gardens created on wasteland areas, which include, for

Figure 3.5   Community garden by Reclaim the Fields Poland, Bartycka St. in Warsaw

example: abandoned plazas (Prinzessinnengärten in Berlin), parks (Fort Bema in Warsaw) or in between blockhouses like in Portimao, Portugal, where despite the fact that the town has a scheme of establishing allotment gardens for the poorest residents, the need to have one's own plot of land to grow vegetables is so great that the list of those waiting for an allotment usually exceeds the number of the available plots by a few dozen.[1] Consequently, the inhabitants set up illegal allotments near their apartments, in their blocks of flats. On the unused land located within the housing estate near the Continente Shopping Centre at Av. das Olímpiadas in Portimao (case study fifteen) are plant beds with tomatoes, beans, lettuce and herbs, hidden among high wild plants, away from the eyes of pedestrians.

The aforementioned examples illustrate that as every gardener takes care of his garden, creates it as continuation and official entrance to the house, every inhabitant of a housing estate in a big city looks after space near his apartment, thus creating his own place of inhabitation. Consequently, a variety of bottom–up interventions create an authentic and specific materialisation of vernacular democracy leading to 'The right to the city' which 'is far more than the individual liberty to access urban resources: it is a right to change ourselves by changing the city' (Harvey, 2008: 23).

Wastelands as inhabited space

The unofficial nature and lack of direct control make wastelands places where activities that do not fit in urban spaces or are removed from them may take place. Therefore, such lands become a shelter for excluded people. In Warsaw, these people are mainly homeless. All the areas subject to the study showed lesser or greater marks left by the homeless, whereas the majority of the studied lands were inhabited to a certain extent.

One of the examples of inhabitation includes an area along the Sielecki Canal (case study nine), a small waterway in the south of Warsaw with sides overgrown with freely vegetating plants such as trees and shrubs, and undergrowth from herbs. Along the thicket, on the border with an open meadow-like area, there is a well-worn path. The inhabitants of the nearby housing estates use it for walks with their dogs or to shorten the way to the areas located on the other side of the wasteland. Every several dozen metres there are small paths leading away from the beaten track, which then disappear in the tight thicket of the undergrowth and crowns of low trees (residents do not go there). The paths go through the bushes to the water canal where two makeshift shelters, as well as plenty of temporary beds with loads of the so-called rubbish, are located. The houses include a dugout and a tent 200 metres further away. There is a small space in their direct vicinity,

---

[1] The data were collected during a conversation with Thomas Panagopoulos, an employee of the University in Faro, as well as during a site inspection at one of the locations of the gardens in the former wastelands conducted on 16 June 2017.

Figure 3.6 Homeless people's habitation on wastelands

namely quasi-front-yards with a firepit, dishes, clothes left to dry, etc. Both of the places are inhabited all year, in winter as well.

Another example of an inhabited wasteland is located in Bemowo district, in the neighbourhood of the old fortification – Fort Bema (case study five). The main path used by the residents of the area has a specific bypass – a path which, at the entrance to the area, goes to the side to form an arch with a length of approximately one kilometre, and finally joins the main path at its end. In its middle, this alternative track goes up a small hill covered with a pile of multicoloured litter. On the hilltop there is a settlement of homeless persons consisting of six shelters set up next to a common yard with a firepit, tables, seats, etc. (see Figure 3.6). Due to the dense tree stand, the people or the buildings cannot be spotted from the outside and it is only after reaching the top that one realises the place is inhabited.

The third example refers to a wasteland located in the Warsaw district that is furthest to the north, namely Bielany. The wasteland is located on the border of a post-industrial area of ironwork (case study six). It is separated with tram railways and a street from the side of the housing estate, and with a tall wall from the side of the ironwork. The area is practically entirely wooded, cut with intersecting paths and a small waterway. Walking along this densely wooded canal, one goes to a small forest glade where are two permanently inhabited houses similar to summer houses. One of the houses has a garden patch with vegetables, as well as a dove-cote and a large pile of construction materials, which were probably brought there from the nearby construction sites. There is a bath, toilet and many old windows piled there. The people living there collect hay – under temporary roofing there is a large pile formed from bundles of hay, which shows that there may be animals reared there, e.g. rabbits.

The aforementioned examples, as well as the remaining lands subject to the study, most of all prove that almost every wasteland is to some extent inhabited by the homeless. Such settlements have not been observed on the wastelands situated at a greater distance from inhabited areas.

The second observation pertains to the structure of space – the inhabited space is totally hidden from the eyes of other users. Reaching such areas requires going off the beaten track, through sometimes dense shrubs and trees, to the furthest land fragments. This spontaneously created spatial structure provides a feeling of privacy and security for the homeless people. Considering the strategy of clearing urban public space from different signs of its informal use, wastelands become one of the few places where homeless persons who cannot, do not want to or do not qualify for official support may find a relatively safe shelter. This type of inhabitation is tolerated by security services and land owners until the presence of such people becomes too evident or troublesome. Staying invisible is in their interest.

Wastelands as places designed from the bottom up

Pursuant to the observations made, as well as on the basis of the inventory of territoriality markers of chosen wastelands, exclusion from the 'official' functioning in urban space seems to constitute the principal value of such areas. Due to the free nature of these lands, they act proactively on the user, thereby allowing subjective perception of space and its grassroots creation (permitted to every user, irrespective of his social status) (Gawryszewska et al., 2016). During her speech at a conference 'Growing in Cities in Switzerland', Stefanie Hennecke (2016) emphasised the creative potential provided by 'dysfunctional' space, which does not in any way imply that it is 'non-functional'. In fact, by the lack of control such space provides the possibility of diversified bottom-up actions, including those which are banned in cities for many reasons but are necessary for the inhabitants to be able to engage in a dialogue with the landscape.

In line with the above-mentioned functions and users, according to our observations, wastelands are filled with man-made small architecture: benches, firepits, stages, playgrounds, places to walk a dog, etc. Often, old or discarded elements which seem to be only rubbish find their second life there in the form of well-worn paths, passages through old roads or concrete plates as well

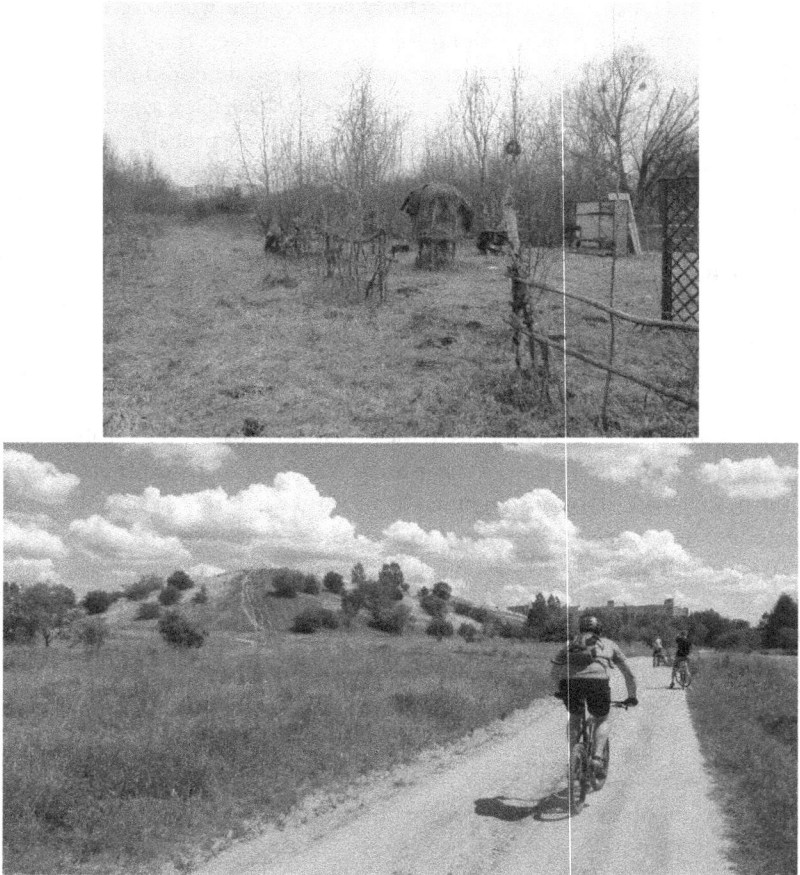

Figure 3.7   Transforming and adapting wastelands

as wildflower beds and rubbish bins and finally a variety of tables and benches or even a professional biking track (case study eight) (see Figure 3.7).

In some cases, local cultural centres are built on wastelands. This was the case for the Jazdów housing estate (case study ten) where a local cultural centre inspired and run by a society of non-governmental organisations was set up in place of the former housing estate. L'espai Germanetes in Barcelona (case study fourteen), Prinzessinnengarten in Berlin (case study thirteen) or Holzpark Klybeck in Basel (case study eleven) are examples of similar places. The hallmark of bottom-up management for all these places are social gardens with specific vernacular aesthetics: elevated plant beds, crops in bags and other casual containers, giving an impression of a 'natural mess'.

When discussing the examples, one must notice that wastelands designed from the bottom up have got their specific character, resulting from the specificity of their development. The image of a wasteland appropriated by its users is some-times the hallmark of communities which decided to take the decisions on their surroundings into their own hands. Familiarity and vernacularism of the land-scape of wastelands evident for each and every passer-by thanks to the freely vegetating greenery 'undisturbed' by municipal services is a message that in such space one may be afforded the luxury of a greater freedom to act.

Wastelands as social benefits under the theory of ecosystem services

Taking into account the variety of landscape values provided by wastelands, their function and benefits being the consequence of active coexistence of people and landscape, in the process of their assessment one may refer to the concept of ecosystem services (CICES, 2012). As stated at the beginning of this chapter, wastelands enable the users to enforce their rights to means to sustain life which are included in the following services: provisioning as well as regulation and maintenance (oxygen production, maintenance of the microclimate, soil remedi-ation and making independent food production possible), as well as the right to dignity, freedom in shaping one's own surroundings and giving them identity, and finally the right to participate in the decision-making process, which fall within the group of cultural services.

As far as the studied wastelands are concerned, both physical and practical use of landscape was observed, walking with dogs, gardening, everyday recre-ation, social meetings promoting social integration, and even inhabitation. Moreover, wastelands are also a place where intangible aspects such as the feeling of attachment to the place, admiring the nature and willingness to preserve it for future generations, are rendered (CICES, 2012).

Another benefit is the feeling of having skills, described in the CICES-Be (Turkelboom et al., 2013) assessment on the example of photographs, which in the case of wastelands include gardening skills, knowledge of herbs, craftwork and small construction works as well as the skill to build new artefacts if needed (Gawryszewska et al., 2016). Wastelands seem to be a perfect tool in shaping the need to participate in the decision-making process and grassroots management, as well as in encouraging creative attitudes that are indispensable in order to build vernacular democracy.

Wastelands as a design problem

Despite the fact that the 'wastelands' referred to in this chapter are commonly deemed as empty and forgotten, they constitute places where both human and non-human actors (Latour, 2010) may find their own space for bottom-up cre-ation. Polish researchers call this phenomenon 'an invisible city' (Krajewski, 2013) regarded as an integral part of the urban tissue which, although present, is invisible for municipal authorities.

The phenomenon of 'an invisible city' may be an inspiration for the transform-ation of unused space. But how can one set directions when it is not obvious who the target group is, or when local communities are not visible or excluded from the society? The present research show that comprehensive observation of what is happening on wastelands is of utmost importance to indicate to local authorities what wastelands for different human and non-human actors (Latour, 2010) mean, why these places are important for an urban landscape and how they could be managed to keep spontaneously created functions and values (Gawryszewska et al., 2016). Unlike the principles of tactical urbanism in which by means of temporary activities the author/designer emphasises spatial values trying to activate space and change its perception, in the case of wastelands this process needs to be started from research on the activities and perceptions that already exist. It should not be presumed that wastelands are places that require 'activation' or a kind of 'repair'.

Designing urban wastelands may be inspired by the example of Park am Gleisdreieck (case study sixteen) opened in 2011 in Berlin. This place used to be abandoned and covered with railways so the city decided to develop this land. The winning design, prepared by Atelier Loidl, did not provide for creating a classical urban park anew but it was based on the spontaneously formed function and aesthetics of the place, which may be observed in the present function of the park. There is a modern skate park or playground, as well as a green field to have a picnic or play games, and finally a spontaneous forest being the characteristic feature of the wasteland aesthetics (Geiger and Hennecke, 2015).

Similar examples can be found in Warsaw. A fragment of Park Kozłowskiego (case study seventeen), where allotment gardens used to be located, was initially intended for a traditional park with lawns and benches. Thanks to the inhabitants' interventions, who knew the area by walking there with their dogs or admiring wild birds, etc., the character of the 'wild allotments' with pergolas overgrown by wild vines, blossoming perennials and high herb fringes was preserved. Only the necessary water-permeable surfaces and new plant supports were built, as well as new benches being installed (see Figure 3.8). Another example is a linear park (case study eighteen) located in the city centre, on the right side of the Vistula river, among a semi-natural marshy meadow, within Natura 2000 protected area. Along the 8.5km promenade, which was set by its users to follow the old, infor-mally used route, no new plants were planted and no new development was introduced, apart from wooden seats, rubbish bins and a water-permeable surface imitating water sand.

The aforementioned parks were set up on spontaneously used wastelands with respect to the local ecosystem and aesthetics. But has the essence of the wastelands been preserved? The essence regarded as the liberty to explore and, most import-antly, to transform land, which provokes the feeling of unrestrained management and agency in creating places full of identity with which their users can identify? Has the problem of homelessness been really solved there? And maybe it is time to develop new forms of urban greenery such as, for instance, micro reserves where

Figure 3.8   New part of Kozłowski Park in Warsaw, a former wasteland on a place of informal allotment garden area

no type of activity connected with plant maintenance is allowed? Certainly, the idea of a grassroots transformation of wasteland in the spirit of 'Do-It-Yourself' or 'Do-It-Together' in the light of contemporary procedures of participatory democracy should not raise doubts. These new strategies need to involve all the present users as well as the homeless, whose presence should be supported by all the possible means, e.g. by building micro houses, as is the case in Jazdów (case study ten).

Conclusion

When speaking of spatial justice with respect to urban wastelands, distributive and performative justice (Jamal and Hales, 2016) may be distinguished. One is when the lands are deemed to constitute a substitute for the designed green areas, the other when wastelands are regarded as the necessary complement of the system of public urban areas. Referring to the deliberations of Peter Marcuse, it may be stated that these values have the character of the commons and their protection corresponds with the commons planning approach (Marcuse, 2009).

Who is therefore the beneficiary of wastelands? The beneficiaries are all the city's inhabitants, especially those underprivileged whose access to the faraway green areas is hindered. At this point, children and the elderly should be taken into consideration since their everyday access to green areas is of special significance. Wastelands are useful even for those who do not use them in physical terms, but who treat them as natural resources, which improve the quality of life in biological terms.

Wastelands are the indispensable complement of the everyday inhabited space since by complementing the structure formed by houses, gardens and undeveloped areas they become a tool of building places and their identities, followed by attachment to the place with which its residents identify as much as with their homes. Finally, wastelands are also places where homeless people may find a semblance of decent life.

Wastelands have formed a vernacular image connected with the character of the plants that grow and freely vegetate there, but also with the equipment made by the users themselves. The connection between the character of such groups of plants and the target users should be noted at this point. Unlike other users, the homeless prefer high bushes and areas almost entirely covered with tree crowns, far away from the beaten tracks and residential premises. Other users wishing to explore lands prefer places in which plants are not higher than their waistlines and with maintained visibility.

Lands that are used informally and transformed from the bottom up, which wastelands undoubtedly are, encourage creative attitudes, which is reflected in social gardens and other centres of social activity that are built there.

These, and the aforementioned values of wastelands, lead to the fact that they render a series of ecosystem services representing all the groups of services listed in the Common International Classification of Ecosystem Services. These services may carry a real economic value. The users are deprived of that value when the land is lost as a result of its development.

Green areas planned in place of wastelands require a new design approach that would preserve their vernacular image and grassroots creation as well as supporting creative attitudes and social participation, which are the key in creating the conditions and procedures for the local vernacular democracy using the idea of the commons.

References

Buczek, A. (2014): Aktualne problemy rozwoju gospodarki przestrzennej na terenach zurbanizowanych w Polsce. http://ucbs.uw.edu.pl/wp-content/uploads/Buczek-MIASTO-IDEALNE.pdf (accessed 26 July 2017).

CICES: Common International Classification of Ecosystem Services (CICES) (2012): http://biodiversity.europa.eu/maes/common-international-classification-of-ecosystem-services-cices-classification-version-4.3 (accessed 5 June 2016).

Council of Europe (2000): European Landscape Convention. www.coe.int/en/web/conventions/full-list/-/conventions/rms/0900001680080621 (accessed 6 April 2018).

Egoz, S., Makhzoumi, J. and Pungetti, G. (2016): The right to landscape: an introduction In: Egoz, S., Makhzoumi, J. and Pungetti, G. (Eds): *The Right to Landscape: Contesting Landscape and Human Rights*. London and New York: Routledge, 1–20.

Gawryszewska, B. J. (2013): *Ogród jako miejsce w krajobrazie zamieszkiwanym*. Warsaw: Wieś Jutra.

Gawryszewska, B. J., Wilczyńska, A. and Łepkowski, M. (2016): Urban wastelands and their potential to deliver CICES community services. In: Tappert, S. (Ed.): *Growing in Cities: Interdisciplinary Perspectives on Urban Gardening Conference*. Basel: University of Applied Sciences, 387–404.

Geiger, A. and Hennecke, S. (2015): Gleisdreieck Park: a modern volkspark. In: Lichtenstein, A. and Mameli, F. A. (Eds): *Gleisdreieck / Parklife Berlin*. Berlin: Transcript Verlag, 230–237.

Harvey, D. (2008): The right to the city. *New Left Review* 53. https://newleftreview.org/II/53/david-harvey-the-right-to-the-city (accessed 23 July 2017).

Hennecke, S. (2016): Adaptation, appropriation and administration of 'dysfunctional' urban open space. Keynote presentation at Growing in Cities: Interdisciplinary Perspectives on Urban Gardening International Conference. Basel, Switzerland (9 September 2016).

Jakubowski, K. (2015): 'Unapparent beauty': the role of urban wastelands for the shaping of a new category of city parks. *Przestrzeń i forma* 24 (2): 145–162.

Jamal, T. and Hales, R. (2016): Performative justice: new directions in environmental and social justice. *Geoforum* 76: 176–180.

Kowarik, I. (2011): Novel urban ecosystems, biodiversity and conservation. *Environmental Pollution* 159 (8–9): 1974–1983.

Krajewski, M. (2013): *Niewidzialne miasto*. Warsaw: Fundacja Bęc Zmiana.

Latour, B. (2010): *Splatając na nowo to, co społeczne. Wprowadzenie do teorii aktora-sieci*. Krakow: Universitas.

Łepkowski, M., Nejman, R. and Wilczyńska, A. (2016): The role of green urban wastelands in 3rd place creation: challenge for urban policy in Poland. In: Jombach, S., Valanszki, I., Filep-Kovacs, K., Fabos, J. G., Ryan, R. L., Lindhult, M. S. and Kollanyi, L. (Eds): *Landscapes and Greenways of Resilience, Proceedings of 5th Fabos Conference on Landscape and Greenway Planning*. Budapest: Szent Istvan Egyetem, 45–53.

Lewicka, M (2011): Place attachment: how far have we come in the last 40 years? *Journal of Environmental Psychology* 31 (3): 207–230.

Louv, R. (2005): *Last Child in the Woods: Saving Our Children from Nature-Deficit Disorder*. Chapel Hill: Algonquin Books.

Marcuse, P. (2009): From justice planning to commons planning. In: Marcuse, P., Connolly, J., Novy, J., Olivo, I., Potter, C. and Steil, J. (Eds): *Searching for a Just City*. Abingdon and New York: Routledge, 91–102.

McCurdy, L. E., Winterbottom, K. E., Mehta, S. S. and Roberts, J. R. (2010): Using nature and outdoor activity to improve children's health. *Current Problems in Pediatric and Adolescent Health Care* 40 (5): 102–117.

Mitchell, D. (2016): Foreword. In: Egoz, S., Makhzoumi, J. and Pungetti, G. (Eds): *The Right to Landscape: Contesting Landscape and Human Rights*. London and New York: Routledge, xxi–xxiii.

Oldenburg, R. (1989): *The Great Good Place: Cafes, Coffee Shops, Community Centers, Beauty Parlors, General Stores, Bars, Hangouts, and How They Get You Through the Day*. New York: Paragon House.

Prüss-Ustün, A., Wolf, J., Corvalán, C., Bos, R. and Neira, M. (2016): WHO report: preventing disease through healthy environments: a global assessment of the burden of disease from environmental risks. http://apps.who.int/iris/bitstream/10665/204585/1/9789241565196_eng.pdf?ua=1 (accessed 23 July 2017).

Rigolon, A. (2016): A complex landscape of inequity in access to urban parks: a literature review. *Landscape and Urban Planning* 153: 160–169.

Soja, E. W. (2009): The city and spatial justice [La ville et la justice spatiale, traduction: Sophie Didier, Frédéric Dufaux]. In: *justice spatiale | spatial justice* | 1, www.jssj.org/wp-content/uploads/2012/12/JSSJ1–1en4.pdf (accessed 7 April 2018).

Stöcker, U., Suntken, S. and Wissel, S. (2014): A new relationship between city and wilderness: a case for wilder urban nature. www.duh.de/fileadmin/user_upload/download/Projektinformation/Kommunaler_Umweltschutz/Wild_Cities/A-case-for-wilder-urban-nature.pdf (accessed 22 July 2017).

Tredici, P. (2014): The flora of the future: celebrating the botanical diversity of cities. https://placesjournal.org/article/the-flora-of-the-future/ (accessed 26 July 2017).

Trzaskowska, E. (2008): The role of the synanthropic plants community in urban recreation places. *Nauka Przyroda Technologie* 2 (4): 1–8.

Turkelboom, F., Raquez, P., Dufrene, M., Raes, L., Simoens, I., Jacobs, S., Stevens, M., Vreese, R., De Panis, J., Hermy, M., Thoonen, M., Liekens, I., Fontaine, C., Dendoncker, N., van der Biest, K., Casaer J., Heyrman, H., Meiresonne, L., Keune, H. and Dufrène, M. (2013): CICES going local: ecosystem services classification adapted for a highly populated country. In: Jacobs, S., Dendoncker, N. and Keune, H. (Eds): *Ecosystem Services: Global Issues, Local Practices*. Boston: Elsevier, 223–247.

Zagospodarowanie przestrzenne (2016): Analiza na potrzeby opracowania diagnozy strategicznej. Program Warszawa 2030, Biuro Architektury i Planowania Przestrzennego Urzędu m.st. Warszawy, Warsaw.

4

Temporary urban landscapes and urban gardening: re-inventing open space in Greece and Switzerland

Sofia Nikolaidou

Introduction

New forms of urban gardening are gaining momentum in cities, transforming the conventional use and functions of open green and public space. They often take place through the informal and temporal (re-)use of vacant land 'that is considered to have little market value' (Schmelzkopf, 1995: 364), as part of greening strategies or social policy. The increased adoption of such forms within urban areas underlines discussions of changing contemporary social and productive urban landscapes by raising important issues, regarding new modes of land-use management, green space governance and collaborative approaches. This chapter mainly focuses on the shifted meanings of the notion of open public space by referring to its openness to a diversity of uses and users that claim it and relates to spatial justice questions of access rights, power relations among actors, negotiations and the so-called right to use and re-appropriate land (Hackenbroch, 2013).

The long tradition of allotment gardens in many European countries has always been a significant element of green open space and urban landscapes. A more flexible approach to urban gardening transforms its conventional characteristics and is adapted to dense urban settings with rather small-scale and temporary interventions that diversify the use and functions of open green and public space. Contemporary forms of gardening initiatives derive from either public actors, grassroots movements or more collaborative governance patterns that combine various groups of stakeholders. This seems to lead to the gradual development of a wide range of social public spaces and urban green areas challenging related planning practices and food sustainability (Nikolaidou et al., 2016).

Various forms of emerging practices and motivations of urban gardening across countries are subjected to the contextual effects of different social transformation processes, levels of urbanisation and industrialisation that affect the availability and use of open space in growing agglomerations. Furthermore a north–south divide can be observed regarding the use of open space and related policies: northern European countries place an emphasis on urban greening, while southern European countries focus more on the socio-economic effects of gardening in the context of crisis and on social inclusion (De Sousa, 2003; Ioannou et al., 2016; Prové et al., 2015).

The need to relate new forms of urban gardening with urban greening strategies and preservation of open spaces is increasing in urbanised cities (Chiesura, 2004) in order to adapt to a growing demand for housing, low open-space availability and diversified needs for open green space in the inner city through the development of long-term scenarios of densification (Nikolaidou et al., 2016). Hence, new flexible forms of small-scale and temporary urban gardens are gaining popularity in green planning practices, especially within dense metropolitan centres where population and economic decline create brownfields (Hula et al., 2016).

At the same time, harsh political and economic conditions and globally induced economic crisis, urban poverty and food insecurity empower the importance of subsistence gardening by enhancing its contribution to the healthy nutrition of cities, even in developed countries (FAO, 2010; Zezza and Tasciotti, 2010). This trend recalls the self-sufficiency gardens that flourished significantly during industrialisation and the world wars in response to severe food crises specifically targeting the poor urban population. In particular, economic decline and negative socio-economic impacts of austerity measures in southern Europe gave a boost to socially oriented policies regarding urban gardening and further mobilised a vibrant urban socio-political movement that symbolically re-appropriates public space.

In this context, food discourses and practices of urban gardening are increasingly recognised as social, environmental and spatial justice issues that generally embrace values of social fairness and equity. Urban gardening is seen as a way to reclaim, create, access and manage urban green space by growing food in urban areas. Therefore it refers to the equal right and opportunities of all citizens to use the resources of urban green space (Wolch et al., 2014) as well as to produce them in an attempt to (re-)appropriate open space (based on Lefebvre's revived notion of the 'right to the city') without locational discrimination and distributional inequalities (Soja, 2009). Discussion about food justice is also centred around access to healthy food and food resource distribution by focusing on the right to food as a component of a more democratic and just society (Wekerle, 2004). Apart from the social and distributive aspects of justice that focus on the (re-)distribution of resources, the notion of spatial justice has a procedural dimension that is closely related to democratisation through inclusiveness and participation in the process of policy elaboration and during implementation (Branduini et al., 2016: 44).

Overall, these new forms of urban gardening re-shape contemporary green space, while allowing the possibility to collectively use space and experiment with commoning practices (Stavrides, 2015). This raises new concerns for planning, design and forms of governance of urban open space. Public spaces regain their strategic importance and are re-invented and re-appropriated through multifunctional and diversified uses (Hackenbroch, 2013), new modes of land-use management and green space governance. Increasing alternative collaboration patterns among several civic and public actors create synergies that foster more inclusive and alternative economic and social functions of public space (Nikolaidou et al., 2016; Prové et al., 2015). Some understand these new participatory processes as an opportunity for citizens to get involved in policy-making and in re-inventing urban spaces (Elwood, 2002; Ghose, 2005). Additionally, it is considered as a significant element in the shift from a pattern of traditional local government to one of local governance that promotes more inclusive processes in decision-making (Geddes, 2006; Philips and Orsini, 2002). However, according to a more critical approach of the consensus-oriented governance model, the politics of 'invited' and state-led participation can in practice 'abuse', 'depoliticise' and control social movements and civil society, thus imposing a context of new power relations (Holston, 1998, Hackenbroch, 2013). Nevertheless, these forms of food provisioning in urban space intersect food geography and civil society with cities, planning, environment, wellbeing and culture and can therefore contribute to various desirable democratic outcomes (Gottlieb and Joshi, 2010; Slocum et al., 2016).

By using examples drawn from Greek and Swiss cases, this chapter advances comparative research under a European perspective. The aim is to call attention to the critical role of the temporary nature of urban gardening initiatives in relation to their multifunctional, spatial and socio-political aspects that affect new configurations of urban green areas and public space as well as related planning practices for spatial justice.

Method and research questions

Based on empirical research in Athens and Geneva, this chapter provides the reader with a comparative macroscopic understanding of the main differences and similarities in urban gardening practices, social and institutional contexts, collaborative governance patterns, motivations, levels of institutionalisation, and how they affect new configurations of urban green areas and public spaces as well as related planning practices through the lens of social and spatial justice. Therefore, this chapter intends to investigate:

- What are the driving factors in each context and what forms of space and governing structures do they generate?
- How do these growing spaces influence the usability and accessibility of open/public space in terms of spatial justice?
- What are the potentials, constraints, future prospects and urban policy implications of such urban gardening projects for sustainable development incentives and urban resilience?

In order to answer these questions in a comparative way, the overall approach is selective and emphasises on the case of municipal initiatives in the two contexts. The method was therefore focused on the analysis of general policy documents and publications that refer to urban gardening and the selected case studies, and the conduction of ten stakeholder face-to-face interviews with key informants: representatives of the Municipality of Geneva (UAC, SEVE, Urban Planning), NGO 'Equiterre', Planning and Social Policy departments in Municipalities of Maroussi and Agios Dimitrios (Athens, Greece). The interviews in Geneva were realised from August 2014 until November 2014 and in Athens, from 2013, with continuous complementary improvements and updates of data until 2017. Interview questions contained main information about the motivations, objectives and future prospects of the project, the actors involved and synergies (participation, organisation, decision-making, funding and space), positive effects and problems faced at different phases of the project.

Emerging trends and policy frameworks of urban gardening in different contexts: urban greening and social cohesion

Greece: urban poverty and social inclusion

In Greece, urban gardening, either in the form of community or municipal gardens, appears very late without pre-existing forms of organised urban farming on individual or collective basis. The great boom was noticed after 2011 with the emergence of municipal allotment gardens. Their appearance coincides with the outbreak of the financial crisis, a social demand for food re-localisation and the parallel activation of citizen movements against the privatisation of public land and natural resources (Nikolaidou and Kolokouris, 2016). Since the onset of the financial crisis, a special emphasis was put on social and economic deprivation, food insecurity and the risk of malnutrition. Apart from self-sufficiency targets in food production these initiatives also address environmental, landscape and cultural functions and the need for quality of life in urban centres (pollution, lack of public spaces, parks and greenery) (Anthopoulou et al., 2015; Ioannou et al., 2016).

In Athens this newly emerging movement deriving both 'from below' and from public actors, has generated innovative forms of alternative collective spaces of sociability and solidarity actions. We can clearly distinguish two main streams that frame the most prominent existing trends in urban gardening:

• Self-governed community gardens that derive from the civil society as alternative forms of protest against controversial neoliberal policies that promote privatisation of public land and natural resources. Usually located without authorisation on misused or abandoned land in the city fringe, their purpose is to claim land rights, social and spatial injustices through alternative forms of production, space appropriation, social interaction and decision-making.

- Spontaneous public initiatives mainly deriving from the local administration as a social policy oriented to combat crisis stress and social exclusion of vulnerable groups (pensioners, unemployed, those on low incomes, single-parent families, etc.) as well as to promote togetherness, social interaction at the neighbourhood level. Hence, municipal initiatives are subsistence gardens for self-production (not commercialised) of fresh organic vegetables while 10 per cent of the production is offered to the 'municipal social grocery'[1] as a response to the impacts of the debt crisis on poverty and income (Anthopoulou et al., 2015; 2018).

Thus, both types of initiatives play a substantial role in urban poverty and food insecurity reduction.

Switzerland: urban densification and open green space management

In comparison to Greece, urban gardening in Switzerland in the form of allotment/family gardens has a longer tradition that dates back to the nineteenth and twentieth centuries and contextually coincides with the development of the industrialisation (Klöti et al., 2016). However, newer forms of urban gardening that have recently arisen in many Swiss cities, contradict and question traditional approaches and large-scale patterns of classical allotment gardens which are no longer supported (Nikolaidou et al., 2016). They arise in a context of urban densification processes, as small-scale, multifunctional and temporary projects with high accessibility and a minimum of infrastructure. These flexible forms of urban gardening (community, intercultural, neighbourhood and guerrilla gardening) are therefore assumed to be more compatible with the current planning paradigm as a strategy to facilitate social interaction and neighbourhood greening while increasing building density in inner cities (Klöti et al., 2016; Nikolaidou, 2014). Thereby, traditionally spacious family gardens have become a central question of urban policies and are either forced out of the inner city, decrease in area in order to preserve more space for development of new residential areas or they are replaced by new forms of gardening in urban areas.

In the city of Geneva, compact city development and densification strategies encourage these new forms of gardening (Ville de Genève, 2009). They are commonly called 'jardins potagers', 'plantages' or 'jardins partagés' and are supported and integrated in the local development agenda by municipalities. Compared to Greece, they are less associated with serving productive functions linked to alimentary questions and self-provision. Embedded within a wider environmental

---

[1] These grocery shops are new social structures that have been developed by municipal and civic actors in a context of rising and provide free food, clothes etc. for 'chronically' and 'new poor' people and families hit by the economic downturn.

discourse of 'City and Nature' (Klöti et al., 2016; Nikolaidou et al., 2016; Ward Thompson, 2002), they are rather concentrated on bringing nature, biodiversity and related leisure activities into the central urban areas, reconciling the goals of urban greening with the need of urban densification while promoting local neighbourhood relations and conviviality.

We can distinguish two main types of 'jardins potagers' that derive either as top-down, bottom-up or collaborative initiatives among several stakeholders:

- Municipal gardens developed at the local neighbourhood scale as a municipal social policy (mainly initiated by the Units for Community Action-UAC).
- Several bottom-up initiatives that are widely supported by the public action as new forms of participation and cooperation between civil society and political-administrative actors (Nikolaidou et al., 2016).

Exploring similarities and differences in open space and governance patterns

The selected case studies

All gardens selected in Athens and Geneva are municipal initiatives and present some key common features as well as some differences concerning size, type, terms of use, infrastructure, etc. Comparison is done according to their effects on three general categories of open space and governance patterns: re-appropriation of vacant land, accessibility and usability of open public space and the degree of public engagement, diversity of actors and participative practices. A brief description of the four selected case studies in Athens and Geneva is presented as follows:

Maroussi, Athens, Greece

Launched in 2012, on a fenced derelict municipal plot of 1,500m², which is divided in forty 25m² plots (see Figure 4.1). Situated in a neighbourhood that has been notably transformed during the last two decades by residential and intense commercial development, especially during the building boom of the Athens Olympic Games that supported the construction of huge malls and extensive venues. After years of disuse, it had been informally transformed into a space for garbage and illegal dumping of building materials. Neighbourhood-based activism and collective actions of residents against the construction of the plot over the years finally mobilised the city administration to transform it into a vegetable garden. Cleaning of the site, deposition of suspended soil and the basic infrastructures (fencing, water supply with water tank) are provided by the municipality. Thereby, a degraded space turned into a friendly and liveable part of the city, a social space for human activities while contributing to the creation of a healthy urban environment.

Figure 4.1 Urban garden of Maroussi, metropolitan area of Athens, Greece

Agios Dimitrios, Athens, Greece

Launched in 2012, it is situated on a fenced city-owned land of 250ha which was formerly used as a bus depot (see Figure 4.2). The land was divided in forty-six plots of approximately 40m² (forty-five plots were allocated to families and one was granted to an NGO, the Center for Vocational Education for Children with Special Needs K.E.E.P.E.A.-'HORIZONS'). In 2013, it was included together with the Social Grocery in the municipal 'Social Structures Against Poverty' with the financial support of the National Strategic Reference Framework (NSRF). Apart from subsistence gardening for the economic relief of households, one of the main targets of the municipality was to upgrade a neglected neighbourhood that has been declining over the years by reusing an abandoned and unsafe plot. Cleaning of the site, soil and basic infrastructure were provided by the municipality with the supplementary role of one non-profit civil partnership in the field of social care (A.M.K.E. 'ANODOΣ') that was engaged to hire one social worker and one general-duty staff member for the garden (Sougela, 2015).

Municipal gardens of UAC Beaulieu, Geneva, Switzerland

Situated in the former horticultural centre that belongs to the Municipal Service of Green Spaces, it has in total forty-nine parcels of 6m² that are allocated to neighbourhood residents, living in a close distance, with a non-renewable contract of two years (see Figure 4.3). It is a municipal initiative developed under the

Figure 4.2   Urban garden of Agios Dimitrios, metropolitan area of Athens, Greece

Figure 4.3   Vegetable gardens of UAC – Beaulieu, Geneva, Switzerland

responsibility and surveillance of the Unit for Community Action (UAC) in the framework of neighbourhood-oriented social policies. These municipal gardens, which were initially created in 2006 on a smaller scale, were formerly situated on public green space in the middle of the park Beaulieu. However, after their relocation inside the horticultural centre of Beaulieu they have doubled their surface area. Since 2013, they are part of a shared public space of the wider collective Beaulieu project. This collaborative initiative run by the 'Collective Beaulieu' comprises eight local associations and has transformed a derelict land into an innovative and a multifunctional gardening site with free access during the whole day. Organic seedlings and vegetables, sales, open garden pickings, honey production, a henhouse and greenhouses are some of the activities available.

Rue du Contrat social, Geneva, Switzerland

Inaugurated in 2012 on a private front yard of a block of flats with free open access, this has fifteen plots of approximately 5m² (see Figure 4.4). The land is allocated to residents of the nearby building that is rented by the 'General Hospice' – an autonomous public organisation responsible for social policy in Geneva – in order to host asylum applicants. It is a collaborative project among the Municipal Social Service-Saint-Jean, the 'General Hospice' and the owner of the land while the space is collectively managed by the participants. According to the UAC, this initiative is considered as a social integration project

Figure 4.4   Jardin Potager – Contrat Social, Geneva, Switzerland

connecting residents of the buildings and their surrounding neighbourhoods mainly targeting asylum seekers and migrant integration. At the same time, it encourages socialisation, participation, intergenerational, intercultural encounters and social diversity while it preserves the green character of the neglected front yards.

Re-activation of vacant land: temporary character and low level of formalisation

Security of land tenure and governance are key aspects of spatial justice, thus it is important to focus on policies, strategies and laws that strengthen land security for urban agriculture or provide land tenure opportunities for collaborative land access. Although municipal gardens are not a policy priority, both cities support their creation by including them in the local policy agenda. In Geneva they are referred to in the cantonal and municipal strategic development plans as a tool for the creation of social green spaces that foster proximity, security, neighbourhood social cohesion and conviviality (Canton de Genève, 2013). In Athens, most of them were co-funded until 2016 by the NSRF and the European Social Fund as a municipal social structure tackling poverty and social exclusion ('Social Structures Against Poverty') (MLSS, 2012). Moreover, according to the recent draft Law on 'land use codification' (under consultation since 2017), 'urban gardening' was proposed as a new land-use category permitted in residential areas, only for personal consumption. Though still not ratified, this revision of the land-use classification system underlines the recent changes in urban land patterns, resource demand and management practices through time and could be related to the potential formalisation of the current urban gardening projects.

Facilitated either by slow real estate development in times of economic instability and budgetary difficulties (Greece), or by densification processes (Switzerland), they arise as a new multifunctional way of management and reactivation of abandoned/misused vacant open spaces while giving the right for re-use of open space to citizens. However, in Athens municipalities seek public brownfields whereas in Geneva strategies comprise broader schemes of a wide range of small-scale public or private lots in disuse, front yard lawns, constructible land waiting for development or spaces within parks/green areas. Nevertheless, the issue of long-term tenure is challenged by the high price of urban land and the many competing uses. In both cases these initiatives remain short-term and low-cost strategies that enable a temporary land access (short-term contracts of one or two years), which is not connected to organised urban revitalisation efforts or urban food policies. Accordingly, because of the unclear policies and the spontaneous management approach, these small-scale efforts are dispersed and excessively susceptible to land-use change in favour of more competitive uses.

Accessibility and usability of open public space as a question of justice

Accessibility and usability of the urban gardening sites are important distributive factors that indicate spatial (in)justice, exclusion/inclusion and (in)equality. The different ways of re-appropriating open green space and vacant land in the two countries have various effects on the access and use issues of the gardens as collective public resources and therefore their inclusiveness/exclusiveness (Nissen, 2008). These effects depend mainly on their location and formal/informal setting, the governance and design of the collective spaces, the multitude of functions, users and actors involved, the openness to the general public via access rights and social events, etc. In all cases, beyond economic and nutritional functions, these spaces are collectively experienced as shared places of socialisation and complex interactions establishing a cooperative feeling among the participants that enhances community bonds. All case studies reflect a high level of internal social diversification among users with different socio-economic backgrounds. However, physical accessibility and social usability of the spaces does not necessarily ensure the inclusive character of the public space (Akkar, 2005). In both countries, municipal gardens are divided into individual plots, which in most cases are not collectively gardened, so land re-appropriation can be considered inclusive for the minority that is taking part and exclusive for all those who are not selected or those who are not able to invest time, knowledge or commitment in the group activity. However, in Geneva, the interplay between the private and public sphere of these spaces is thought to be more open to the wider public due to their multifunctionality, diversified activities and open spatial structures as parts of public parks, open garden picking by all residents, intercultural aspects, (e.g. Beaulieu garden is a free-access, multi-user, multi-actor and multifunctional space). In Greece, fencing and locking/surveillance measures impede an all-day free access to passers-by or neighbours resulting in a rather uneven access to public space that might increase temporal social and spatial inequalities.

Public engagement, diversity of actors and participative practices

In terms of procedural justice, a major difference identified between the cases examined in the two countries concerns the degree of collaborative and participatory design processes in all stages of their implementation. The municipality of Geneva strategically supports new forms of collaboration and partnerships involving a broader set of public, private and civic actors, in order to enable participatory processes in urban development projects. These partnerships usually involve horizontal collaboration between different services of the municipal administration as well as broader and constant collaborations with associations, grassroots movements, NGOs and other representatives of the civil society or private actors that take part in the negotiation of space (such as in the case of the

Collective Beaulieu). The participatory approach is promoted mainly through the municipal 'Service Agenda 21' for the sustainable development and the 'UAC' who are key actors for implementing urban gardening initiatives through the active participation of residents. Their approach is to adapt to the existing demand of citizens, instead of imposing top-down projects. Hence, they have external collaborations with associations, NGOs and collectives that are interested in setting up new gardens (Nikolaidou, 2014).

In opposition to Geneva, the Greek examples are clearly top-down, conceived on municipal level with no participatory processes in space governance or initial sharing of the aim of the garden. However, there are many cases where vacant lots were subject to residents' claims against their construction, before their transformation to vegetable gardens (see the case of Maroussi). Therefore, though municipal practice was top-down designed they were successful in terms of green space and urban landscape enhancement of neglected places that gather people from the neighbourhood. Thus, participation of gardeners mainly consists in self-organisation of their individual plot or the activities and the management of the garden. Local municipalities administratively and financially support urban gardens in city's neighbourhoods, while since 2012, they are assumed to collaborate with civic actors in order to receive funds from 'Social Structures Against Poverty'. This structure has the aim to alleviate the socio-economic and psychological problems of urban dwellers, showing an increased sensitivity to vulnerable social groups affected by the multiple effects of the crisis on income, unemployment, labour insecurity, etc. Beneficiary NGOs with the necessary expertise and staff in the field of social care are invited for the creation of a Social Corporate Scheme for the new urban gardening projects (see the case of Agios Dimitrios). Facing the economic crisis, issues of social justice are mainly related to plot selection criteria and fair policy by giving priority to vulnerable socio-economic categories.

Concluding remarks

Either driven 'from below' or 'from above', either following the outbreak of the financial crisis, or other social, political and environmental motivations, urban gardening initiatives can redefine household livelihoods in both cities as a means of food security and healthy food access, improve the environment, local food systems, family budget and living standards (Philander and Karriem, 2016). They also have a transforming effect on physical and social dynamics of public space as well as on the conventional dominant forms of economic and social cooperation and play an important role in the creation of new shared/collective identities, partnerships, relationships and ethics of solidarity among urban dwellers. By claiming open access to fresh, qualitative, healthy and affordable food and more sustainable land use, these practices also reflect a social demand for food re-appropriation and re-localisation of food systems (family self-sufficiency, food safety, organic production, employment and income generation, etc.). They foster collective practices, civic engagement and local activism and facilitate new forms of socio-political participation and perceptions of inclusiveness that can combat spatial injustice.

However, despite their growing popularity the comparative study revealed that municipal gardens are short-term social actions rather than long-term sustainable urban planning tools. In Greece, this temporary character is embedded within a wider discourse on urban resilience in times of economic decline and consequent real estate collapse that assume municipal support. In Switzerland it is rather connected to densification policies and the challenge to maintain open green spaces in the city. Planning aspects in both cases involve low formalisation and opportunistic facilitation of the use of vacant lots, though there are first steps for legitimisation through integration to the city's sustainable agenda and land-use planning. This political recognition of collective action and shared forms of public space management create more opportunities for the development of innovative social practices that improve social wellbeing and justice (Amin, 2006). However, it is a question how this ongoing trend can combine mixed-use neighbourhoods with new productive green spaces and be perceived as green infrastructure for long-term inner-city revitalisation and ecological, economic and social urban development. Informal land management through gardening practices on undeveloped land has the potential to facilitate social and spatial justice either by addressing temporarily urban social inequalities or by helping embed social vulnerabilities in neighbourhoods (Hochedez and Le Gall, 2016). Thus, until now these alternative socio-temporal practices face several institutional limitations that inhibit long-term spatial processes that could lead to a more stable incorporation of issues of equity and social justice. Nevertheless, all these shared practices in urban spaces are locally defined solutions that combine food provision with social inclusion and urban greening. They can be perceived as a promising collective experiment across time and space that could result in building sociality, civic engagement and space commoning, thus increasing the resilience and social equity of urban planning (Amin, 2006; Stavrides, 2015; Wekerle, 2004).

References

Akkar, M. (2005): Questioning 'inclusivity' of public spaces in post-industrial cities: the case of Haymarket bus station, Newcastle upon Tyne. *METU Journal of Faculty of Architecture* 22 (2): 1–24.

Amin, A. (2006): Collective culture and urban public space. www.publicspace.org/en/text-library/eng/b003-collective-culture-and-urban-public-space (accessed 14 September 2017).

Anthopoulou, Th., Kolokouris, O., Nikolaïdou, S. and Partalidou, M. (2015): Aux arbres citoyens! Le mouvement d'agriculture urbaine, une forme participative d'appropriation de l'espace. *Options Méditerranéennes* B (7): 339–349.

Anthopoulou, Th., Nikolaidou, S., Partalidou, M. and Petrou, M. (2018): The emergence of municipal gardens in Greece: new social functions of agriculture in times of crisis. In: Soulard, C. T., Perrin, C. and Valette, E. (Eds): *Toward Sustainable Relations Between*

Agriculture and the City: Urban Agriculture. Cham: Springer, 181–199. doi: 10.1007/ 978-3-319-71037-2_11

Branduini, P., Perrin, C. and Puente Asuero, R. (2016): Spatial justice and heritage enhancement in the urban gardening. In: International conference *Growing in Cities: Interdisciplinary Perspectives on Urban Gardening*, 9–10 September, Basel, Switzerland. www1.montpellier.inra.fr/wp-inra/jasminn/wp-content/uploads/sites/ 6/2016/02/Branduini-et-al-2016.pdf (accessed 14 September 2017).

Canton de Genève (2013): Plan directeur cantonal 2030. A14: Promouvoir de nouvelles formes de jardins familiaux et encourager la création de plantages. Geneva: République et Canton de Genève.

Chiesura, A. (2004): The role of urban parks for the sustainable city. *Landscape and Urban Planning* 68 (1): 129–138.

De Sousa, C. A. (2003): Turning brownfields into green space in the City of Toronto. *Landscape and Urban Planning* 62 (4): 181–198. doi:10.1016/S0169-2046(02)00149-4

Elwood, S. (2002): Neighborhood revitalisation through 'collaboration': assessing the implications of neoliberal urban policy at the grassroots. *GeoJournal* 58 (2–3): 121–130.

FAO (2010): Fighting poverty and hunger: what role for urban agriculture? *Policy Brief, Economic and Social Perspectives* 10. www.fao.org/docrep/012/al377e/al377e00.pdf (accessed 18 November 2017).

Geddes, M. (2006): Partnership and the limits to local governance in England: institutionalist analysis and neoliberalism. *International Journal of Urban and Regional Research* 30 (1): 76–97.

Ghose, R. (2005): The complexities of citizen participation through collaborative governance. *Space and Polity* 9 (1): 61–75.

Gottlieb, R. and Joshi, A. (2010): *Food Justice*. Cambridge, MA: MIT Press.

Hackenbroch, K. (2013): Negotiating public space for livelihoods: about risks, uncertainty and power in the urban poor's everyday life. *Erdkunde* 67 (1): 37–47.

Hochedez, C. and Le Gall, J. (2016): Food justice and agriculture. *justice spatiale – spatial justice*. Université Paris Ouest Nanterre La Défense: UMR LAVUE 7218, Laboratoire Mosaïques, Food justice and agriculture. www.jssj.org/article/justice-alimentaire-et-agriculture/ (accessed 12 October 2017).

Holston, J. (1998): Spaces of insurgent citizenship. In: Sandercock, L. (ed.): Making the invisible visible. A multicultural planning history. Berkeley: 37–56.

Hula, R. C., Reese, L. A. and Elmoore, C. J. (Eds) (2016): *Reclaiming Brownfields: A Comparative Analysis of Adaptive Reuse of Contaminated Properties*. USA: Routledge.

Ioannou, B., Moran, N., Sondermann, M., Certoma, C. and Hardman, M. (2016): Grassroots gardening movements: towards cooperative forms of green urban development? In: Bell, S., Fox-Kämper, R., Keshavarz, N., Benson, M., Caputo, S., Noori, S. and Voigt, A. (Eds): *Urban Allotment Gardens in Europe*. New York: Routledge, 62–89.

Klöti, T., Tappert, S. and Drilling, M. (2016): Was für Grün in der Stadt? Politische Aushandlungsprozesse um städtische Grün- und Freiräume am Beispiel des urbanen Gärtnerns in Schweizer Städten. *Standort. Zeitschrift für Angewandte Geographie* 40 (2): 123–128.

MLSS – Ministry of Labor and Social Security (2012): Call for the operational program 'Human resources development' – Axis: 'full integration of the total human resources in a society of equal opportunities' (AΔA:B45AΛ-Θ2Δ in Greek). Athens: Hellenic Republic. http://old.dad.gr/Documents/2012/prokhryjeis/%CE%92443%CE%9B-6%CE%A15-signed.pdf (accessed 28 May 2016).

Nikolaidou, S. (2014): Emerging forms of urban gardening in Geneva. STSM Report. Basel: Urban Allotment Gardens. www.urbanallotments.eu/fileadmin/uag/media/ STSM/STSMReport_SN.pdf (accessed 28 September 2015).

Nikolaidou, S. and Kolokouris, O. (2016): Transition movements in Greece: an alternative green solution to the crisis? In: International Conference on *Urban Autonomy and the Collective City – Towards the Collective City*, 1–2 July, 2016, Athens, Greece.

Nikolaidou, S., Klöti, T., Tappert, S. and Drilling, M. (2016): Urban gardening and green space governance: towards new collaborative planning practices. *Urban Planning* 1 (1): 5–19.

Nissen, S. (2008): Urban transformation from public and private space to spaces of hybrid character. *Sociolog-ickýčasopis* 44 (6): 1129–1149.

Philander, F. and Karriem, A. (2016): Assessment of urban agriculture as a livelihood strategy for household food security: an appraisal of urban gardens in Langa, Cape Town. *International Journal of Arts and Sciences* 9 (1): 327–338.

Phillips, S. and Orsini, M. (2002): Mapping the links: citizen involvement in policy processes. *CPRN Discussion Paper No. F | 21*. Canadian Policy Research Networks Inc. (CPRN). http://rcrpp.org/documents/ACFRJK8po.PDF (accessed 15 May 2016).

Prové, C., Kemper, D., Loudiyi, S., Mumenthaler, C. and Nikolaidou, S. (2015): Governance of urban agriculture initiatives: insights drawn from European case studies. In: Lohrberg, F., Licka, L., Scazzosi, L. and Timpe, A. (Eds): *Urban Agriculture Europe*. Berlin: Editions Jovis, 64–69.

Schmelzkopf, K. (1995): Urban community gardens as contested space. *Geographical Review* 85 (3): 364–381.

Slocum, R., Cadieux, K. and Blumberg, R. (2016): Solidarity, space, and race: toward geographies of agrifood justice. *justice spatiale – spatial justice*. Université Paris Ouest Nanterre La Défense, UMR LAVUE 7218, Laboratoire Mosaïques Food justice and agriculture, 9. https://halshs.archives-ouvertes.fr/halshs-01507278/document (accessed 25 February 2017).

Soja, E. W. (2009): The city and spatial justice. *justice spatiale – spatial justice* 01, September.

Sougela, S. (2015): The contribution of urban agriculture to the social inclusion of vulnerable social groups: the example of the municipal vegetable garden in Agios Dimitrios. Master's thesis. Athens: Panteion University.

Stavrides, S. (2015): Common space as threshold space: urban commoning in struggles to re-appropriate public space. *Commoning as Differentiated Publicness, Footprint* 16: 9–20. doi: 10.7480/footprint.9.1.896

Ville de Genève (2009): Genève 2020 – Plan directeur communal de la Ville de Genève. Renouvellement durable d'une ville-centre. Ville de Genève: Rapport de synthèse.

Ward Thompson, C. (2002): Urban open space in the 21st century. *Landscape and Urban Planning* 60 (2): 59–72.

Wekerle, G. R. (2004): Food justice movements: policy, planning, and networks. *Journal of Planning Education and Research* 23 (4): 378–386.

Wolch, J. R., Byrne, J. and Newell, J. P. (2014): Urban green space, public health, and environmental justice: the challenge of making cities 'just green enough'. *Landscape and Urban Planning* 125: 234–244. doi:10.1016/j.landurbplan.2014.01.017

Zezza, A. and Tasciotti, L. (2010): Urban agriculture, poverty, and food security: empirical evidence from a sample of developing countries. *Food Policy* 35 (4): 265–273.

5

Urban gardening and spatial justice from a mid-size city perspective: the case of Ortobello Urban Garden

Giuseppe Aliperti and Silvia Sarti

Introduction

The concept of justice is strongly related to present-day conditions that are constantly influenced by class, race and gender, and are able to generate a locational discrimination on certain groups of the population (Soja, 2009). Starting from the 1970s, the term *spatial justice* has been introduced in order to describe this kind of phenomenon. Spatial justice has been initially investigated by focusing on the territorial dimension of urban politics (O'Laughlin, 1973; Pirie, 1983; Reynaud, 1981; Soja, 2009). In early 1980s, the interest in investigating spatial justice considerably increased and scholars actively approached the topic. The term spatial justice became almost exclusively associated with the work of geographers and planners in Los Angeles (Soja, 2009).

Los Angeles was the most important metropolitan region in the United States considering the production of unjust geographies and spatial structures of privileges. These characteristics have played a fundamental role in the strategies and activism of labour and local community groups (Soja, 2009). The increasing number of metropolitan areas worldwide suggests that more in-depth investigations into these metropolitan neighbourhoods are needed in order to explain the complex social dynamics emerging in these new contexts. As a matter of fact, the majority of the existing studies provided analyses and investigations focused on metropolitan settings. However, the issue of spatial justice also involves smaller urban settings.

We propose the analysis of a case study based in Italy. The relevance of the study relies on the prevalent composition of the Italian urban sites characterised by a majority of medium-size cities. In this context, our study aims at analysing how spatial justice/injustice is developed and managed in mid-size cities. In particular, we propose to focus on the dynamics generated within the local community through the promotion of urban gardening projects in order to examine how these initiatives are able to influence spatial justice. The investigated group of people potentially subjected to the spatial injustice is formed by the residents and the local retailers.

According to Certomà and Notteboom (2015) urban gardening is a tool that has been used as manifestation of the 'right to the city' claim since the 1970s (Schmelzkopf, 2002; Staeheli et al., 2002), and it is able to foster the empowerment of people in alternative uses, forms and functions of public spaces (Brenner and Theodore, 2005; Hardman and Larkham, 2014; Tornaghi, 2014). We propose to analyse an urban community garden case study developed in Perugia, a small/ mid-size city located in the centre of Italy. The project is named 'Ortobello Urban Garden' and it is based in the historical city centre of the city.

In the following sections, we introduce the theoretical background that has been used in order to shape the study. We therefore refer to the main themes that have been successively analysed through the development of a qualitative investigation. We also offer a description of the case study in order to explain the general features of the analysed urban gardening project. Later, we present the adopted methodology and we provide the emerging findings proposing three different perspectives: one of the promoters of the urban gardening initiatives; one of the residents; and one of the retailers. The chapter concludes by highlighting final results with the aim to facilitate a discussion, define new research opportunities and clarify research limitations.

Theoretical background

Community gardens emerged in many nations and in both urban and rural areas during the 1990s (Ferris et al., 2001). Their number increased due to the development of cities and consequent land scarcity, and they are now recognised to be an international phenomenon (Ferris et al., 2001). Academic research investigated urban gardening to analyse in more depth the causes and the social effects generated by their implementation. The investigations mainly focus on two areas (CoDyre et al., 2015). One is represented by the research stream that focuses on the impact of urban gardening on the community development (Glover et al., 2005; Roubanis and Landis, 2007; Saldivar-Tanaka and Krasny, 2004). The second one refers to the research stream that investigates the potential production of self-provisioning gardens in the developed world (CoDyre et al., 2015). Our study contributes to the first research stream analysing the impact that urban gardening is able to produce on the quality of life, urban security and community engagement in the specific setting characterised by the small/mid-size city. The perspective is linked to the concept of spatial justice. Therefore, we aim to evaluate how this urban gardening project influenced the locational discrimination of the people that live within the investigated area.

Recently, the development of community gardens has emerged as a significant phenomenon that contributes to the beautification and greening of many neighbourhoods and fosters a spirit of community cooperation (Schukoske, 1999). In turn, such sense of community, namely community cooperation, facilitates the re-development of the cities, contributing to the increasing of urban security and generating other social effects. Ferris et al. (2001) state that the differences between a community garden and a private garden are ownership, access and degree of democratic control. The consideration of these elements seems to be fundamental in order to identify and categorise the forms of urban gardening. The involvement of the local community plays a key role for the success of urban gardening. In particular, a successful initiative will allow citizens to contribute to its creation, development and improvement. De facto, citizens will be able to see the urban garden as a public service, in which they may have an active role of intervention. Citizens' involvement in the realisation and the use of urban gardening may be linked to the concept of co-production (Glover et al., 2005). According to Crompton (1999), co-production is the process in which community groups participate jointly with a public actor in the production of services that will be used and enjoyed by the community itself. Focusing on urban gardening initiatives, they can be promoted by both public and private stakeholders that collaborate with the final aim to provide a service to the community. According to the Resource Mobilization Theory (Jenkins, 1983), there is the need of the presence of a group able to secure collective control over the resources needed for collective action. Therefore, even if urban gardening is promoted by public institutions or private citizens, it seems to be always necessary to analyse how the resources have been collected and later invested in order to reach the collective aim. This is in line with the concept of resource mobilisation promoted by Jenkins (1983) that, in addition, suggests also to analyse the extent to which outsiders increase the group's pool of resources.

Our contribution proposes an investigation about the processes that were behind the creation of the urban gardening initiatives realised in Perugia (Italy), considering its urban and social effects and the stakeholders' engagement processes. In particular, our qualitative study takes into consideration different perspectives of several stakeholders that are involved in the process as well as promoters, institutions, local retailers, citizens and universities. We therefore investigate how the Ortobello project has been created and maintained during the years. Later, we focus on the effects that have been generated, by analysing expected and achieved results. In the next section, we start this investigation process by providing a more in-depth description of the initiative.

The 'Ortobello Urban Garden' case

Perugia is the capital city of the Umbria region in Italy and has approximately 167,000 inhabitants. The city has a vast historical, artistic and cultural heritage, hosting internationally important museums, multiple annual festivals and events, and is the birthplace of two renowned Italian Renaissance painters. The city is characterised by the presence of two universities[1,2] and several art-related educational institutions.

The presence of this multitude of universities and academies shaped the image of the city as a lively modern and innovative cultural centre. Despite that, the inner city has been subject to demographic changes and the social fabric is constantly changing. A constantly increasing number of residents tended to leave the central neighbourhoods of the city, replaced by temporary residents composed of students and new citizens coming from foreign countries. A report provided by the National Institute for Statistics (ISTAT, 2017) refers to the fact that the inner city of Perugia has a higher number of unused buildings compared to the peripheral areas (ISTAT, 2017). The combination of these phenomena – the depopulation of local residents and the abundance of properties to rent – have attracted mainly students and foreign citizens to live in the historic centre of Perugia. As a result, this area is mainly populated by young people, such as undergraduate students, living alone or in shared flats (ISTAT, 2017); whereas foreign citizens are mostly present in the neighbourhood of the railway station and in the historic centre (ISTAT, 2017).

The new social fabric generated by the issue of depopulation has been characterised by a second phenomenon related to the presence and development of criminality. Criminal activities (especially drug-dealing) emerged in some neighbourhoods, such as the historic centre and the area close to the main railway station (Ministero dell'Interno, 2015). Thus, the perception of increased crime among citizens generated an additional incentive to leave these areas for peripheral residential neighbourhoods. In sum, it created a vicious circle between local residents abandoning the centre of the city and temporary residents (students and foreign citizens) willing to rent unused buildings in that area. This has allowed the crime to continue, pushing additional residents to leave the historical centre.

---

[1] The University of Perugia, founded in 1308, has sixteen departments and about 22,000 students in 2015/16 (MIUR, 2017).

[2] The University for Foreigners was established in 1921 and is the oldest university oriented to promoting and teaching the Italian language and culture to foreign students, with about 1,000 students in 2015/16 (MIUR, 2017).

The 'Ortobello Urban Garden' project

In order to tackle the depopulation issue and seek to increase spatial justice for all citizens, multiple initiatives for the revitalisation of the inner city have been conducted both at institutional and citizen levels. For instance, local authorities are trying to combat this unpleasant phenomenon by defining a political strategy that recognises the crucial role of individuals and their rights in the community (Regione Umbria, 2015). At the same time, citizens began to promote initiatives aimed at increasing urban liveability.

The 'Ortobello Urban Garden' project, pursuing a community engagement approach, is the result of one of these attempts. It represents a good example of co-production (Glover et al., 2005) including the proactive participation of the local community. The initiative has been promoted by a local association, Associazione Borgo Bello, and a centre for higher education, the Umbra Institute, with the support of local government and academia. The municipality of Perugia provided patronage, the University of Perugia, University for Foreigners of Perugia and the Umbra Institute provided scientific knowledge and started collaborative projects involving students (see Figure 5.1).

This urban garden initiative has been developed since 2013 and was formally realised in 2015. It is part of a more structured project named 'C.A.R.O Vicolo' aimed at revitalising the whole area through communicating, activating, retraining and hosting community-oriented initiatives. It is located in different parts of the Borgo Bello neighbourhood that represents one of the most characteristic areas of the historic centre of Perugia. The name of the initiative, 'Ortobello', or 'Beautiful Garden', expresses the main objective of the project. By stimulating the local community, it aims to create a network of people that take care of the community garden together. It represents an urban regeneration project, born with the aim of strengthening sense of community, conviviality and social wellbeing. The philosophy of the project is: 'By cultivating gardens, we cultivate community!'.

The Ortobello project consists in craftily constructed green area installations for the planting of different species of plants, including vegetables, aromatic and ornamental, strategically placed in the alleys of Borgo Bello neighbourhood, in the historic centre of Perugia. The installations are mainly created using materials from reusing and recycling practices. Despite the use of recycled materials, considerable attention has been paid to creating design installations as decorative elements for the neighbourhood. Thus, the urban space has been equipped through vertical (see Figure 5.2) and ground-level installations (see Figure 5.3). In addition to the creation of the urban gardens, 'social areas' have been developed in neglected places of the neighbourhood in order to increase the liveability by creating community spaces able to foster social interaction (see Figure 5.4).

Figure 5.1   Students' engagement at Borgo Bello neighbourhood, Perugia – Project Ortobello

Methodology

Our study offers a qualitative analysis of a single case study in order to investigate the effects on local spatial justice generated by urban gardening initiatives in more depth. Referring to spatial justice, the proposed perspective aims at investigating the effects on the local community and, in particular, it focuses on residents and local retailers.

The methodology of the case study is widely applied in literature and highly recommended in studying contemporary events over which the researcher has little or no control (Yin, 1994) and in exploring an emerging area of research

Figure 5.2 Vertical garden at Borgo Bello neighbourhood, Perugia – Project Ortobello

where few previous studies have been conducted (Madanipour, 2010;Yin, 1994). For these reasons, a single case study has been deemed as the most appropriate methodology to assess the effect of urban gardening initiatives on local spatial justice within an Italian mid-size city, despite potential weaknesses related to generalisability (Donmoyer, 2000; Flyvbjerg, 2006).

Qualitative data collection mechanisms including in-depth interviews and content analysis of existing documentation were used to collect evidence about the project and its effects on local spatial justice. Data were collected through semi-structured interviews using an open-ended interview protocol.Three levels of investigation have been identified:

- Promoters of the 'Ortobello' initiative.
- Residents of the Borgo Bello neighbourhood and the historic centre of Perugia.
- Retailers of the Borgo Bello neighbourhood and the historic centre of Perugia.

Interviews were conducted during July 2016, gathering information from a sample of thirty-four individuals: two promoters of the initiative, twenty residents and twelve retailers. Respondents were randomly selected.

Figure 5.3 Green areas installations at Borgo Bello neighbourhood, Perugia – Project Ortobello

A case study protocol was designed, one for each of the categories of respondents involved. The interviews lasted from sixty to ninety minutes with the members of the organisation that promotes the initiative and from twenty to thirty minutes with residents and retailers. All interviews were audio recorded and transcribed verbatim. The main contents of the interview protocol are summarised in Table 5.1.

Findings: stakeholders' perspectives

In the data collection process, we deeply investigated the perspectives of multiple stakeholders involved in the project. In order to gather evidence about the effects of the urban gardening project on local spatial justice, we adopted an inclusive approach taking into account three main actors: the promoters, the residents and the retailers.

Figure 5.4   Community furnishings at Terrazza del Cortone, Perugia – Project Salotto con vista

The promoters' perspective

First, we interviewed the individuals who launched the idea and promoted the Ortobello project. This step has been necessary in order to identify the composition of the group of actors that were able to secure collective control over the resources needed for collective action (Resource Mobilization Theory – Jenkins, 1983). It has been confirmed that the Ortobello urban gardening represents a bottom-up initiative, born from the need to recover residual urban spaces and finally giving them new social life. To this aim, it was implemented in a three-step process:

- Promoting the idea of urban gardening among possible stakeholders.
- Recreating the available unused urban space, providing vertical gardens, green areas and plants.
- Engaging people, local associations, local businesses and retailers in playing an active role in taking care of such community spaces and guaranteeing the necessary amount of resources to increase the sustainability of the project over the years.

According to the organisers, the initiative has been successful for several reasons. First, it has generated a strong and stable collaboration with the

Table 5.1 Interview protocol

Promoters of 'Ortobello Urban Garden'

Case study: understanding of Ortobello project, by identifying promoters, financiers, audience, mission

Role of institutions: the extent to which the local institutions have been involved in the implementation of the Ortobello project

Motivations: understanding of the determinants that driven the development of the Ortobello project in relation to motives and aims

Expected/achieved results: the extent to which the Ortobello project had an impact in improving local conditions and expected results for current actions

Stakeholder engagement: the extent to which stakeholders have been involved in the project with regard to residents, retailers, tourists, universities and schools, institutions, volunteering associations and others

Assessment tools: understanding of the measures adopted for assessing the impact of the Ortobello project and benchmarking activities

Future objectives: understanding of future projects and replication in other neighbourhoods in Perugia

Residents

Knowledge about urban gardening project: the extent to which the respondents are familiar with the concept of urban gardening, not related to the case of Ortobello

Knowledge and involvement about Ortobello project: the extent to which the respondents are familiar with the Ortobello urban gardening project, established in the neighbourhood of Borgo Bello in Perugia and the extent to which respondents are involved in the initiative

Benefits: the extent to which respondents perceive benefits generated by the Ortobello project in terms of security, valorisation and liveability and other aspects

Criticisms: the extent to which respondents perceive criticisms caused by the Ortobello project in terms of presence of crowd, insects, cleaning and other aspects

Retailers

Knowledge about urban gardening project: the extent to which the respondents are familiar with the concept of urban gardening, not related to the case of Ortobello

Knowledge about Ortobello project: the extent to which the respondents are familiar with the Ortobello urban gardening project, established in the neighbourhood of Borgo Bello in Perugia

Benefits: the extent to which respondents perceive benefits generated by the Ortobello project in terms of commercial improvement, security, valorisation and liveability and other aspects

Criticisms: the extent to which respondents perceive criticisms caused by the Ortobello project in terms of presence of crowd, insects, cleaning and other aspects

---

universities that are actively involved in maintaining the installed gardens and in animating these places. Second, the project is growing up with additional community-engagement activities organised within the same restored areas with the aim to increase the quality of life of the citizens, guarantee the liveability of the neighbourhood and attract visitors and tourists. Among other future plans, the commitment to recovering a panoramic terrace of the city, named Terrazza del Cortone, was highlighted. The initiative, called *Salotto con vista* or *Living room with a view*, aims at recuperating the panoramic terrace to be used as an outdoor space for theatre shows, concerts, art appreciation events and astronomical observations.

With regard to the social effects on the community, it has been claimed that the initiative has led to at least three beneficial consequences.

- *Regeneration of urban sites*. One of the main evident effects is the attempt of urban regeneration. Ortobello garden has turned existing neglected urban sites into new places for the community, where people may interact, communicate and cultivate social relations, along with flowers and plants.
- *Sense of security*. The initiative has increased the perceived sense of security in the Borgo Bello neighbourhood. The creation of these community places has enhanced the sense of liveability of the neighbourhood, creating opportunities for social aggregation.
- *Sense of belonging*. Making places enjoyable has enhanced the perceived sense of belonging to a shared project and to the neighbourhood and consequently to the city.

Despite these positive effects, the promoters of Ortobello project recognised some criticisms related to the community engagement. The involvement of citizens, retailers and local institutions has been problematic. Even though the urban garden has been appreciated and the recovered urban sites have been utilised by citizens, the engagement process has been slow. Retailers have not shown a high level of interest in the initiative and local government has been only partially proactive. Similarly, only a small proportion of residents actively joined the initiative.

Therefore, it has been emphasised that the interaction between the community and the urban spaces need to be constantly animated. Individuals tend to not activate an autonomous and spontaneous interaction with public spaces. Thus, the implementation of continuous engagement processes aimed at animating and maintaining the urban sites appear to be necessary. Finally, the necessity to attract financial resources able to ensure the medium- to long-term sustainability of the project has been identified by the promoters as one of the biggest challenges.

The residents' perspective

From the sample of residents that have been interviewed, it emerged that the Ortobello project is generally well-recognised, as well as the local association that co-promoted the urban gardening initiative. This finding indicates the active presence of the association in the neighbourhood.

However, the residents have confirmed only a partial achievement of the targets identified by the promoters. In particular, with regard to the regeneration of the neighbourhood, the residents declare that the activity brought a temporary enhancement to the general architecture of the area, recognising that the interventions have been promoted through the Ortobello project. However, the necessity to constantly maintain the urban garden to keep it in a good condition has been identified as a limitation of this positive effect. For instance, one respondent stated: 'I like these gardens. However, this garden is not looked after. I think this initiative should be maintained in a better way' (female, thirty-seven years old).[3]

This issue is again associated with the need for resources and their management. In addition, most of the interviewees demonstrated that, even if they were able to recognise the presence of the installations, they were not adequately informed about the fact that the urban gardening was a community-oriented initiative that could become sustainable also through the support provided by every single citizen, including them.

With regard to the security perceptions, residents generally expressed concerns about the level of criminality present in Perugia, although declaring that it is limited to some zones of the city. The positive impact generated by the urban gardening initiative is partially perceived. In some cases, it has been reported as a sort of 'inverse' effect generated by the impossibility to constantly control all the areas that have been regenerated. For instance, the praiseworthy renovation of the Terrazza del Cortone seems to generate two different effects depending on the ability to sustain the project over time. It is a place of aggregation able to increase the sense of belonging of the local community and increase the attractiveness for the tourists visiting the city. At the same time, according to the residents' comments, during the period with no maintenance or with no events organised, some places that were renovated by the urban gardening initiative are perceived as not safe due to the criminality issue (e.g. drug dealing). As declared by a resident of Borgo Bello neighbourhood: 'The terrace now is very beautiful. During the day, I like to walk there and enjoy the wonderful view. I think it is a good service for the city. However, during the night I'm scared to go to the terrace as I don't feel safe' (male, sixty-two years old).[4]

In addition, the sense of belonging to the community seems to be strong when referring to the city or to the neighbourhood. However, even if residents seem to be prone to ideally support the urban gardening initiative, in the fact there is no strong participation in the project. As confirmation, an interviewee states: 'Yes, I know these gardens. I like the fact that the neighbourhood is full of these nice

---

[3] 'Questi giardini mi piacciono molto. Tuttavia, a volte sembrano abbandonati. Andrebbero curati maggiormente.'

[4] 'La terrazza ora è bellissima. Di giorno, ci passo a piedi e ammiro il panorama che da lì è fantastico. Credo che sia una buona cosa per la città. Invece, di notte, non mi sento sicuro e mi spaventa andarci.'

urban installations. However, I've never participated to the maintenance and, honestly, I don't know who is in charge to do it' (male, forty-three years old).[5]

In some cases, residents complained about the number of initiatives conducted in the centre of the city that generate traffic and parking issues. The residents asked for better event management and, where possible, for the events to be located in different areas of the city, in order to reduce the impact on their daily lives. This finding highlights the fact that residents feel that they are overexposed to events and festivals and that better event planning is needed, for instance: 'During the last years, too many events have been organized in Borgo Bello. It is impossible to have a normal life here. Do we really need this additional urban gardening project to bring even more people to visit this overcrowded area?' (female, fifty-six years old).[6]

The retailers' perspective

The retailers' perspective is partially similar to the residents' perspective. All the interviewed retailers know about the local association and they are enthusiastic about the activities that are frequently organised in the neighbourhood. A small share of retailers (20 per cent) seems to know that one of the promoters of the project is also the centre for higher education, the Umbra Institute. They generally recognised that the neighbourhood has improved in recent years and that criminality is decreasing, even though it is still present and perceived as an urgent problem. They are aware of the urban gardening project. However, retailers declared that the installations of urban gardens did not have a direct economic impact on their commercial activities. Nevertheless, they admitted the social and aesthetic impact of this initiative in improving the liveability of that area of the city. It has been underlined that: 'The Borgo Bello is now safer due to the several events that are organized in the area allowing a continuous flow of people. The urban gardening may contribute to make the neighbourhood more attractive. The feeling of insecurity related to crime activities is now higher in other areas of the city' (male, fifty-two years old).[7]

Most of the retailers are conscious of the different perspectives of some of the citizens referring to the risk of overcrowding the area. However, they highlighted two different positive aspects emerging from this situation. The first is economic, as

---

[5] 'Conosco questi giardini e mi piace il fatto che il quartiere ora è pieno di gradevoli istallazioni urbane. In realtà, però, non ho mai partecipato attivamente al mantenimento e sinceramente, non so chi se ne occupi.'

[6] 'Negli ultimi anni, sono stati organizzati troppi eventi in questo quartiere, Borgo Bello. È impossibile condurre una vita normale qui. Ne avevamo davvero bisogno di questo ulteriore progetto di orto urbano, che porta ancora più persone a visitare questa zona già sovraffollata?'

[7] 'Il quartiere Borgo Bello ora è più sicuro grazie ai numerosi eventi che sono stati organizzati in questa zona che generano un continuo passaggio di persone. Il progetto di orto urbano può aver contribuito a rendere il quartiere più attrattivo. La percezione di insicurezza connessa alle attività criminali ora è sentita maggiormente in altre zone della città.'

the constant presence of people during the day and the night time increases their revenue. The second one refers to crime, as this constant presence of people also discourages drug-dealing activities in the area. The presence of the regenerated areas, created by the Ortobello project, is perceived as an additional activity able to attract new tourists and customers from different parts of the city. For instance, it has been claimed: 'The gardens are just a part of the process of renovation of the city. I think this is a good initiative even if it is not the main reason behind the increased level of attractiveness of the area' (female, sixty years old).[8]

Conclusion

Our research analyses a case study of urban gardening promoted by a local association of residents and a centre for higher education with the aim of valorising the central neighbourhoods of Perugia through participatory planning interventions and requalification of urban sites.

The initiative, generated by a participatory approach, has included several actors within the process of implementation. In particular, the urban gardening process involved promoters, residents, retailers, local government and universities. However, our study is mainly focused on the first three categories as we intend to measure the impact for citizens and commercial activities.

The Ortobello initiative has been developed with the aim to regenerate the neighbourhood of Borgo Bello, in Perugia (Italy). This objective has been identified due to the necessity to bring new life to the area and limit spatial injustice. In particular, from this perspective, the revitalisation of several narrow streets and squares had the final aim to increase the liveability of the district, offering to the residents new community areas for social interaction, and to the retailers the opportunity to benefit from a livelier neighbourhood, characterised by the increasing presence of visitors and potential customers.

The urban gardening project is generally perceived as a good initiative by the community. Indeed, both the categories of citizens interviewed – residents and retailers – have recognised the presence of a positive aesthetic impact. The main benefit associated with the Ortobello project concerns the capacity of regenerating urban spaces and contributing to enhance the attractiveness of the area. Simultaneously with further events and festivals organised at the institutional level, the neighbourhood attracts visitors and generates important tourist flows. From this perspective, the urban gardening project represents the perfect tool to make the Borgo Bello neighbourhood more pleasant.

Considering the three different perspectives adopted – promoters, residents, retailers – it seems that the success of the project has been ambivalent. Despite the

---

[8] 'I giardini urbani sono parte di un processo di rinnovamento della città più ampio. Credo che sia una buona iniziativa anche se ritengo che non sia la ragione principale del miglioramento del livello di attrattività del quartiere.'

fact that urban gardens and social areas have been created and people interact in those places, it seems that community engagement has been limited. The need to continuously animate these urban spaces by identifying new and more effective strategies in order to engage with the local community has been recognised. The urban gardens are mainly perceived as public places and thus less related to an autonomous interaction. The majority of the respondents demonstrated an awareness about the existence of the urban gardens. However, it is still not very clear to the residents and retailers who is in charge of their management and maintenance. This highlights a scarce or ineffective communication strategy from the promoters of the project. Further investigation could focus on this issue in order to identify the most effective way to communicate and engage all the stakeholders living in that area.

A further key element that emerged from this case study concerns the resource management. In particular, in order to maintain the urban gardens in good condition, a crucial element seems to be the ability to collect financial resources through the identification and involvement of several stakeholders. From this perspective, the local government may provide a concrete organisational support. However, in order to obtain this support, it is expected to be able to provide reports and data about achieved goals, highlighting social and urban improvement. In this sense, a critical point emerged, since the organisers neither develop nor adopt any form of measurements to check the achieved results. This element may represent a limitation with regard to the project management and to the necessity to communicate the achieved goals to the institutions and community.

A research limitation refers to the selection of the categories that have been analysed. We included in the investigation three main stakeholders, exploring the perspectives of promoters, residents and retailers. Further investigation may consider other stakeholders involved, such as universities and local governments, in order to put in evidence their perceptions and enrich additional elements to analyse in more depth the roles and perceptions of the different actors involved in the process.

In conclusion, the Ortobello project has had a good impact on the local community. However, the positive effects may be enlarged, implementing a strategy for monitoring all the typologies of initiatives realised. In order to do that, an increasing flow of resources – human, economic and organisational – is needed. A more concrete engagement from the community may guarantee the achievement of future results.

Acknowledgements

The authors would like to thank the community of respondents for their valuable collaboration and are grateful to the Associazione Borgo Bello, Raymond Lorenzo and Viviana Lorenzo for sharing images of the project Ortobello.

References

Brenner, N. and Theodore, N. (2005): Neoliberalism and the urban condition. *City* 9 (1): 101–107.

Certomà, C. and Notteboom, B. (2015): Informal planning in a transactive governmentality: re-reading planning practices through Ghent's community gardens. *Planning Theory* 16 (1): 51–73.

CoDyre, M., Fraser, E. D. and Landman, K. (2015): How does your garden grow? An empirical evaluation of the costs and potential of urban gardening. *Urban Forestry & Urban Greening* 14 (1): 72–79.

Crompton, J. L. (1999): Beyond grants: other roles of foundations in facilitating delivery of park and recreation services in the US. *Managing Leisure* 4 (1): 1–23.

Donmoyer, R. (2000): Generalizability and the single-case study. In: Gomm, R., Hammersley, M. and Foster, P. (Eds.): *Case Study Method: Key Issues, Key Texts.* London, Thousand Oaks and New Delhi: Sage, 45–68.

Ferris, J., Norman, C. and Sempik, J. (2001): People, land and sustainability: community gardens and the social dimension of sustainable development. *Social Policy and Administration* 35: 559–568.

Flyvbjerg, B. (2006): Five misunderstandings about case-study research. *Qualitative Inquiry* 12 (2): 219–245.

Glover, T. D., Parry, D. C. and Shinew, K. J. (2005): Building relationships, accessing resources: mobilizing social capital in community garden contexts. *Journal of Leisure Research* 37 (4): 450–474.

Hardman, M. and Larkham, P. J. (2014): *Informal Urban Agriculture: The Secret Lives of Guerrilla Gardeners.* New York: Springer.

Istituto nazionale di statistica (ISTAT) (2017): Percorsi evolutivi dei territori italiani – 60 anni di storia socio-demografica attraverso i dati censuari. Italian National Institute for Statistics. www.istat.it/it/archivio/198306 (accessed 18 June 2017).

Jenkins, J. C. (1983). Resource mobilization theory and the study of social movements. *Annual Review of Sociology* 9 (1): 527–553.

Madanipour, A. (2010): Whose public space. In: Madanipour, A. (Ed.): *Whose Public Space? International Case Studies in Urban Design and Development.* Abingdon: Routledge, 237–262.

Ministero dell'Interno (2015): Relazione sull'attività delle forze di polizia, sullo stato dell'ordine e della sicurezza pubblica e sulla criminalità organizzata. www.camera.it/leg17/494?idLegislatura=17&categoria=038& (accessed 18 June 2017).

MIUR (2017): Anagrafe Nazionale Studenti. http://anagrafe.miur.it/index.php (accessed 18 June 2017).

O'Loughlin, J. V. (1973): Spatial justice for the black American voter: the territorial dimension in urban politics. Doctoral dissertation. Pennsylvania State University.

Pirie, G. H. (1983): On spatial justice. *Environment and Planning A* 15 (4): 465–473.

Regione Umbria (2015): Nuovo Piano Sociale. www.regione.umbria.it/notizie/-/asset_publisher/54m7RxsCDsHr/content/nuovo-piano-sociale-regionale-avviata-fase-concertazione-e-partecipazione-assessore-barberini-equita-centralita-della-persona-e-dei-territori-innovazi?read_more=true (accessed 18 June 2017).

Reynaud, A. (1981): *Société, espace et justice: inégalités régionales et justice socio-spatiale* (Vol. 6). Paris: Presses universitaires de France.

Roubanis, J. L. and Landis, W. (2007): Community gardening project: Meredith college students explore sustainability, organics. *Journal of Family and Consumer Sciences* 99 (3): 55–56.

Saldivar-Tanaka, L. and Krasny, M. E. (2004): Culturing community development, neighborhood open space, and civic agriculture: the case of Latino community gardens in New York City. *Agriculture and Human Values* 21 (4): 399–412.

Schmelzkopf, K. (2002): Incommensurability, land use, and the right to space: community gardens in New York City. *Urban Geography* 23 (4): 323–343.

Schukoske, J. E. (1999): Community development through gardening: state and local policies transforming urban open space. *NYUJ Legis. & Pub. Pol'y* 3: 351–392.

Soja, E. W. (2009): The city and spatial justice. *Spatial Justice* 1: 31–38.

Staeheli, L., Mitchell, D. and Gibson, K. (2002): Conflicting rights to the city in New York City's community gardens. *GeoJournal* 58: 197–205.

Tornaghi, C. (2014): Critical geography of urban agriculture. *Progress in Human Geography* 38: 551–567.

Yin, R. K. (1994): *Case Study Research Methods*, 2nd edn. California: Sage.

6

Community gardening for integrated urban renewal in Copenhagen: securing or denying minorities' right to the city?

Parama Roy

Introduction

Community gardening has been identified as a means of resistance to social injustice (McKay, 2011) and specifically to neoliberal[1] agendas and associated outcomes (Roy, 2010). At the same time, community gardens have also been identified as neoliberal artefacts (Pudup, 2008) that are used for gentrifying neighbourhoods (Quastel, 2009) or for compelling communities to compensate for State-retrenchment through grassroots community development projects, casting those who are unable to participate as undeserving of citizenship rights (Ghose and Pettygrove, 2014). While sufficient research on community gardening and its relevance to civil society – especially within the current market-driven political-economic condition – exists, the subtle similarities and differences between the extensively explored US (and to some extent UK) experience and that from the rest of the global North is only beginning to unfold as more scholars focus on these issues in the European State context (Certomà et al., 2016; Follman

---

[1] The post-1970s political-economic shift from a welfare-driven to a more market-driven and market-centric thinking and action, particularly in the United States and United Kingdom and later in other parts of the global North and South, has been described as neoliberal(ism) (see Brenner and Theodore, 2002). In this chapter, the term is used to underscore the competitive and entrepreneurial workings of the State and its unjust implications for the vulnerable population. Given the focus on competition, efficiency and profit-making, neoliberalism is critiqued for working in favour of the rich and the powerful, while further disempowering the poor and increasingly taking away from the rights of the common citizen (see further elaboration of this point in the next section).

and Viehoff, 2015; Rosol, 2010). This work not only adds empirical knowledge on community gardens in new geographic settings, but also theoretically advances our understanding of multiple and multifaceted neoliberalisms (Peck and Tickell, 2002) and their diverse manifestations in shaping socio-environmental and spatial justice through such everyday environmentalism (Milbourne, 2012). This chapter contributes to that end by highlighting the contradictory ways in which the dynamic Danish political-economy, strongly rooted in welfare-driven policies and increasingly moulded by global pressures of neoliberalism, is shaping urban community gardening practices and their impact on social and spatial justice for minority groups.

Community gardening is increasingly used by the Danish Integrated Urban Renewal (IUR) programme as a tool for dealing with issues of social cohesion. The IUR is mandated with uplifting the most socio-economically disadvantaged neighbourhoods in Danish cities. This chapter explores a gardening effort case study from Copenhagen in order to examine what state-initiated efforts mean for minority groups' (the homeless and ethnic minorities') rights to the city (Purcell, 2002; 2013a; 2013b), particularly within a traditionally welfare-driven but increasingly neoliberalised urban context. This work draws primarily on qualitative empirical research conducted between 2012 and 2015, when the author followed the Sundholm district urban renewal process as a participant observer. During this time the author conducted archival data analysis of planning documents, newspaper articles and website material, and carried out thirty-eight in-depth semi-structured interviews with individuals associated with the project (including five local planners, three social service workers, two local police officers, two representatives of local non-profit organisations, six active residents of Sundholm district and twenty citizen gardeners using the Sundholm garden, out of which three were homeless and ten were ethnic minorities). While attempts were made to reach out to more of the area's homeless, this group remained unresponsive. Local social workers explained that this was likely due to their lack of trust and their concern that they will be misrepresented. The Sundholm garden case study was chosen strategically. This urban garden and district renewal effort was heavily advertised in social media and in the local, national and European planning arenas as an exemplary case of inclusive planning (Sundholmsvej Omradeløft, 2009). It partnered with the EU-funded USER project, which intended to support efforts across nine European cities to plan and maintain public spaces by involving multiple and contending users including tourists, citizens, beggars and the homeless (USER, 2012). Not only was the garden space advertised as a space where citizens of all backgrounds are welcome, these citizens were also invited to be part of the process of planning the new neighbourhood space. As such, this case study presents an opportunity to evaluate the socio-spatial implications of a state-led but user-centric gardening effort that claims to be inclusive in protecting users' right to the city.

Theoretically informed by neoliberal urbanism (Brenner and Theodore, 2002; Peck and Tickell, 2002) and the right to the city literature (Harvey, 2008; Purcell,

2002) and empirically guided by a Danish case study, this chapter demonstrates how a dualistic policy focus – i.e simultaneously welfare- and market-driven – creates a complex scenario which at once secures and denies minorities' right to the city. While the Sundholm community garden on the one hand offers an add-itional open green space and provides a platform for neighbourhood minorities, particularly immigrant communities, to become politically active and connected, on the other hand it also restricts how and when homeless residents can use the garden space and its surrounding area. The chapter concludes by suggesting that the effectiveness of such state-initiated but community-led gardens in addressing concerns of social and spatial justice is likely to be ambiguous within such a political-economic context where traditional welfare-driven priorities intersect with emerging neoliberal policy trends in complex ways. Ultimately, market-driven policies and programmes are implemented at the ground level by local planners and street bureaucrats (Agger and Poulsen, 2017). As such, awareness among implementers about how broader political-economic shifts and associated impacts on urban renewal processes restrict minority rights to the city can be helpful to achieving more empowering community gardening experiences and other similar community-driven efforts for the traditionally disadvantaged.

Theoretical framework: using the right to the city concept as a measure of socio-spatial justice

Over the past couple of decades, the concept of the right to the city has become increasingly popular – within academia (Harvey, 2008; Marcuse, 2009; Mitchell, 2003; Purcell, 2002) as well as within policy-making and advocacy circles (Purcell, 2013a; 2013b; UNESCO, 2006; UN-HABITAT, 2010; United Nations Center for Human Settlements, 2001; Worldwide Conference on the Right to Cities Free from Discrimination and Inequality, 2002). This increasing engagement jus-tifies the multiple interpretations of what the right to the city encompasses. Henri Lefebvre, the urban sociologist who first developed the concept, presented the most radical interpretation (Purcell, 2013a). For Lefebvre, the right to the city was not about incrementally adding to existing liberal-democratic rights. Rather, he imagined the right to the city 'as a cry that initiated a radical struggle to move *beyond* both the state and capitalism' and as 'an essential element of wider polit-ical struggle for revolution' (Purcell, 2013a: 142). Contemporary scholarly and policy usage are rarely as radical. Despite considerable diversity within contem-porary interpretations and operationalisation of the right to the city concept, everyone seems to agree that it is ultimately about recognising the rights of urban inhabitants, irrespective of their nation-state citizenship or property rights. In other words, ensuring urban inhabitants' right to the city calls for challenging the capitalist mode of production of space that prioritises exchange value (hence property rights of owners) over use value (Purcell, 2013a). As such, the right to the city concept aims to challenge capitalist class relations and therefore can be operationalised as a tool for recalibrating social relations, inequalities and related spatial implications.

While there are multiple formulations of the right to the city, in this chapter I specifically follow Harvey's interpretation. According to Harvey, the right to the city is 'not merely a right of access to what already exists, but a right to change it after our heart's desire' (Harvey, 2003: 939). This definition highlights two aspects: the first relates to urban inhabitants' ability to access and use urban spaces and the second relates to urban inhabitants' ability to produce and change those spaces as per their needs and concerns. Instead of accepting how state planners, property speculators, developers and/or urban elites produce city spaces, all urban inhabitants are then expected to play a more empowered and active role in socio-political decision-making processes. This could be achieved through participation in elections, through planning-related public engagement processes or through local organisations. In this sense, the physical access to and use of right to city spaces symbolise a state of spatial justice, while the processual access to the socio-political realm where urban inhabitants can actively mould production of urban space and claim some degree of shaping power over the process of urbanisation (Harvey, 2008) symbolises social justice. As such, in this chapter I intend to operationalise the concept of the right to the city as a measure of or proxy for social and spatial justice, and to explore how the state-initiated community gardening effort in Sundholm district shapes, secures and/or denies neighbourhood homeless groups' and ethnic minorities' ability to:

- Use and just be in the physical space of the garden (a public space).
- Translate this into access to the political, urban governance space where they can voice their needs and have a say in (re)producing this and other spaces in the neighbourhood and the city.

The right to the city and community gardens

The relevance of the right to the city concept within urban research and activism has particularly strengthened in response to neoliberal capitalism. Pointing out the interconnections between neoliberal political-economic shifts and corresponding changes in urban governance (such as the rescaling of urban governance, the shift from redistribution-based to competition-based policy-making and the greater involvement of non-state and quasi-state bodies), scholars have suggested that emerging governance configurations tend to further disempower urban inhabitants with respect to their role in urban decision-making (Purcell, 2002; Tickell and Peck, 1996; Ward, 2000). This is particularly true for already disenfranchised groups such as the poor, ethnic minorities, the homeless, the LGBT community, etc. Within this context, the right to the city concept has offered a reasonable framework to think about resisting neoliberal urbanisation or at least challenge the disempowering implications of neoliberal urbanisation (depending on how radically the idea is interpreted) and formulate strategies to empower urban inhabitants (Holston and Appudurai, 1999; Isin, 2000; Sandercock, 1998; Soja, 2000; Worldwide Conference on the Right to Cities Free from Discrimination and Inequality, 2002).

As such, community-based urban organisations are increasingly guided by this concept of securing communities' right to the city (Purcell and Tyman, 2015), sometimes explicitly and sometimes implicitly. Purely grassroots as well as state-supported local initiatives forming neighbourhood watch groups, food cooperatives or community gardening efforts present examples of bottom-up attempts to mobilise local inhabitants and to take control of neighbourhood spaces. Community gardening scholarship has indicated how these initiatives have increasingly emerged as ways for communities to resist neoliberal retrenchment of the state, challenging neoliberal inequalities especially within marginalised neighbourhoods (Ghose and Pettygrove, 2014) and for claiming rights to space for racially and economically marginalised citizens (Staeheli et al., 2002). In fact, while community gardens have had a long history (Smith and Kurtz, 2003), these practices have proliferated immensely as a commonplace community response to neoliberalisation at the local urban scale (Baker, 2004).

On the one hand, community gardens have been discussed as spaces of empowerment for citizens in general and marginalised citizens in particular. On the other hand they have also been identified in many instances as artefacts of neoliberalism. For example, Pudup (2008) points out how state-initiated garden projects are often meant for coaxing incarcerated, socially unwanted individuals to think and behave like citizen-subjects who do not question, but instead comply with, the existing neoliberal socio-political system. Furthermore, since neoliberal and entrepreneurial states promote certain kinds of public spaces and tend to control who uses these spaces and how (Rosol, 2012), conflicts over garden spaces have proliferated (Smith and Kurtz, 2003; Staeheli et al., 2002). Those garden practices/spaces that are seen as threats or barriers to capital accumulation and revenue generation are therefore subject to eviction and severe restrictions by state agencies within neoliberal political-economic regimes (Irazabal and Punja, 2009; Smith and Kurtz, 2003). While community garden practices in some instances are discouraged by state authorities and private interests, in other cases entrepreneurial states may actively encourage community gardens with the intention of attracting capital investments and gentrifying neighbourhoods (Domene and Saurí, 2007; Quastel, 2009). This further signifies the sort of tension between use value and exchange value of urban land discussed earlier as the main issue inspiring the right to the city concept. As such, there is greater scepticism regarding such gardening efforts initiated and supported by state authorities within the global neoliberal political-economic context. But how can we understand the real implications of state-initiated yet community-driven gardening efforts in a dynamic political-economic context like Copenhagen in Denmark – which currently does not fit neatly into its traditional image of a welfare system, nor is it as distinctively neoliberal as the United States or the United Kingdom? The next section elaborates on the Danish context and the nature of its urban governance.

Implications of global neoliberalism on Danish urban governance

Denmark, like most Scandinavian countries, is rooted in a strong social democratic post-war welfare regime. The Danish state has long been committed to providing universal social benefits for all and continues to spend substantial amounts on social expenditure (Eurostat, 2014; Roy, 2018). Furthermore, it has invested and continues to invest in environmentally sustainable urban growth dependent on public transportation, while protecting its green and blue infrastructures (Copenhagen European Green Capital, 2014; Danish Ministry of the Environment, 2007; Technical and Environmental Administration, 2012) and encouraging broad civic involvement in urban planning processes (Agger et al., 2016). However, this relatively strong socio-environmentally progressive state context is increasingly reshaped by the global trends of neoliberalisation. Although Denmark joined the neoliberal bandwagon late, definitive shifts have been noticed within Danish political-economic norms and urban governance values since the 1990s. Moving away from a redistributive development strategy to making Copenhagen the regional capital and the primary growth engine, the Danish state has abandoned its earlier universal growth agenda.

In the last couple of decades, 'an entrepreneurial urban politics, more accommodating towards investors and developers, has been implemented here [in Copenhagen, Denmark]' (Larsen and Lund Hansen, 2008: 2433). As such, Andersen and Pløger (2007) describe Danish urban governance as 'dual' in character – where entrepreneurial discourses and practices are increasingly entangled with the traditional welfare-driven state's workings. This in its turn seems to have inspired a similar dualism within Denmark's Integrated Urban Renewal (IUR) programme. On the one hand, the IUR programme emphasises its primary agenda as the upliftment of disadvantaged neighbourhoods by involving local residents. This is supported by the programme's claim to help those who are in need and give them the opportunity to access equal social, economic and environmental benefits so that Danish cities can be more cohesive (Technical and Environmental Administration, District Development, 2010). On the other hand, the IUR programme also celebrates its success to revert the development of non-profit housing and render the renewed neighbourhoods more attractive to employed middle-income residents (Jensen and Munk, 2007). This makes such renewal efforts resonate with state-led gentrification projects (Lees, 2008). A similar duality is reflected in Copenhagen municipality's aim to ensure that 20 per cent of investment in housing goes to non-profit housing for the poor while at the same time working to gentrify neighbourhoods. As such, the head of the municipal planning bureau explains that, in order to make the city economically sustainable (i.e. suitable for the economically well-off), the city's housing policy (ironically titled *housing for all*) must aim to remove the less economically resourceful or the 'trash' from the city (Larsen and Lund Hansen, 2008)! Within such dualistic urban governance and urban renewal context, state-initiated community gardening practices present a new set of meanings for the socio-spatial rights of minority citizens in disadvantaged neighbourhoods.

Securing the right to the city by claiming the right to a neighbourhood community garden

Sundholm, the district and the institution

Sundholm district is situated in south-east Copenhagen (see Figure 6.1). The district is named after the Sundholm Institute, located in the north-western corner of the district (see Figure 6.1). Built in the early eighteenth century as a labour camp for the destitute (USER, 2012), Sundholm still houses several social institutions that provide services to the homeless. As such, the place continues to be 'a sanctuary' for Copenhagen's homeless, with 200 to 300 homeless visiting or loitering in Sundholm every day, and making use of the resources (USER, 2012: 56). Sundholm district, which makes up the larger area around the Sundholm Institute, was identified as one of Copenhagen's 'disadvantaged' neighbourhoods and targeted for an IUR in 2008 (Technical and Environmental Administration, District Development, 2010). The area is believed to have deteriorated in its socio-economic character over the last fifteen years, with increasing social problems such as crime and vandalism (Unified Plan, 2008). Data from the Statistical Bank of Copenhagen Municipality (2012–13) show that the district has a higher percentage of people who are unemployed (5 per cent), live on social security (15 per cent) and belong to non-Western ethnic backgrounds (23 per cent) compared to the city average (4 per cent, 11 per cent and 14 per cent for the three parameters, respectively).

Among a variety of other efforts, Sundholm district renewal is particularly lauded for its Sundholm community garden project, which is situated inside the Sundholm institutional area (see Figure 6.1). Sundholm garden was created with the explicit purpose of fostering social cohesion. Therefore, planners played an active role in recruiting a group of Pakistani and Turkish women, as well as Sundholm's homeless (who were guided by a social worker from Activity Center, an agency providing the homeless with employment opportunities) to join and work in the garden alongside Danish and other Western-immigrant locals. In the following section, I highlight the positive and negative implications of the garden space for the district's homeless and ethnic minorities in terms of their right to the city's physical and socio-political space. To address the possible dismissal of the disempowering implications simply as unwanted effects of well-intended planning, I begin by highlighting the explicit and implicit motivations driving the garden project.

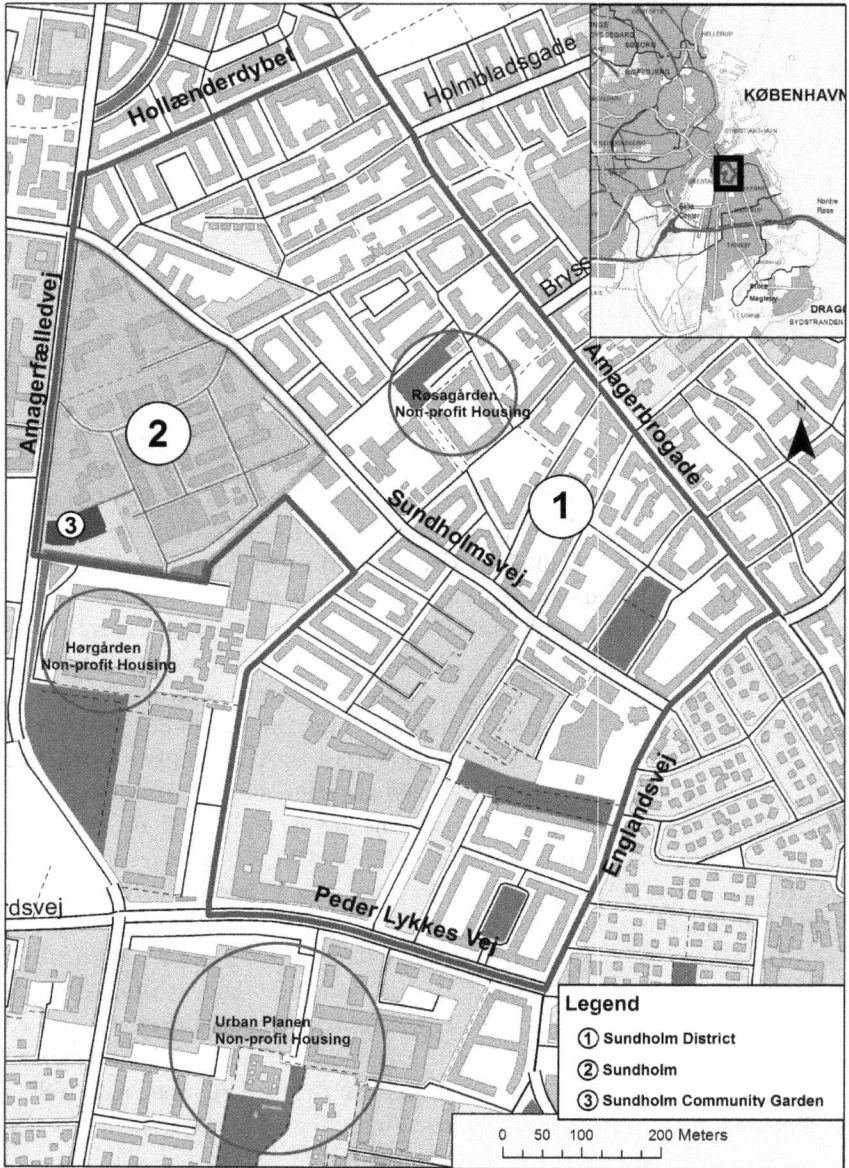

Figure 6.1   Map of study area

Sundholm garden: competing motivations

Sundholm garden was inspired by the dual nature of the Danish state and urban policies, including its IUR programme and local planners' and citizens' socio-political

Figure 6.2   Sundholm urban garden

values and aspirations. As such, it reflects interesting ambiguities in its motivations. One planner explained that the Copenhagen municipality was interested in investing in public green infrastructures like pocket parks and community gardens in its effort to ensure that all its citizens have access to a green/blue space within ten minutes of walking distance. This is commonly presented as a matter of achieving a cohesive city environment where everyone, irrespective of class or ethnicity, enjoys environmental equality (see Figure 6.2, which reflects the diversity of the Sundholm gardeners) (Technical and Environmental Administration, District Development, 2010). However, we should also recognise that this motivation is likely to be associated with Copenhagen's aspiration to become a European Green Capital, which it achieved in 2014 (Copenhagen European Green Capital, 2014). Undoubtedly, such titles of greenness and sustainability are effective branding tools in the hands of contemporary entrepreneurial cities competing for comparative advantage in the global market for capital (Roy, 2018).

Another motivation behind developing Sundholm garden, as highlighted by the urban renewal planning team, is one of building a space of socio-cultural integration. As such, the garden was presented as 'a socially and culturally inclusive urban garden, where excluded groups meet the "normal" civil society, to achieve a more tolerant and understanding view of "the others" and thereby underpin the coexistence of the very different groups of users existing in Sundholm' (Sundholm District Urban Renewal Office, 2014: 3). Therefore, in addition to providing access to the physical space, providing opportunities for greater acceptance and interaction across social and cultural barriers – and hence greater social justice – was also seen as an important function of this space.

Finally, Sundholm garden was also seen as an important means to changing the neighbourhood image. Given that the municipality was building middle-income housing in the vicinity and had plans to develop many of the other available lots into middle-income housing in the area, one planner explained how it was important to 'build something social before the physical development' that showed that this is a safe place. Sundholm garden, therefore, was also about creating a cleaner and more beautiful space (compared to before, when it was a glass-ridden abandoned space used uniquely by the homeless), which presented an image of a diverse yet cohesive space, where Danes, non-Danes and the socially neglected homeless could all coexist. This new image lift was necessary in order for the municipality to attract middle-income home owners and renters into the neighbourhood.

Sundholm garden: ambiguous implications for minorities' right to the city

These multiple motivations have meant that Sundholm garden is a space that to varying degrees offers environmental equality, social cohesion, greater market-ability and comparative advantage – all at the same time. While this may seem like a win-win outcome, a closer look at the implications in terms of ethnic immigrants' and homeless' right to the city suggests otherwise. In the next section, I examine:

*   The minority communities' access and ability to use Sundholm garden.
*   The extent to which such physical access translates into greater access to the city's social and political spaces of interaction and decision-making.

This latter development is fundamental to achieving a higher order of the right to the city as discussed in the theoretical section.

Access to physical space

Most of the ethnic immigrants living in Sundholm district live in apartments with little access to open green spaces. While Sundholm district has a number of parks, such as Saeterdals Parken and Scotlands Plads, they were unkempt, unsafe and underutilised. The Sundholm urban renewal process refurbished these existing parks, in addition to creating new green areas like the Sundholm garden and Nabohavn, another small community garden that mostly involved ethnic immi-grant girls from surrounding social housing projects. As immigrant women were purposefully recruited into the Sundholm garden, it undoubtedly contributed positively towards ethnic immigrants' access to such physical resources. One Pakistani woman acknowledged, 'I think this is a wonderful thing that the

Kommune [meaning municipality] is doing for us … so that we can come out and do something productive'. During a discussion with a group of ten Pakistani and Turkish women working in the garden, all agreed that coming to the garden was their only chance to get out of their small apartments and enjoy nature hands-on. Interestingly, few ethnic immigrant men were included in the Sundholm garden project, which could be explained in part by the gendered nature of gardening practice in general (Parry et al., 2005) and also by the fact that planners might have found it easier to recruit ethnic immigrant women than young ethnic men and boys – who are generally perceived in the neighbourhood as the more 'problematic group'. Overall, however, one could argue that ethnic minority groups in the district now have better access to green spaces as a result of the garden, and can claim their right to this neighbourhood space.

Unfortunately, homeless groups' access to the garden is a bit more limited. In principal, they are welcome in the garden. Twelve out of a total of sixty gardening boxes are kept aside for the homeless and are maintained by the Activity Center, which is also in charge of recruiting interested homeless to participate in gardening. However, very few homeless individuals actually use the garden. Several of them are unhappy about losing free space as a result of the renewal process. One of the local planners explained, 'it's obvious that homeless people are feeling the pressure from outside with all the new buildings and they feel that they are being pushed away from a space that was formerly theirs. The garden, of course they like it, mostly those who use it for gardening, but it used to be just a wild area, so that they could camp and now there is less and less space for that. So, some of the free space they have had disappears now and they react to that, no doubt about it'. In the process of urban renewal, then, the area's homeless lost their claim to this space that they previously enjoyed. This spatial injustice cannot be fully understood in isolation from the renewal efforts' contribution to cleansing of other green spaces in the area, pushing the homeless into specific corners of the neighbourhood (Roy, 2018). Furthermore, only those who are ready to participate like responsible citizens or neoliberal subjects (Barron, 2017; Ghose and Pettygrove, 2014; Pudup, 2008) by working productively in the garden are welcome, while those loitering or sleeping in the garden are politely asked to move on by Activity Center social workers – or, if required, by local police officers. Overall, the Sundholm garden therefore fits well with the city's aim to transform the image of the area into a more clean and safe place with staged and manageable diversity while subtly imposing restrictions on people and behaviours that might threaten its economic development goals for the neighbourhood.

Access to socio-political city spaces

Sundholm garden brought together a group of people from varied backgrounds who are unlikely under normal circumstances to share a common space, let alone interact freely together. In a neighbourhood where ethnic relations have been strained to say the least, where Danish residents commonly feel that 'since the immigrants have come, it [the neighbourhood] has changed … It has become worse' (interview with an elderly Danish woman, January 2015), and where non-Danes express that, '[t]hey (the Danes) don't like us, we don't like them' (interview with Pakistani teenage boy, September 2014), Sundholm garden has indeed provided a space for some degree of reconciliation. A sense of understanding and acceptance, if not friendship, has developed – at least among those who use the space. One of the gardeners said, 'I have got many new friends through the urban garden. Today, we do not only meet there (in the garden) but we also do other things together. I feel that I have become part of a community of active people, and we pop up with new ideas of what we can do together' (Social Response, 2014: 29). During participant observation sessions, it was obvious how easily discussions around different types of crops being grown in the garden for different ethnic recipes led to more open discussions around religious and cultural differences, offering an effective means of fostering greater socio-cultural understanding and tolerance. Generally held negative perceptions and stereotypical images of the homeless were also challenged in the garden space. One Pakistani gardener explained how her and others' attitude towards Sundholm's homeless people had evolved: 'You can see here, how wonderfully she has made this fence here. She is also homeless. Like her there are many others who have done nice things here … While we may think that the homeless are addicted and cannot do anything … that perception changes when you see them do productive things.'

As such, gardening practices in Sundholm garden have opened new opportunities for the diverse group of neighbourhood users to share a space, interact and even develop a sense of acceptance and understanding of each other. In addition, local planners who initiated the garden played an important role in handing greater decision-making power and opening channels to get connected with the city's decision-making and political space in innovative ways. First and foremost, they made sure that users eventually form a formal association to make decisions regarding the garden space when the renewal period of five to seven years ends (Agger et al., 2016). On various occasions these planners also attempted to politically empower the garden users. For instance, on one occasion local planners brought the ballot to the garden, in an effort to encourage citizens who avoid participating in the polls to do so and to recognise the importance of voicing their needs. On another occasion, local planners helped garden users write to their local mayor to invite him to the garden and convince him to fund a social activist who would be in charge of keeping the homeless community involved in the garden. One planner explained the motivation behind this effort by saying that, 'having the citizens invite the politicians is a very important tool, both to empower people, to show that they can actually do this, so that when we [planners] are not there anymore, they can still do this' for meeting other community needs. These intentional efforts on the part of the planners to use the garden space as a venue for developing linking social capital (Szreter and Woolcock, 2004; also, see Agger et al., 2016) played an important part in developing key socio-political networks that the garden users can use in the future for the sake of governing the garden space as well as for meeting other community concerns (Agger et al., 2016). Now, as a result of such efforts, garden users have better exposure to and linkages with the city's political space, agencies and representatives.

However, perhaps not surprisingly, homeless garden users were not able to extract the benefits of these new political connections to the same extent as Danish and non-Danish users. This is partly because very few homeless remain involved in the gardening, and the ones who do are represented by the Activity Center. Their ability to get involved or represent themselves more directly is complicated by issues of addiction, mental health conditions and pressure to meet immediate needs such as food, shelter, etc. As such, the extent to which Sundholm garden contributed to greater socio-political empowerment and hence social justice is differential for ethnic minorities and the homeless community.

Conclusion: differential socio-spatial implications of gardening practices for minorities

Substantial research on community gardening has highlighted how it can some-times contribute to greater civic empowerment and social-environmental justice, while at other times it can emerge as a means to reinforcing neoliberal forces and relations that enhance existing inequalities. Analysis of the Sundholm urban garden using a right to the city framework suggests that whether such practices empower or disempower urban inhabitants depends partly on the political-economic context and national and local state priorities, partly on the aspirations and values of local planners and street bureaucrats working on the ground and partly on the characteristics of the different user groups. As such, the dual Danish governance context presents competing motivations for the development of projects like the Sundholm garden. The state's welfare-bent, which is supported by local planners' compassionate intentions on the one hand, developed Sundholm garden as a space for social interaction, acceptance and political empowerment for the disadvantaged. At the same time, the state's entrepreneurial-bent shaped Sundholm garden as a means to uplifting the image of the place as a diverse yet safe area for potential middle-income residents to live in. These competing motivations lead to ambiguous and differential social and spatial implications for different minority groups in the neighbourhood.

For ethnic minorities, Sundholm garden provided physical access to a new city space while offering opportunities for gaining access to the city's socio-political decision-making space. For the neighbourhood's homeless, however, physical access to the garden itself remained limited by the imposition of specific behavioural norms and expectations. Sundholm garden, therefore, to a certain extent secured both the right of use and the right of shaping urban spaces for ethnic minorities while largely denying those rights to the homeless.

This chapter presents some important lessons for future community gardening scholarship and practice. First and foremost, it highlights the essential need to understand the political-economic history and context of a place and its institutional environment when examining the implications of community garden practices for communities' right to the city. As we have seen in this case study from Denmark, a specific manifestation of neoliberalism represented by the dual urban governance in Copenhagen shapes state-initiated yet community-led gardening practices with some empowering and some disempowering results for marginalised members of the community. This chapter also underscores the need to recognise that the challenges faced by different disadvantaged groups are diverse and hence the efforts that prove to be empowering for one group may not be so for others. Finally, this case study also points to the need to emphasise the role that local planners and street bureaucrats play in using community garden projects for more socio-spatially just results. While these individuals ultimately work within their broader political-economic context, their values and aspirations to, for instance, 'empower' citizens or 'challenge social inequality' can be extremely effective for extracting positive implications for minorities' right to the city. Therefore, a good understanding of the broader context, strategic mobilisation of the right to the city concept and intentional effort of planners and citizens can better ensure community gardens' role in fostering greater socio-spatial justice in cities.

References

Agger, A. and Poulsen, B. (2017): Street-level bureaucrats coping with conflicts in area-based initiatives in Copenhagen and Malmo. *Scandinavian Political Studies* 40 (4): 367–387.

Agger, A., Roy, P. and Leonardsen, Ø. (2016): Anchoring network-based community projects in Copenhagen. *Planning Theory and Practice* 17 (3): 325–343.

Andersen, J. and Pløger, J. (2007): The dualism of urban governance in Denmark. *European Planning Studies* 15 (10): 1349–1367.

Baker, L. E. (2004): Tending cultural landscapes and food citizenship in Toronto's community gardens. *Geographical Review* 94 (3): 305–325.

Barron, J. (2017): Community gardening: cultivating subjectivities, space, and justice. *Local Environment* 22 (9): 1142–1158.

Brenner, N. and Theodore, N. (Eds) (2002): *Spaces of Neoliberalism: Urban Restructuring in North America and Western Europe*. Malden, MA: Blackwell Publishers Ltd.

Certomà, C., Hardman, M., Ioannou, B., Morán, N., Notteboom, B., Silvestri, G. and Sondermann, M. (2016): Grassroots movements: towards cooperative forms of green urban development? In: Bell, S., Fox-Kamper, R., Keshavarz, N., Benson, M., Caputo, S., Noori, S. and Voigt, A. (Eds): *Urban Allotment Gardens in Europe*. New York: Routledge, 62–90.

Copenhagen European Green Capital (2014): Copenhagen European Green Capital 2014: a review. http://ec.europa.eu/environment/europeangreencapital/wp-ontent/uploads/2013/02/Copenhagen-Post-Assessment-Report-2014-EN.pdf (accessed 30 December 2015).

Danish Ministry of the Environment (2007): Spatial planning in Denmark. http://naturstyrelsen.dk/media/nst/attachments/planning_260907_ny6.pdf (accessed 11 April 2015).

Domene, E. and Saurí, D. (2007): Urbanization and class-produced natures: vegetable gardens in the Barcelona Metropolitan Region. *Geoforum* 38: 287–298.

Eurostat (2014): *Eurostat Statistical Books: Living Conditions in Europe.* Luxembourg: European Union.

Follmann, A. and Viehoff, V. (2015): A green garden on red clay: creating a new urban common as a form of political gardening in Cologne, Germany. *Local Environment* 20 (10): 1148–1174.

Ghose, R. and Pettygrove, M. (2014): Actors and networks in urban community gardens. *Geoforum* 53: 93–103.

Harvey, D. (2003): The right to the city. *International Journal of Urban and Regional Research* 27 (4): 939–941.

Harvey, D. (2008): The right to the city. *New Left Review* 53: 23–40.

Holston, J. and Appadurai, A. (1999): Introduction: cities and citizenship. In: Holston, J. (Ed.): *Cities and Citizenship.* Durham, NC: Duke University Press, 1–20.

Irazabal, C. and Punja, A. (2009): Cultivating just planning and legal institutions: a critical assessment of the south central farm struggle in Los Angeles. *Urban Affairs* 31 (1): 1–23.

Isin, E. (2000): Introduction: democracy, citizenship and the city. In: Isin, E. (Ed.): *Democracy, Citizenship and the Global City.* New York: Routledge, 1–21.

Jensen, E. H. and Munk, A. (Eds) (2007): *Kvarterløft: 10 Years of Urban Regeneration.* Denmark: The Ministry of Refugees, Immigration and Integration Affairs. www.nyidanmark.dk/NR/rdonlyres/8B65A41E-79E6-4227-B08B-1B5A641CC27E/0/10_years_of_urban_regeneration.pdf (accessed 3 March 2015).

Larsen, H. G. and Lund Hansen, A. (2008): Gentrification gentle or traumatic? Urban renewal policies and socioeconomic transformations in Copenhagen. *Urban Studies* 45 (12): 2429–2448.

Lees, L. (2008): Gentrification and social mixing: towards an inclusive urban renaissance? *Urban Studies* 45 (12): 2449–2470.

Marcuse, P. (2009): From critical urban theory to the city. *City* 13 (2–3): 185–197.

McKay, G. (2011): *Radical Gardening.* London: Frances Lincoln Limited.

Milbourne, P. (2012): Everyday (in)justices and ordinary environmentalisms: community gardening in disadvantaged urban neighborhoods. *Local Environment* 17 (9): 943–957.

Mitchell, D. (2003): *The Right to the City: Social Justice and the Fight for Public Space.* New York: Guilford Press.

Parry, D., Glover, T. D. and Shinew, K. J. (2005): Mary, Mary quite contrary, how does your garden grow? Examining gender roles and relations in community gardens. *Leisure Studies* 24 (2): 177–192.

Peck, J. and Tickell, A. (2002): Neoliberalizing space. In: Brenner, N. and Theodore, N. (Eds): *Spaces of Neoliberalism: Urban Restructuring in North America and Western Europe.* Malden, MA, Oxford, UK and Carlton, Australia: Blackwell Publishers Ltd, 33–57.

Pudup, M. (2008): It takes a garden: cultivating citizen-subjects in organized garden projects. *Geoforum* 39: 1228–1240.

Purcell, M. (2002): Excavating Lefebvre: the right to the city and its urban politics of the inhabitant. *GeoJournal* 58: 99–108.

Purcell, M. (2013a): Possible worlds: Henri Lefebvre and the right to the city. *Journal of Urban Affairs* 36 (1): 141–154.

Purcell, M. (2013b): The right to the city: the struggle for democracy in the urban public realm. *Policy & Politics* 43 (3): 311–327.

Purcell, M. and Tyman, S. K. (2015): Cultivating food as a right to the city. *Local Environment* 20 (10): 1132–1147.

Quastel, N. (2009): Political ecologies of gentrification. *Urban Geography* 30 (7): 694–725.

Rosol, M. (2010): Public participation in post-Fordist urban green space governance: the case of community gardens in Berlin. *International Journal of Urban and Regional Research* 34 (3): 548–563.

Rosol, M. (2012): Community volunteering as neoliberal strategy? Green space production in Berlin. *Antipode* 44 (1): 239–257.

Roy, P. (2010): Analyzing empowerment: an ongoing process of building state-civil society relations, the case of Walnut Way in Milwaukee. *Geoforum* 41: 337–348.

Roy, R. (2018): 'Welcome in my backyard' ... but on my terms: making sense of homeless exclusion from renewed urban spaces in Copenhagen. *GeoJournal* 83: 289–304.

Sandercock, L. (1998): The death of modernist planning: radical praxis for a postmodern age. In: Friedmann, J. and Douglass, M. (Eds): *Cities for Citizens: Planning and the Rise of Civil Society in a Global Age.* New York: John Wiley & Sons, 163–184.

Smith, C. and Kurtz, H. (2003): Community gardens and politics of scale in New York City. *Geographical Review* 93 (2): 193–212.

Social Response (2014): Fortællinger fra et områdeløft – og anbefalinger til arbejdet med netværksbaseret byudvikling. https://issuu.com/sofiebwinther/docs/fort__llinger_ fra_et_omr__del__ft (accessed 23 April 2018).

Soja, E. (2000): *Postmetropolis.* Malden, MA: Blackwell.

Staeheli, A. L., Mitchell, D. and Gibson, K. (2002): Conflicting rights to the city in New York's community gardens. *GeoJournal* 58 (2/3): 197–205.

Statistical Bank of Copenhagen Municipality (2012–13): www.dst.dk/en/Statistik (accessed January 2014).

Sundholmsvej Omradeløft (2009): Kvarterplan 2008–2013, Sundholmsvejkvarterets Omradeløft. www.kk.dk/da/borger/byggeri/byfornyelse/omraadefornyelser/Sundholmskvarteret (accessed 5 February 2013).

Sundholm District Urban Renewal Office (2014): Urban gardening for social inclusion: a report for EU-USER project.

Szreter, S. and Woolcock, M. (2004): Health by association? Social capital, social theory, and the political economy of public health. *International Journal of Epidemiology* 33: 650–667.

Technical and Environmental Administration (2012): Integrated urban renewal in Copenhagen, 2012. http://kk.sites.itera.dk/apps/kk_pub2/pdf/870_hHa1d53AJZ. pdf (accessed 19 March 2015).

Technical and Environmental Administration, District Development (2010): Policies for disadvantaged areas in Copenhagen (2010). www.kk.dk/da/Om-kommunen/ Indsatsomraader-og-politikker/Publikationer.aspx?mode=detalje&id=869 (accessed 24 November 2013).

Tickell, A. and Peck, J. (1996): The return of the Manchester men: men's words and men's deeds in the remaking of the local state. *Transactions of the Institute of British Geographers* 21: 596–616.

UNESCO (2006): *International Public Debates: Urban Policies and the Right to the City.* Paris: UNESCO.

UN-HABITAT (2010): *The Right to the City: Bridging the Urban Divide.* Rio de Janeiro: World Urban Forum, United Nations.

Unified Plan (2008): Boligsocial helhedsplan for Sundholmsvejkvarteret. VIBO, AAB, Lejerbo, Hovedstadens Almennyttige Boligselskab. www.sundholmskvarteret.dk/picture/upload/file/Helhedsplan%20Sundholmsvej%20ENDELIG.pdf (accessed 3 February 2013).

United Nations Center for Human Settlements (2001): *Policy Dialogue Series: Number 1 Women and Urban Governance*. New York: UNCHS (Habitat).

USER (2012): USER changes and conflicts in using public spaces, base line study URBACT II. http://urbact.eu/fileadmin/Projects/USER/outputs_media/baselineUSER_01.pdf (accessed 2 March 2013).

Ward, K. (2000): A critique in search of a corpus: re-visiting governance and re-interpreting urban politics. *Transactions of the Institute of British Geographers* 25: 169–185.

Worldwide Conference on the Right to Cities Free from Discrimination and Inequality. (2002): Conference in Porto Allege, Brazil, February.

7

Limits to growth? Why gardening has limited success growing inclusive communities

Hannah Pitt

Introduction

As this collection's introduction highlights, heavy expectations are placed on urban gardens' ability to advance social and spatial justice. Community is central to these: as outcomes of garden practices, it is taken as evidence of social inclusion as people form relationships of trust and mutual-dependence. As both mode of garden activity and mechanism of its achievements, community is seen to represent an inclusive approach to addressing injustice, hence much attention to *whether* urban gardens form communities. Instead I ask *what kinds* of communities are made and whether they can tackle inequality, questioning the success of community as both process and product of gardens' potential to challenge injustice. Answering these questions requires attention to activities forming garden communities and their spatiality – how extensive are these place-based relations and can they effect change rooted elsewhere? I challenge simplistic treatments of links between garden, community and place, and propose gardens produce communities of interest-in-place. Case studies demonstrate how facets enabling gardens to form communities result in exclusivity, unintentionally limiting who has access to their benefits. Informed by relational geographies, I apply a spatial lens to focus on gardens' limits in building inclusive communities where people belong regardless of differences, and benefits are fairly distributed. This suggests communities formed through collective place-making struggle to extend across space and time, limiting their potential to reduce social inequalities. Achieving wider change requires work to push spatial relations across time to imagine a better future, across space towards neighbours, social justice movements and structural causes of injustice. First, I outline the need for a relational approach to gardens' spatiality and its relationship to community; the third section details how case study gardens in the UK formed communities. Subsequent sections consider expectations around community, and then explore how ideals were not met and perspectives from outsiders. A spatial perspective is applied to illuminate how community-forming processes were limiting in terms of social inclusion, before the conclusion outlines implications for the operation of urban gardens if they are to advance urban justice.

What is the relationship between community, place and gardens?

The idea of community is central to the operation and analysis of urban gardens, as a product of garden practices and a mode of delivering benefits. But urban gardening literature tends to lack clarity on the nature of community, or treats it simplistically and idealistically, as a homogeneous coherent unit (Neo and Chua, 2017). Studies increasingly highlight how communal experiences within urban gardens are far from ideal, including conflict and inequalities (Aptekar, 2015; Tan and Neo, 2009). Other work unravels meanings of community and demonstrates it as performed through social relations (Drake, 2014). I build on these foundations to question the nature of community developed through gardening, without assuming it is inevitable or ideal, using a relational understanding. From a relational perspective, place and community do not exist prior to activity or relationships but are generated by them, so are always in process (Massey, 2005). If community forms around a garden it is a result of social practices taking place there, with the relationships it comprises a potential mechanism for achieving benefits (Drake, 2014).

Previous work on urban gardens includes problematic assumptions about links between place and community. Early advocates presented urban gardens as countering social isolation and individualism, re-building communities dismantled by urban decline (Hynes, 1996; Irvine et al., 1999). This narrative assumes urbanisation dissolved close-knit community, replacing local interaction with relations at a distance (Day, 2006). This appeal to lost community has been criticised as romantic nostalgia for impossible ideals (Amin and Thrift, 2002), assuming a single version centred on direct personal interactions incapable of adapting to new social conditions (Day, 2006). Because this prioritises local face-to-face relationships, gardens where different people meet and become familiar are celebrated for fostering social inclusion (Beilin and Hunter, 2011; Colding and Barthel, 2013; Firth et al., 2011). From this perspective place is a platform on which social relations develop rather than a product of them, without considering how relations emerge or are influenced by spatial form.

Writing on urban gardens can imply inevitable, unproblematic relationships between place and community, and that those sharing a place equate a unified community. This roots community in place, prioritising local direct relations over spatially extensive connections through interest or identity. This conception has been challenged on multiple grounds, particularly its homogenising effects (Young, 2010). Geographers argue there is no essential relationship between place and community (Massey, 1994). There are non-spatial identities around which communities form, whilst neighbours do not necessarily equal a community (Massey, 1994; Staeheli, 2008). If place is produced through ongoing processes of relating (Massey, 2005), community is similarly constituted through relationships as groups come together (Rose, 1997), cannot be fixed and includes multiple identities (Young, 2010). Treated relationally, garden communities may or may not arise through processes of coming together (Drake, 2014); their form and outcomes vary between garden-places (Kurtz, 2001).

Relational understandings which complicate the links between community and place have been influential in human geography (Jones, 2009), but alternative narratives are enacted through policy. These affect urban gardens linked to community development programmes either as projects directly supported by policy initiatives (Milbourne, 2011), or as symptoms of neoliberal rollback (Pudup, 2008). As community-based attempts to drive urban change (Drake, 2014), gardens enact positive imaginaries of place-based communities. The community development policy relevant to my case studies is Communities First, a poverty reduction programme targeting Wales' most deprived wards. It focused on local people identifying problems and delivering solutions, and assumed strong communities capable of action (Adamson and Bromiley, 2008). Like other place-based policies, it assumed place-based communities exist and located responsibility to tackle poverty within them (Amin, 2005). Such programmes fetishise community, attribute it agency and idealise it as cooperative with resources to effect change (Day, 2006). They suggest stronger community relations alter experiences of injustice, hence projects like gardens which strengthen local connections are encouraged.

These visions influence how gardeners interpret and enact community because policy is part of the context in which people come to understand it (Charles and Davies, 2005). Community development approaches championing bottom-up participation are also favoured by urban gardens (Hou et al., 2009; Saldivar-Tanaka and Krasny, 2004), allowing projects to secure public funding. But community-focused strategies have been criticised as inadequate solutions to poverty and inequality, micro-scale action on macro-injustices. If global political-economic processes cause injustice, situating solutions at the community level cannot address its roots in state and capitalism (Amin, 2005). If community action has limited impact on problems not caused by community-level processes, gardens may also have limited effects on injustice. Critical perspectives on urban gardens question their potential – as site-based initiatives – to effect justice. Relationships fostered through gardening may be superficial, confined to the garden, or to a select group (Corcoran and

Kettle, 2015; Veen et al., 2015). Community gardens have limited impact on cohesion if they reinforce pre-existing social divisions or benefit the more privileged (Aptekar, 2015; Glover, 2004). They may be ill-equipped to advance social justice or tackle inequality because, like community-focused poverty-alleviation programmes they align with, they represent micro solutions to macro problems (McClintock, 2014). Garden projects are often marginal so struggle to impact structural causes of injustice embedded in neoliberal cities (Tornaghi, 2017), constrained in their capability to challenge problematic power-relations (Ghose and Pettygrove, 2014).

To fully understand urban gardens' impacts we need to consider their context, look within and beyond, hear from people on a garden's outskirts and ask how non-garden aspects of gardeners' lives are changed. These endeavours are aided by a relational perspective which does not assume a place creates an inclusive community, and recognises spatially extensive processes which may limit place-based attempts to dismantle injustice. Viewed relationally a place comprises relations connecting local and global, with porous boundaries open to change, and is not tied to one community identity (Massey, 2005). Communities produced by ongoing social relations are complex and varied, with differences underlying any appearance of unity (Panelli and Welch, 2005; Staeheli, 2008). Gardens vary in the type of communities they develop, or whether this happens at all (Firth et al., 2011; Veen et al., 2015). That people congregate at a garden site does not necessarily demonstrate community has formed which depends on relationships' qualities (Pitt, 2018).

Place and community are connected, but not in ways often suggested in relation to urban gardens. The garden is not where community takes place, rather material space and social relations constantly interact (Pitt, 2013). Nor can garden communities be identified as place-based or interest-based, the former being those founded on local relationships and led from within a neighbourhood rather than by an outside agency (Firth et al., 2011). Relational place means gardens led by distant organisations are also place-based, but with spatial relations stretching beyond the immediate neighbourhood. Communities are not of place *or* interest as the two are connected: those who place-make together become community (Gray, 2000). Gardeners share interest in a place, and the shared experience of making it is crucial to becoming community (Pitt, 2013). I argue these characteristics have implications which undermine expectations of gardens' potential to advance social justice. Spatial dynamics, which enable formation of garden communities, limit their ability to foment social inclusion, examined next through empirical examples.

How do gardens form communities?

Relationships between place, community and gardens were explored through researching three case studies in Wales, UK:

- Garden one – large site in a post-industrial town, operated by a community development charity.
- Garden two – small inner-city garden, linked to a community centre operated by a social housing provider, managed by a voluntary committee.
- Garden three – on a farm in a rural town, operated by volunteers to permaculture principles.

Gardens one and two were in areas of high deprivation targeted by a Communities First poverty alleviation programme. The research entailed over a year of ethnographic fieldwork, including regular participant observation alongside staff and volunteers. In total thirty-two people associated with the case studies were interviewed, with additional discussion with neighbours not directly involved in the gardens. Volunteers at Garden two requested a survey of local residents through a questionnaire, which received thirty-three responses. Interview transcripts, fieldnotes and survey responses were analysed thematically (for full methodology and results, see Pitt, 2013).

Numerous studies offer evidence of urban gardens developing community (e.g. Teig et al., 2009; Veen et al., 2015). At the case-studies gardeners suggested similar signs of community, meaning 'people who regularly see each other with a common kind of goal, common pass time' (volunteer, Garden three). Relaxed amongst familiar company people demonstrated feelings of comfort and safety typical of community (McMillan and Chavis, 1986). Being comfortable to 'rely on' fellow garden volunteers is why volunteer John[1] felt the group at Garden two were a community. Conversely, not feeling supported at Garden one was interpreted as lack of community spirit: 'you always imagine a community project to be nurturing, but it's not' (trainee). Participants commonly expressed an expectation of grassroots participation because the gardens were *community* initiatives. Gardens two and three were felt to encapsulate this, being 'created by the community for the community', whilst Garden one was the opposite because it was not led by local people. The manager told me no one wanted 'to really get involved or get involved in the planning of it' because the Association had 'micro-managed' it instead of involving local residents in decisions. These contrasts show a garden's organisation influences the nature of relationships, with top-down approaches limiting collective responsibility (Firth et al., 2011).

Variations between the three gardens demonstrate that whether community forms depends on how people relate at a garden (Drake, 2014). Simone, a volunteer at Garden three, recognised this aspect of community:

> When I first thought of doing it and calling it a community garden I thought it meant for *the* community that is already there. But actually what it is, is *a* community that comes out of this place, that is born of the people that end up coming here. Do

[1] All names are pseudonyms.

you see what I mean? It's actually different. The *community* of this garden is – that is *the* community. Rather than the garden is for that community over there [pointing towards town] … It's an ongoing process … because we all come here and do things and spend time together then we're a community here.

Her comment encapsulates a shift in thinking from community as a pre-existing entity served by a garden, to understanding it as processes of relating developed through collective gardening practices. If community is ongoing processes, what is it about gardens that fosters these relationships? Three factors emerged from the case studies.

Space to gather

To Simone, Garden three was important as the town's first 'outdoor space where people can gather' so people could 'just be outside and have somewhere that they can congregate'. Volunteer Graham suggested Garden one should capitalise on the power of space to 'bring people together' by being somewhere people can 'hang out'. A place where people can gather facilitates encounters (Amin and Thrift, 2002); urban gardens as shared public spaces are often celebrated for such potential to foster community (Firth et al., 2011). One-off encounters do not necessarily result in deep connections, but gardens support repeat encounters over time so a sense develops of belonging together.

Feeling comfortable together

Gardens are outdoor spaces offering feelings of escape which seems to put people at ease amongst strangers. Toni, a trainee at Garden one, wondered if this was why people of all ages got on: 'we just, you know, work as a team and people pitch in and stuff. Whether it's coz you're outside as well. You haven't got to sort of – you can behave – you're not sort of restricted are you as [to] your behaviour, you're not in an office'. In outdoor spaces people seem less self-conscious about the awkwardness of getting along with others: 'when I'm outdoors I don't kind of feel [laughs] I don't feel like me, the sense of self drops away a lot' (trainee, Garden one). Volunteers at Garden two suggested this openness brought different people together in a way not possible elsewhere, they 'find more connections with people they wouldn't normally connect with'. Gardens can dissolve differences between people through a focus on the common pursuit of gardening (Corcoran and Kettle, 2015), although I outline below limits to their ability to bring diverse people together.

Working together

Perhaps the strongest force driving garden relations was the necessity to cooperate on practical tasks. All three sites were gardened collectively, meaning gardening work was completed by volunteers working together, so required negotiation. Practical work helped a sense of community develop, first, because tasks encouraged and enabled people to relate:

> Physical work is great. If you're working together with a group of people indoors somewhere you can drive each other up the wall. But there's something about – even if you're working in a large group and you're all rabbiting on about something different or you're disagreeing, something about doing physical work and being outdoors, it just dissolves. (Trainee, Garden one)

This sense of community was built on what people did together and how, not shared characteristics (Eizenberg, 2011). Focusing on work eased the formation of relationships by giving strangers a common ground for conversation; silence was eased by focusing on a task obviating awkward eye contact. Cooperation produced material things which reinforced relationships: 'you get the sense of ownership, and pride in developing something beautiful, and functional, and you get to share those feelings with everyone else involved' (volunteer, Garden two). Having cooperated in place-making, gardeners shared pride in the results and had enduring reifications of their relationships (Wenger, 1998). This required individuals to feel they had influence (McMillan and Chavis, 1986), hence lack of participation at Garden one inhibited sense of community. As communities of shared interest in place practical work was central to membership.

Idealised expectations of community

The three groups exhibited signs of coming together through collective place-making experiences, and stated their garden's community comprised whoever took part, implying open access for all. But this view was sometimes in tension with a contradictory vision of *the* locally rooted community, pre-existing to be served by a garden. John said volunteers constitute Garden two's community but he felt it should be otherwise: 'the objective behind it was that it was for the people of [neighbourhood], that's the point of having the garden. And I feel a bit that if the people of [neighbourhood] aren't going to come here and help out then it's kind of missing its objective'. He and other regular volunteers were not residents of this neighbourhood, so sometimes suggested they were not the target community. Being connected to the Communities First programme, the garden 'should' support disadvantaged people – those living in a deprived neighbourhood – which the volunteers did not identify as.

Normative versions of community as place-bound are embedded in policy and practice, which is problematic if they lead to assumptions of harmonious unity which could mean tensions go ignored or gardeners being ill-prepared to manage them. Community entails conflict (Staeheli, 2008), as Rachel, designer and trainer for Garden two, often saw:

one of the key factors is to have a group that gets on well together and is able to resolve any issues or problems easily and has mechanisms for doing so. It's not enough to say 'oh calm down Doris have a cup of tea' or whatever it might be coz Doris will still feel quite disgruntled. I think you have to have ways and means of dealing with issues that arise.

In her view, groups benefit from training to manage such issues: 'kind of community development and community engagement training and listening and speaking and respecting others' views'. Bringing people together does not automatically form a cohesive functional group, so systems for resolving differences and making decisions are required, but idealistic visions of community suggest these are not necessary. Idealising community may lead gardeners to expect that differences will not be an issue, especially as it is commonly said gardens bring diverse people together (Colding and Barthel, 2013; Hou et al., 2009). In practice, the groups were fairly homogenous in age, background and ethnicity. Simone thought 'like-mindedness' helped her garden function, suggesting the garden community was not bringing together diverse people. The likelihood of *everyone* getting on is very small, as Rachel noted: 'it's always a tension'. But gardeners focused on positive dimensions of community not on conflict and gave no account of the negotiation required to overcome differences (Aptekar, 2015).

Other problematic dimensions of garden communities are explored next, but it is important to emphasise how the processes and relations comprising community are place-based. First, feeling part of a community is associated with being in a shared space with shared attachments. This collective sense of belonging is strongest where there is collaborative participation in place-making. Cooperation results in gardens which reify relations so returning there reinforces the sense of shared endeavour as gardeners can see traces of their work. A garden community was not there prior to a garden being made, nor were garden relationships wholly determined by the garden-place. But neither is community divorced from place as experiencing their particular garden-place together is fundamental to gardeners' communing. These are communities of shared interest-in-place. This has implications for their potential to foster inclusion as illuminated by applying a spatial lens to their limitations. These communities are spatially limited as belonging is confined to the space and time of being in the garden. Working together to make a garden establishes relationships tied to being there (Corcoran and Kettle, 2015). Co-gardeners from the case studies tended not to see each other elsewhere or do things not associated with gardening; conversation focused on garden matters. Occasionally a group went from Garden two to another garden or event and it felt strange to be together somewhere else as belonging together centred on their garden or gardening; the usual cues for relationships – cups of tea, working – were missing. If gardeners bond through shared connections to a place and cooperating in place-making, non-gardeners in the vicinity may not be affected, affecting garden communities' inclusivity.

How inclusive are garden communities?

Research suggests not everyone is equally welcomed into garden communities, as exclusivity may be necessary to allow groups to congregate safely (Kurtz, 2001; Staeheli, 2008). Pre-existing divisions are reinforced, or new ones emerge (Glover, 2004; Kingsley and Townsend, 2006; Tan and Neo, 2009). Few previous studies consider perspectives from people not directly involved in garden communities, but whether all local residents have equal opportunities for inclusion affects how socially just they are. I surveyed residents of streets directly adjacent to each garden regarding their awareness and experiences of them. Discussions revealed several reasons people were not using them, the first being lack of awareness. Just less than half of neighbours of Garden two knew of it whilst all those asked about Gardens one and three were aware of them. This was associated with visibility: Garden two was surrounded by buildings, invisible from the street, whilst passers-by could see the other gardens. Not all who were aware of a nearby garden realised they could visit or get involved; some said they did not understand their function or organisation. False impressions of what gardens were for led some to assume they were not intended for them. One neighbour of Garden one imagined the produce was only for 'needy people'. A trainee there encountered a local resident who assumed people working there were doing community service following a criminal conviction.

Those aware a community garden was available to them suggested three main reasons for not participating. First, were those interested in visiting or helping out who felt unable to because of their personal situation. This included lack of time, limited physical ability, and as one put it 'I'm too bloody old'. Second, were those who had no interest in a garden or associated activities: 'it's not my cup of tea' or 'it's not for me'. Some self-excluded because they would rather garden in a personal space, or expressed interest in occasional events but not regular volunteering. Although gardening is claimed as levelling and accessible (Firth et al., 2011), not everyone enjoys getting involved (Guthman, 2008). Finally, were those deterred by who they knew or assumed to be involved. One neighbour of Garden two said she would not want to go because 'everyone would be a stranger'. Another said she had seen who went to the garden and did not want to join because 'it is full of foreigners'. An older neighbour felt he would not fit in amongst youngsters there. People seem to prefer interacting with those like themselves (Glover et al., 2005) so voluntary participation might only attract certain people.

These findings suggest the gardens' communities were not inclusive in the sense of being accessible to all potential members: there were limits to who was and could be included. Processes of exclusion – particularly lack of promotion – prevented some from joining, although this was not always problematic for excluded parties, particularly as some enacted self-exclusion. Neo and Chua (2017) suggest exclusion is not inherently bad, rather we should consider why barriers are created around participation to help gardens function. There were positive effects of bounding, for example at Garden two the regular group remained committed because they enjoyed gardening together and functioned as a cohesive group. The site's physical boundary protected their work from vandalism, and ensured children could play safely; as Neo and Chua suggest, limiting access was in some regards necessary. But to fully explore exclusion we need to ask not just why it is employed, but its implications, including those beyond the garden community. The case studies suggest three repercussions of exclusive communities.

Bringing people in

Each garden intended to be open to everyone, but it takes active effort to bring people in (Teig et al., 2009). Garden two volunteers were prompted by the neighbourhood survey to run and promote events to attract non-gardeners, but this required work and funding, with limited success expanding their community. Gardens can develop a core membership which is difficult for newcomers to penetrate (Bendt et al., 2012; Kingsley and Townsend, 2006). Rachel often encountered this: 'You form bonds which is necessary – but then that sometimes makes it difficult to be open to others and for a group to evolve and have a flow through of people leaving, people coming, joining, leaving. That's another tension which needs to be resolved.' Some Garden two volunteers hinted they preferred a small number of regulars who knew each other. The struggle to attract enough volunteers was constant at all three sites; involvement averaged less than a year with very few involved for more than two years. Such turnover makes a constant in-flow of participants vital for longevity, but is challenging in terms of effort to recruit people, then integrate them into an established group (Hou et al., 2009). Exclusivity leaves a garden community vulnerable as sustainability depends on attracting participation, whilst lack of equal access for all could be regarded as unjust.

Outside foes

Most non-gardeners expressed neutral or positive feelings towards gardens, but a minority felt quite negative. Two neighbours of Garden three disagreed with how it was set up as they had wanted the site to offer allotments. One said he never saw anyone working there and it looked neglected: 'they're obviously not doing it'. A neighbour of Garden one suggested the project attracted excessive funding not put to good use, whilst others mentioned the Association's negative reputation, or criticised its ways of working. This site suffered vandalism, thefts and arson, physical damage with obvious and financial repercussions for the garden and gardeners. Critical attitudes may be less immediately damaging, and in some cases were based on misunderstanding: Garden three looked neglected because permaculture practices leave dead plants in situ. But clearly not all residents supported the gardens' aims or operations, suggesting they do not meet all local people's needs. It is conceivable this makes it difficult to demonstrate the broad support required to attract funding and recognition, undermining project sustainability.

Limited success

Authors claim gardens enhance the wider community including people not directly involved (Saldivar-Tanaka and Krasny, 2004; Teig et al., 2009). But benefits arising from these gardens were concentrated with those inside their communities, meaning wider objectives were not achieved. Community enhancement depends on involving a critical mass of individuals who benefit through direct participation (Alaimo et al., 2010); those who were excluded could not benefit. Garden two sought to green the neighbourhood and promote environmentalism amongst residents, but few participated or were aware of this. Realising these limits, volunteers sought opportunities to garden on street spaces visible to people during daily life: 'because you're enriching what they see, you're enriching the areas they walk past every day' (volunteer, Garden two). Volunteers at Garden three took up guerrilla gardening around town to reach more people with its sustainable food objectives. Both communities recognised that benefits were concentrated with gardeners, whilst achieving wider aims meant working outside the garden, extending the scale of place-making.

More challenging were ambitions around employability and economic regeneration of organisations hosting Gardens one and two as Communities First partners. Community involvement is rarely a path to paid employment for the socially excluded (Amin, 2005). The housing association did not expect Garden two to contribute to employability which was addressed through other activities. Garden one provided training and work experience to help young people secure employment, however, 'there are not endless jobs in that sector' so 'people need to have their expectations managed' (staff, funder). The garden had only one full-time employee, with other partial posts dependent on project funding and subject to constant review. Job insecurity severely affected morale, whilst pressure to deliver project targets meant little time to foster personal or community development. Garden activities offered limited stop-gap solutions to local people's problems (Lawson, 2005). Unemployed gardeners gained temporary improvements to wellbeing but their fundamental problems were not alleviated (Pitt, 2014). This is symptomatic of place-based initiatives which do not target complex structural factors behind deprivation so have limited impact (Amin, 2005). Communities First focused within deprived communities, failing to develop connections outwards or shift the locus of power and economy so inequality persisted (Adamson, 2010). As site-specific activities within this approach, community gardens were similarly incapable of dismantling more extensive causes of inequality and injustice, structurally embedded within capitalist cities (Tornaghi, 2017). Using gardens for poverty and inequality objectives is limited by the exclusivity and place-based nature of their communities.

Spatiality of exclusive communities and implications for injustice

The case studies suggest community as product and process of gardens has limited potential to challenge urban injustices. The product – garden communities – are exclusive if they do not offer everyone within a neighbourhood equal access to their benefits. The process – community's ability to assist those experiencing injustice – is limited by the scale of benefits and solutions enabled. Communities based on relationships formed through collective place-making struggle to extend across space and time to have effects beyond the garden. A spatial lens helps make sense of the repercussions of this, demonstrating why exclusion matters in relation to injustice. First, participating in place-making is central to processes of communing at a garden, building communities of interest-in-place. Whilst more people might be encouraged to visit, few local residents would engage in gardening, hence participation in processes forming garden communities remains limited. Occasionally passing or visiting does not promote the belonging to place and community fostered by participation. So a garden might only form weak ties between neighbours, with only active place-makers becoming a community. If involvement in place-making is significant to a sense of community then the resulting relationships are tied to being in that place, and do not affect other aspects of urban life.

Second, no place is fully bound (Massey, 2005), so a garden-place community is always connected to elsewhere and draws things from all over (Pitt, 2013). These connections bring in vital resources – funding, external support and a supply of voluntary labour (Hinchcliffe, 2007). Not only is it inevitable that a garden's boundary is porous, it is essential. The challenge is regulating comings and goings so enough useful resources are pulled in, whilst adverse ones such as vandals are not. Regulating inclusion is, therefore, a constant part of making garden communities, but these decisions are not always made collectively or transparently. Fairer distribution of power to decide matters of exclusion would foster more equitable garden communities.

Third, because a garden is connected to other places and influenced by forces stretching across great distances it will struggle to effect all the changes it might desire (Pitt, 2014). Not all problems faced by members of a garden community are caused within the garden, so garden-centred action will not necessarily impact them. Whilst some may be content to focus on immediate garden tasks, others aspire to target root causes of injustice (e.g. Reynolds and Cohen, 2016). Making progress with this requires alliances between sites and with other progressive movements (Tornaghi, 2017). Viewed spatially, this means making connections across garden boundaries by building outward-looking relationships. It requires a garden community to move beyond the present, towards the future as collective political action requires a shared vision of a desired future for community members to work towards (Pitt, 2017). A key value of gardens as spaces of encounter is people working out how they want to live together (Purcell and Tyman, 2015). In relation to urban justice, such shared understandings should imagine alternative futures as without a vision of a just future, a garden community's political potential is limited by lack of agreed changes to pursue. Discussing issues such as injustice is therefore an essential aspect of more progressive garden activity (Reynolds and Cohen, 2016). If they are to work towards more just cities, garden relations must extend across time to consider possible futures and across space towards the causes of injustice.

Conclusion

I began by asking what kinds of communities are made through collective urban gardening and whether they can be a basis for tackling inequality. As process and product of gardens, community has limited capacity to foster social justice. Garden communities can be unintentionally exclusive, so not everyone can access benefits accrued there. By exploring how gardens form communities of interest-in-place and perspectives from beyond the garden I demonstrated inherent limits to their social impacts. A spatial lens on these communities shows membership through participation in place-making, belonging tied to being in the garden. Although exclusion can help gardens function, I argued the importance of considering negative repercussions of exclusion, including those affecting non-gardeners. These are significant because exclusion limits a garden's ability to secure support and participation, or to make progress tackling inequality and injustice. Garden project activities concentrated at the micro-level have limited impact on injustices rooted in forces beyond the immediate community. Benefits concentrate with relatively select groups of core participants, whilst those excluded from participation – albeit unintentionally – gain little.

Building relationships within a garden fosters forms of social inclusion, which cannot challenge the roots of injustice, suggesting a need for connections spanning spatio-temporal limits on communities of shared interest-in-place. These limits on gardens' ability to grow social inclusion and justice should be acknowledged to highlight action required to overcome them. First, it urges garden leaders to set out with a non-idealised vision of community; not expecting positive relations as inevitable or easy they can prepare for the skilled work of facilitating communing and negotiating differences. Deliberate effort is required to draw in those who do not see themselves as belonging, and to manage inevitable tensions within communities. Second, for those aspiring to impact urban injustices it prompts realism about what can be achieved by a garden-place, drawing attention to activity required to target structural causes rooted elsewhere. Not all garden initiatives seek wider effects on causes of social exclusion. Those which do need to question how to reach those with power to make change, through deliberate work to push garden relations outwards to embrace neighbours, to link gardens into a social movement, and connect to other activities addressing causes of inequality.

References

Adamson, D. (2010): Community empowerment: identifying the barriers to 'purposeful' citizen participation. *International Journal of Sociology and Social Policy* 30: 114–126.

Adamson, D. and Bromiley, R. (2008): *Community Empowerment in Practice: Lessons from Communities First.* York: Joseph Rowntree Foundation. www.jrf.org.uk/report/community-empowerment-practice-lessons-communities-first (accessed 16 April 2018).

Alaimo, K., Reischl, T. and Ober Allen, J. (2010): Community gardening, neighborhood meetings, and social capital. *Journal of Community Psychology* 38: 497–514.

Amin, A. (2005): Local community on trial. *Economy and Society* 34: 612–633.

Amin, A. and Thrift, N. (2002): *Cities: Re-imagining the Urban.* Cambridge: Polity Press.

Aptekar, S. (2015): Visions of public space: reproducing and resisting social hierarchies in a community garden. *Sociological Forum* 30: 209–227.

Beilin, R. and Hunter, A. (2011): Co-constructing the sustainable city: how indicators help us 'grow' more than just food in community gardens. *Local Environment* 16: 523–538.

Bendt, P., Barthel, S. and Colding, J. (2012): Civic greening and environmental learning in public-access community gardens in Berlin. *Landscape and Urban Planning* 109: 18–30.

Charles, N. and Davies, C. A. (2005): Studying the particular, illuminating the general: community studies and community in Wales. *The Sociological Review* 53: 675–690.

Colding, J. and Barthel, S. (2013): The potential of 'urban green commons' in the resilience building of cities. *Ecological Economics* 86: 156–166.

Corcoran, M. P. and Kettle, P. C. (2015): Urban agriculture, civil interfaces and moving beyond difference: the experiences of plot holders in Dublin and Belfast. *Local Environment* 20: 1215–1230.

Day, G. (2006): *Community and Everyday Life.* London: Routledge.

Drake, L. (2014): Governmentality in urban food production? Following 'community' from intentions to outcomes. *Urban Geography* 35: 177–196.

Eizenberg, E. (2011): Actually existing commons: three moments of space of community gardens in New York City. *Antipode* 44: 764–782.

Firth, C., Maye, D. and Pearson, D. (2011): Developing 'community' in community gardens. *Local Environment* 16: 555–568.

Ghose, R. and Pettygrove, M. (2014): Urban community gardens as spaces of citizenship. *Antipode* 46: 1092–1112.

Glover, T. (2004): Social capital in the lived experiences of community gardeners. *Leisure Sciences* 26: 143–162.

Glover, T., Shinew, K. and Parry, D. (2005): Association, sociability, and civic culture: the democratic effect of community gardening. *Leisure Sciences* 27: 75–92.

Gray, J. (2000): Community as place-making: ram auctions in the Scottish borderland. In: Amit, V. (Ed.): *Realizing Community.* London: Routledge, 38–59.

Guthman, J. (2008): Bringing good food to others: investigating the subjects of alternative food practice. *Cultural Geographies* 15: 431–447.

Hinchcliffe, S. (2007): *Geographies of Nature.* London: Sage.

Hou, J., Johnson, J. and Lawson, L. (2009): *Greening Cities Growing Communities.* Seattle: University of Washington Press.

Hynes, H. (1996): *A Patch of Eden: America's Inner-City Gardeners*. White River Junction: Chelsea Green.

Irvine, S., Johnson, L. and Peters, K. (1999): Community gardens and sustainable land use planning: a case study of the Alex Wilson Community Garden. *Local Environment* 4: 33–46.

Jones, M. (2009): Phase space: geography, relational thinking, and beyond. *Progress in Human Geography* 33: 487–506.

Kingsley, J. and Townsend, M. (2006): Dig in to social capital: community gardens as mechanisms for growing urban social connectedness. *Urban Policy and Research* 24: 525–537.

Kurtz, H. (2001): Differentiating multiple meanings of garden and community. *Urban Geography* 22: 656–670.

Lawson, L. (2005): *City Bountiful: A Century of Community Gardening in America*. Berkeley: University of California Press.

Massey, D. (1994): *Space, Place and Gender*. Minneapolis: University of Minnesota Press.

Massey, D. (2005): *For Space*. London: Routledge.

McClintock, N. (2014): Radical, reformist and garden-variety neoliberal. *Local Environment* 19: 147–171.

McMillan, D. and Chavis, D. (1986): Sense of community: a definition and theory. *Journal of Community Psychology* 14: 6–23.

Milbourne, P. (2011): Everyday (in)justices and ordinary environmentalisms: community gardening in disadvantaged urban neighbourhoods. *Local Environment* 17: 943–957.

Neo, H. and Chua, C. (2017): Beyond inclusion and exclusion: community gardens as spaces of responsibility. *Annals of the AAG* 107: 666–681.

Panelli, R. and Welch, R. (2005): Why community: reading difference and singularity within community. *Environment and Planning A* 37: 1589–1611.

Pitt, H. (2013): Growing together. PhD thesis. Cardiff University. http://orca.cf.ac.uk/53953/1/2013pittehphd.pdf (accessed 16 April 2018).

Pitt, H. (2014): Therapeutic experiences of community gardens: putting flow in its place. *Health & Place* 27: 84–91.

Pitt, H. (2017): An apprenticeship in plant thinking. In: Bastian, M. (Ed.): *Participatory Research in More-than-Human Worlds*. London: Routledge, 92–106.

Pitt, H. (2018): Questioning the cultivation of care through connecting with more than human communities. *Social and Cultural Geography* 9 (2): 253–274.

Pudup, M. (2008): It takes a garden: cultivating citizen-subjects in organized garden projects. *Geoforum* 39: 1228–1240.

Purcell, M. and Tyman, S. K. (2015): Cultivating food as a right to the city. *Local Environment* 20: 1132–1147.

Reynolds, K. and Cohen, N. (2016): *Beyond the Kale: Urban Agriculture and Social Justice Activism in New York City*. Athens: University of Georgia Press.

Rose, G. (1997): Performing inoperative community: the space and resistance of some community arts projects. In: Pile, S. and Keith, M. (Eds): *Geographies of Resistance*. London: Routledge, 184–202.

Saldivar-Tanaka, L. and Krasny, M. (2004): Culturing community development, neighborhood open space, and civic agriculture: the case of Latino community gardens in New York City. *Agriculture and Human Values* 21: 399–412.

Staeheli, L. (2008): Citizenship and the problem of community. *Political Geography* 27: 5–21.

Tan, L. and Neo, H. (2009): Community in bloom: local participation of community gardens in urban Singapore. *Local Environment* 14: 529–539.

Teig, E., Amulya, J., Bardwell, L., Bucehnau, M., Marshall, J. and Litt, J. (2009): Collective efficacy in Denver, Colorado: strengthening neighborhoods and health through community gardens. *Health and Place* 15: 1115–1122.

Tornaghi, C. (2017): Urban agriculture in the food-disabling city: (re)defining urban food justice, reimagining a politics of empowerment. *Antipode* 49: 781–801.

Veen, E. J., Bock, B. B., Van den Berg, W., Visser, A. J. and Wiskerke, J. S. C. (2015): Community gardening and social cohesion: different designs, different motivations. *Local Environment* 21: 1271–1287.

Wenger, E. (1998): *Communities of Practice.* Cambridge: Cambridge University Press.

Young, M. (2010) [1986]: The ideal of community and the politics of difference. In: Bridge, G. and Watson, S. (Eds): *The Blackwell City Reader.* Oxford: Blackwell, 228–236.

8

Is urban gardening a source of wellbeing and just freedom? A Capability Approach based analysis from the UK and Ireland

Alma Clavin

The world in which we live is not only unjust, it is, arguably, extraordinarily unjust.
(Sen, 2006: 237)

Introduction

Individuals attach different meanings, values and derive different wellbeing benefits from their environment. Alkire (2008) states that in addition to individual action, the process of improving human wellbeing often requires sustained, collective action of people. The neoliberalisation of urban governance may, however, limit opportunities for individual and collective freedoms in urban areas (Harvey, 1990). As wellbeing goals may be individually, socially and politically influenced, so too are the values and reasoning behind why individuals become involved in urban gardening activities. Such urban activity may enhance both the sustainable and just use of urban resources.

In examining the opportunities and freedoms valued in engaging with urban gardening activity, one must look to the varying conceptions of freedom. Harvey (2005) writes of a lack of serious debate as to which of several divergent concepts of freedom might be appropriate to our times. He goes on to state that 'obliged to live as appendages of the market and of capital accumulation rather than as expressive beings, the realm of freedom (generally) shrinks before the awful logic and hollow intensity of market instruments' (Harvey, 2005: 185). Focusing on the potential of community gardens to encourage such an expressive mode of being, this chapter adopts the Capability Approach (CA) (Alkire, 2003; Nussbaum, 2000; Sen, 1999), a freedoms based approach to evaluating human wellbeing.

This work builds on research by Clavin (2011) in which positive wellbeing benefits for active adult users of community garden sites were examined. In a further examination of this topic, here, the CA is used to examine wellbeing impacts and associated valued freedoms of three different user groups: passive adult users; active youth and child users. Taking into account the critiques of Sen's work, the CA is reconceptualised and the freedoms and associated unfreedoms that these user groups value in using the community garden sites are examined. The aim is to understand how these urban gardening projects may reject the market ethic and practices that neoliberalisation imposes, producing a particular idea of justice in urban environments – one that has freedom at its core.

Urban gardening and the production of urban space

Community gardens are an example of how the distribution of benefits and burdens in society may impact on social justice – bridging notions of both distributive and social justice in urban areas. A socio-spatial approach (Harvey, 1990; Lefebvre, 1991 [1974]; Smith, 1984) to unjust and uneven urban development has influenced a number of authors in their examination of urban community gardens. The results have shown both positive agency and wellbeing benefits of these spaces (e.g. Clavin, 2011) and also more critical accounts of how the spaces are limited in their ability to truly enhance political freedoms, overcoming asymmetric power relations (Certomà and Tornaghi, 2015; Rosol, 2012; Schmelzkopf, 1995). The development of urban community gardens generate local and participative forms of neighbourhood-level politics and group activity in times of political/economic crisis, but Schmelzkopf (1995) asserts that at the end of the crisis, although the problem of the urban poor and disadvantaged persists, governments generally withdraw their support and focus instead on profitable real estate development on the former plots. Sites are often then clawed back by local authorities and speculative developers during times of economic recovery. Examples include Dolphin's Barn community garden in Dublin, Ireland that was closed in 2007 and in the UK, the Eastern Curve Community Garden in Dalston, in the borough of Hackney, London that has been under threat of relocation. In addition to issues of security of tenure, some well-intentioned urban food growing initiatives may be seen as light green, weak approaches to urban sustainability and urban food poverty reduction, rather than a true oppositional discourse of practice (Eizenberg and Fenster, 2015), therefore seen to continue neoliberal forms of both unsustainable and uneven development.

In order to examine how community gardens may enable individuals and groups to be more expressive beings and to overcome such unsustainable and uneven development, the CA is operationalised to examine not just the positive wellbeing benefits of community garden sites but also ideas of injustice, with a focus on unfreedoms and counterfactuals – what could be done differently. Specific types of community garden sites are examined – those that are ecologically designed (with minimum waste and energy inputs/outputs). In this way the CA is operationalised in an intentionally designed sustainable urban context.

In the same way that the CA broadens the conceptual space to evaluate wellbeing, the sustainable design of community gardens provides an opportunity for individual values relating to sustainability to be developed, affirmed, encouraged and realised. Using the CA in this context further develops the theory and language of Sen and his contemporaries within the discipline of sustainability. In this context the CA examines not merely the existence of sustainable resources for individuals but what such resources enable people to do or be.

The Capability Approach (CA)

The CA uses a value-based conception of wellbeing. The approach takes into account the freedom that people have to achieve the beings, doings and havings that one values and has reason to value, looking to individuals as agents of change in enhancing/changing their own wellbeing. It focuses particularly on the individual's ability to achieve the things that they value and have reason to value. The core concepts within the capability framework are 'functionings' which are the 'beings' and 'doings' people value and have reason to value; capability – different combinations of functionings that one can achieve or choose from, and human agency – a person's ability to pursue and realise the goals that he/she values. These concepts are used to broaden the informational space for evaluative judgements affecting different dimensions of human wellbeing. A number of critiques of Sen's work and the CA, on how wellbeing can be accurately and justly evaluated and measured, have come from within the Human Development and Capability Association itself.[1] Specifically, a number of authors consider how the CA can be truly and justly evaluated and expressed in an individualistic, neoliberal economy.

The CA and individualism

A focus on individual wellbeing has been recognised and explored by a number of authors of the CA (e.g. Alkire, 2008; Robeyns, 2008). Robeyns (2008: 30) argues that the CA adopts what is called 'ethical individualism' in that individuals are the ultimate units of moral concern in evaluating wellbeing. In this way, the concerns

[1] See the Human Development and Capability Association website (www.hd-ca.org) which details thematic groups using various methodological approaches for the greater understanding of human capabilities.

of the group are not celebrated without taking into account individual agency and 'unfreedoms'. However, Robeyns also asserts that the CA does not suffer 'ontological individualism', i.e. society is nothing more than the sum of individuals and their properties, nor does it advocate 'methodological individualism', that all social phenomena can be explained by individuals and their properties (Robeyns, 2008).

Here, although the starting point for evaluating ideas of wellbeing in community gardens is the individual user, there is an attempt to overcome the focus on the individual by reconceptualising the CA in the context of ecological design and ecological sustainability, wherein individuals are seen as part of rather than apart from their environment (Bateson, 1979; Marten, 2001; Orr, 1992). Furthermore, a focus on counterfactuals and unfreedoms to some extent addresses what users would like to see done differently in their urban environment, whether that is within the garden and local environment itself or on a more political level both locally and globally.

The CA and neoliberalism

In critiquing the neoliberal debasement of the concept of freedom, Harvey (2005) critiques what he sees as Sen's assumption that a liberal-style market will afford freedoms to individuals. Specifically he asserts that Amartya Sen's *Development as Freedom* (1999) wraps up important social and political rights in the mantle of free market interactions. 'Without a liberal-style market, Sen seems to say, none of the other freedoms can work' (Harvey, 2005: 184). He asserts that some do seek a world of mutual support but ultimately we are embedded in an economic mentality transformed under capitalism rather than as expressive beings (Harvey, 2005: 185).

Sen has written about the absolute core of poverty, which goes beyond the mere inequality of having less than others. This core may be reconstructed as living a life in unfreedom (Sen, 1983). In developing a methodology for evaluating wellbeing where participants may be in a state of unfreedom – passivity and conformity in a neoliberal economy, the critical social science approach of overcoming a 'false consciousness' may also be applicable. This is akin to Sen's identification of the process of 'adaptive preference'. Originally introduced by Elster (1983), the issue of adaptive preference formation was adopted by Sen (1999) and Nussbaum (2000) in their critique of utilitarianism – whereby the moral worth of an action is determined solely by its utility in providing happiness. Sen's broader informational space of functionings and capabilities for evaluating wellbeing is based on a critique of utilitarianism and its alleged insensitivity to the problem of adaptive preferences. The use of the CA to evaluate wellbeing in community gardens, spaces used for mutual support and alternative modes of being in urban environments, may provide insight into how such expressive modes of being may be realised.

The CA and measuring wellbeing

In measuring wellbeing or quality of life, authors often cite a 'list' or 'indicators' or 'dimensions' of wellbeing which are the ingredients of human wellbeing. Such lists may be deliberately incomplete. Max-Neef (1993: 20) states of his list that 'Fundamental human needs are finite, few and classifiable'. It may be offered as one person's opinion of what may be universally true. Another author states: 'It does not matter if you disagree with my list' (Griffin, 1996: 30). Such lists may also be used, revised and offered as a best attempt at a general account (Finnis, 1980).

One may argue that by deciding on the capabilities that are going to count for purposes of social justice, we are already imposing a comprehensive notion of the good life (Robeyns, 2008). But Robeyns also questions whether it is possible to construct a theory of justice that is truly and completely independent of any comprehensive ideas (e.g. Rawls (1971) conceptualises citizens as free and equal moved by higher order interests). The crucial question is whether it is possible to select capabilities without imposing a comprehensive notion of the good life. Martha Nussbaum (2007) has proposed and defended what she takes to be a universal list of capabilities.[2] Thus, the objection that capability theories of justice could indirectly endorse a comprehensive notion of the good life may perhaps be relevant here. Nussbaum's list is also prone to objections of perfectionism (Robeyns, 2005 in Robeyns, 2008: 406).

The CA and theories of justice

Some philosophers would argue that to be able to assess what constitutes wellbeing or the 'good life', individuals need to know what is actually possible (Qizilbash, 1998). Campbell (1976) suggests that individuals judge their own situation in various life domains according to standards of comparison based on aspiration, expectations, feelings of what would be just, reference group comparisons, personal needs and personal values. Layard (2005) also refers to reference group comparisons when evaluating one's own life circumstances.

Harvey (2005) states that those with wealth and power avidly support certain conceptions of rights and freedoms while seeking to persuade us of their universality and goodness. Ideal theory (Rawls, 1971) may sharpen our thinking on justice and serves as a guide, but it does not tell us how to reach the ideal of justice. Moreover, in practice ideal theory too often makes theoretically distorting assumptions about human nature or societal conditions, resulting in theories that provide little guidance for dealing with actual cases of socio-economic injustice (Robeyns, 2008). According to Robeyns, most of Sen's writings are concerned with how to think about justice in the non-ideal world we currently inhabit

---

[2] For a full list of ten capabilities see Nussbaum (2007). Alkire (2002) also provides a commentary on Nussbaum's ten central capabilities and other authors' lists/dimensions of human development.

and Sen is concerned not with an ideal theory like Rawls but with developing a non-ideal theory on justice, with greater direct relevance for pressing issues of injustice (Robeyns, 2008). A theory of justice that can serve as the basis of practical reasoning must include ways of judging how to reduce injustice, and advance justice, rather than aiming only at the characterisation of a perfectly just society (Sen, 2010: ix).

For Sen, human society is dynamic and perfect justice and perfectly just institutions are unrealistic. His 'realization-focused comparison' (Sen, 2010: xvi) is a practically oriented approach to justice, in which justice is concerned with the lives people end up leading, not just the institutions and rules within which people make choices. This realisation focused notion of justice is multidimensional, pluralistic and comparative as it focuses not just on institutions but on various features of human society, which are dynamic. Specifically, the focus is on reducing acts and features of injustice, rather than pursuing the ideal of justice or perfect human institution.

Operationalising the CA

Whilst taking the above critiques into account, here the CA is operationalised in five ecologically designed urban gardening projects in the UK and Ireland. The sites chosen are specifically designed with ecological principles and associated features: Eglantine, Belfast (UK); Scotswood, Newcastle (UK); Easton, Bristol (UK); Shanakill, Kerry (Ireland); Moulsecoomb, Brighton (UK).

For the purpose of the study, ten dimensions of wellbeing were derived from the abundant literature on wellbeing; wellbeing and green space provision; wellbeing and nature and are used here to evaluate wellbeing in community garden sites. The ten dimensions are stimulation; social wellbeing; mental restoration; physical health; expression; spiritual wellbeing; enjoyment; psychological wellbeing; purpose; and security.[3] Employing qualitative, visual methods in the form of semi-structured interviews (adult participants); photo elicitation (child participants) and a video-walkabout method (youth participants), an examination of the wellbeing benefits of these urban spaces was carried out in 2009/10. A set of beings, doings and havings that users value and have reason to value in using the sites were established. Clavin (2011) documented the wellbeing impacts on adult users in these community garden sites. Building on this work, here, a variety of other user groups are examined – twenty-five passive users (users who pass by or have views of the site, but have not been actively involved in site activities); eleven youth users and twelve child users.

Rather than establishing a comprehensive idea of wellbeing in these spaces, the original ten dimensions of wellbeing were refined for each different user

---

[3] See Clavin (2011) for a detailed account of the ten dimensions of wellbeing.

group while taking into account counterfactuals and unfreedoms realised in using these urban spaces. The revised lists are detailed in Tables 8.1, 8.2 and 8.3 for adult, youth and child users respectively.

A focus on unfreedoms

Sen has advocated the need to re-evaluate the framework of wellbeing to encompass a much wider concept that centres on freedom. In keeping with Sen's ideas on adaptive preference, Samuels (2005) terms the practical constraints to ever expanding freedoms 'unfreedoms' – barriers that could exist in economic, social or political realms of society. Such a focus on unfreedoms may provide us with insight into concerns about social and spatial (in)justice in everyday environments.

The concept of unfreedom in this context may unpack the extent to which site activities can lead to more 'expressive beings' (Harvey, 2005: 185) – providing opportunity for mutual support to enhance human wellbeing and not to simply live in a state of unfreedom – as appendages of the market. Valued freedoms (and associated unfreedoms) are used as the unit of analysis here – they are the freedoms users value and have reason to value in using the site, or indeed in the case of passive users, in choosing not to use the site. Further analysis of these valued freedoms provides insight into bridging ideas of individual and collective wellbeing – just freedoms.

Adult capabilities and functionings

Out of the ten capabilities derived from the literature, eight were found to have most impact on adult users, in the five community garden sites examined (Table 8.1).[4] A number of key functionings and associated valued freedoms (and unfreedoms as detailed below) were identified by passive site users – those living nearby or those pass through/near the community gardens. This group also describes why they do not actively participate in the site (see Figure 8.1).

Unfreedom: limited access to green space and wildlife

Both active and passive adult user groups viewed the site as having high amenity and wildlife value. One passive user attributes the wildlife in his own garden to its location beside the Scotswood community garden site: 'We have newts, frogs, bats, and foxes in our garden. There are six types of dragonfly. Many of these are because we are beside the garden site. We get grey crested newts in our garden that come from the site. We also get hover moths. I hunt and fish but I would not harm the newts' (Passive Scotswood user 3). For some passive users, the aesthetic stimulation

---

[4] See Clavin (2011) for further details of analysis of these ten capabilities.

Table 8.1 Adult capabilities and functionings

Capabilities	Functionings
Stimulation	Stimulating the mind – new ideas and ways of thinking
	Having a sense of longevity and time passing
	Sensory stimulation
	Feeling of vitality
Purpose	Having an aim
	Having a sense that something is important
Psychological wellbeing	Learning, communication and thought
	Gaining cognitive skills
Mental restoration	Having opportunities for short term recovery
Social wellbeing	Participation in social life and cultural activities
Expression	Feeling a sense of ownership
	Having opportunities for political expression (choice and opportunity)
Security	Feeling of safety and freedom to use the local environment
	Having control of resources
Enjoyment	Being active

Source: Clavin, 2011.

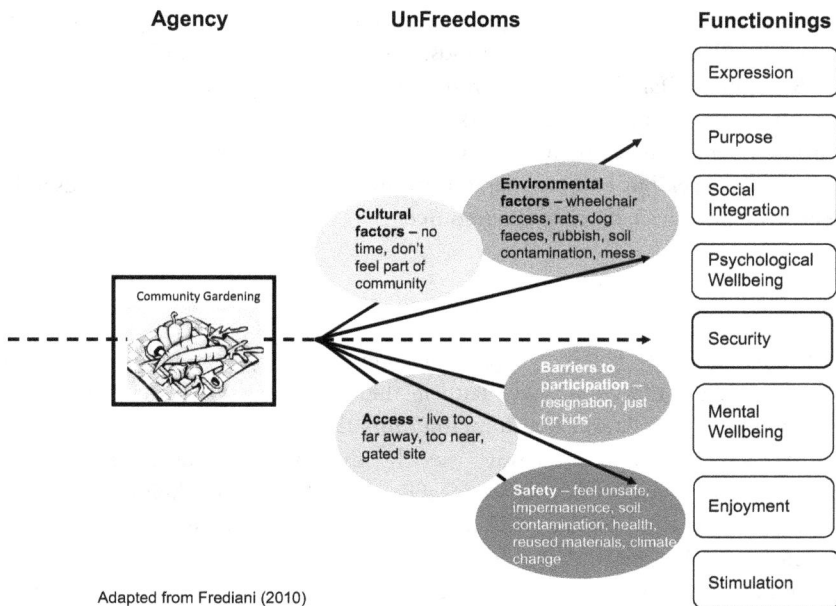

Figure 8.1 A number of unfreedoms and associated functionings of wellbeing – why the passive users did not actively use the community garden site

of the site varied. In Moulsecoomb one passive user sees the woodland site behind the garden as 'ugly and very steep and very open' (Passive Moulsecoomb user 2). In Eglantine, one passive user, when giving an opinion about the aesthetic benefits of the site, stated: 'it depends if you know what you are looking at' (Passive Eglantine user 4). This may imply that having a level of understanding or any knowledge of the site may affect how one sees it aesthetically.

Users felt that the sites were of benefit as part of wildlife corridors in their urban areas. One passive user stated: 'It is important to have green corridors in the city. There are badgers and foxes. I believe that it is important to keep wildlife. We need insects and flowers for pollination' (Passive Easton user 1). There was also a belief amongst passive users that in urban areas, green spaces were not a priority in terms of land use but rather viewed as in-fill development. For example, another passive user in Easton stated: 'The space does benefit the local area because other-wise there would be a factory there. There are already many warehouses in the area at present' (Passive Easton user 5).

Unfreedom: lack of local resources for children

In the Easton site one passive adult user stated: 'I have brought my children to the site because it is free [of charge]. Kid's activities are very costly and my kids complain that there is not enough to do' (Passive Easton user 4). Both passive and active users valued sites which had children's activities and events provided a safe, regularly supervised space which is free of charge and part of the community. Others felt that the site was just for kids, impeding their participation.

A number of families in the surrounding area of the Shanakill and Scotswood sites in particular did not use the site themselves but their children attended organised events there. Such a passive adult user in Shanakill stated: 'My child goes once a week but I would like if it was more often' (Passive Shanakill user 3), desiring greater availability of the resource.

Unfreedom: lack of opportunity for political expression

In Easton one user stated: 'People don't get involved [in community garden activity] because they don't have faith in the local authority. People have been let down so much. Easton is a dumping ground for the local authority' (Passive Easton user 1). In Eglantine passive users living adjacent to the site did not use the site actively because they did not feel they could influence their environment in any way and they felt they had not been included in decision-making about the sites. A passive user in Eglantine stated: 'It is not our property to use' (Passive Eglantine user 1), while another stated: 'People will look to the government to fix their problems rather than trying to fix them themselves' (Passive Eglantine user 2). In Easton, a passive user felt unsafe in the area and feels disempowered to participate in local politics and stated: 'We just make our own place, our own home secure' (Passive Easton user 1).

A number of passive users stated that they did not use the site because they had no time, or don't feel part of the community. Some felt that they lived too far away from the site and conversely others felt that they did not want to use the site as it was too near to their home, they wanted to go further afield for a day of restoration and activity.

Unfreedom: feelings of fear and concerns for safety

A passive user in Eglantine stated: 'It is not safe. The willow is over six feet tall; there could be anything in there.' Another stated: 'It feels unsafe as there is no lighting.' Passive users in Moulsecoomb also felt that lighting would improve a sense of safety, as more people would use the site if it was lit and she would use the site more often if more people were around. Another passive user stated that the trees in the site enhance a feeling of safety 'when there are less trees, there is more need for security' (Passive Scotswood user 3). Environmental factors impeded passive users from being more active in the site, e.g. lack of wheelchair access in some sites (steep ground in some allotment sites) and fears of soil contamination and other 'mess', such as dog faeces, rubbish and rats.

Figure 8.1 depicts a number of unfreedoms noted by passive users, i.e. why passive adults felt they could not or would not use the community gardens. The unfreedoms described include cultural, environmental factors and users detail barriers to participation, issues of access and unfreedoms associated with safety and security.

Youth capabilities and functionings

Youth users (between age thirteen and nineteen) in Moulsecoomb, Shanakill and Scotswood visited the sites on a weekly basis. The functionings most impacted on for youth users were explored using video-walkabout method (Pink, 2007) are detailed in Table 8.2. A number of freedoms and associated unfreedoms are detailed below.

Unfreedoms: lack of opportunity to access nature and biodiversity

Youth users identified a deficit in local green space. The functionings of stimulation found to be most influential in youth wellbeing were experiencing sensory stimulation; a sense of longevity and time passing. Having a sense of longevity and time passing was most influenced by learning about and maintaining plants, and noticing change in pond life through the year. Sensory stimulation can be broken

Table 8.2 Youth capabilities and functionings

Capabilities	Functionings
Stimulation	Having a sense of longevity and time passing
	Sensory stimulation
Purpose	Having an aim
Psychological wellbeing	Learning, communication and thought
	Gaining cognitive skills
Social wellbeing	Participation in social life and cultural activities
Expression	Feeling a sense of ownership
	Having opportunities for political expression (choice and opportunity)
Enjoyment	Experiencing pleasure

Source: Author's elaborations.

down into tactile; visual; gustatory; audio; and olfactory stimulation. Having diversity in pond life and also plant types, site activities, recycled site materials to reuse were found to bring multiple stimuli to the youth user.

The key functionings of purpose were having an aim and a sense that the site and site activities are important. These included opportunities to interact with nature and wildlife that the site provided and the freedom to be actively involved in a local green space, particularly for children and disabled groups.

Unfreedoms: inability to shape one's life

Youth users felt that site activity helped them to shape their everyday lives. The functioning of having capacity to shape one's life included the valued freedoms of having a choice of a different type of green space and learning environment – of learning in an outdoor space. A sense of ownership was found in planting, building and participating in artwork in the sites. Set maintenance tasks enabled a sense of care of youth users. Tasks may be of individual, e.g. individual beds in Moulsecoomb, or of a collective nature, e.g. building ponds or other structures together. There was a sense of ownership in displaying artwork made of recycled materials in the site in Shanakill. This was particularly the case for the Alternative Centre for Education students in Moulsecoomb. Opportunities to be creative involved working with arts and crafts in Moulsecoomb and Scotswood but also opportunities to be both creative and destructive were valued in both sites in the form of building temporary structures in Moulsecoomb and then destroying them and smashing old materials to create art form recycled materials in Shanakill.

Key functionings of psychological wellbeing for youth users included learning communication and thought and cognitive skills of being resourceful; being challenged and enhancing self-esteem. Learning involved mainly learning about and gaining skills of growing plants and building low-tech structures with natural materials. Having a variety of indoor and outdoor growing spaces enables this. Cognitive functionings of psychological wellbeing include being resourceful and being challenged. Values in being resourceful included using solar water heating, building with natural materials and use of multiple functions such as the pond (e.g. for leisure and pest control). Building with natural materials also enabled users to feel challenged. The functioning of self-esteem was enabled by completing building tasks and also in participating in off-site competitions such as the Shanakill artwork made from recycled materials. Activities seen as important to youth users were composting, organic food growing methods and using the compost toilet – examples of how the site does not pollute other environments.

Child capabilities and functionings

Child users aged between eight and twelve years in Moulsecoomb, Scotswood and Shanakill usually visited the sites on a weekly basis. Participant-led photography and photo elicitation methods (Harper, 2002; Rose, 2007) used showed overwhelmingly that the most valued activities are those related to a stimulating environment, which enabled them to take part in activities with other children and gave them a goal or sense of purpose while at the same time being fun. The key functionings that were most impacted on are summarised in Table 8.3.

Unfreedom: lack of opportunity to access nature

Flowers growing on the site brought a sense of security in Shanakill as a child user takes a photograph of marigolds in a raised bed in the site, stating: 'I chose these because they are colourful and because they are mostly the only flowers around

Table 8.3 Child capabilities and functionings

Capabilities	Functionings
Stimulation	Stimulating the mind – new ideas and ways of thinking
	Having a sense of longevity and time passing
	Sensory stimulation
	Having variety
Purpose	Having a sense that something is important
Psychological wellbeing	Gaining cognitive skills
Social wellbeing	Participation in social life and cultural activities
	Establishment of friendships and social networks
	Having a sense of community
Enjoyment	Having fun

Source: Author's elaborations.

here. Other flowers planted in the estate have been destroyed by people' (Shankill child user 2).

Having physical contact with plants and eating the plants enabled stimulation. Waiting for the plants to grow enhanced a sense of longevity and time passing. The capability of purpose included having a feeling of achievement and a sense that something is important. A feeling of achievement also came from participating in shared tasks. Reusing and recycling, particularly in composting activities, and using the compost toilet and use of natural pest control such as the pond features enabled the feeling that something is important. Many children felt features of the site such as natural habitats, solar energy, the compost toilet and reusing and recycling to be important and enhance eudemonic element of wellbeing for the child users.

Social wellbeing bore the key functioning of participation in social life and cultural activities. Children valued making items from recycled materials, eating together and sitting by the fire. The site provided the valued freedom of having a space to relax, particularly by the pond, and it also acted as a 'zone one' communal hub, enhancing relaxation and mental restoration.

Unfreedom: having little to do/see

The sites presented opportunities for new adventures and new types of local activities. Functionings of enjoyment included being in contact with a diversity of plant, flowers, trees and vegetable beds, and having fun in site activities. These included creating site features such as scarecrows and murals from recycled material, building with natural materials and taking part in these activities with friends. For children, enjoyment involves short-term affective or hedonic functionings and valued freedoms.

For the functionings of psychological wellbeing, being challenged and learning and adapting new skills were enabled by older children (ten to twelve years old) working hard in building structures and taking home the yield in the form of flowers and vegetables. This involves cognitive elements and experiences.

The capability of expression bore the functioning of a feeling of ownership, caring for and loving the site, and having opportunities for exploration and discovery. Having one's own growing plot enabled a feeling of ownership. Caring for and loving the site included the valued freedoms of a diverse site with activities such as making arts and crafts from recycled materials. The Scotswood site in particular has a focus on interacting with bugs and creatures – enhancing exploration and discovery. The children showed pride in their achievements, the achievements of others, and of their space. They had a sense of the importance of reusing and recycling; using features such as composting waste and an on-site compost toilet in the Moulsecoomb site.

For all groups, the sites are novel and help to address a deficit of green space, biodiversity and amenity in their local environments. The presence of the sites enhance fear for some passive users in that they are unaware or ill-informed about what is taking place there. Passive adult users and youth users spoke of how the sites were catalysts to expose frustrations and inabilities to make decisions about one's life and one's local environment. For children and youths, the sites provide opportunities for new types of activities and access to nature, compared to other more formalised neighbourhood and school spaces and activities. Overall, these ecologically designed community garden spaces expose and unlock freedoms for these user groups. Individual and collective wellbeing are bridged, enhancing a sense of both freedom and justice that goes beyond the individual user.

Conclusion

The work of critical geographers such as Harvey can set thoughts in motion to identify and unpack injustices in our urban environments. In taking into account the critiques of Sen's work, the CA is reconceptualised here and the varying converging and diverging freedoms/unfreedoms that users value in using the community garden sites are examined in a critical manner, exploring how such spaces may produce a different ethic, and a different idea of justice.

The idea of justice plays a meaningful role in how – and how well people live their everyday lives. For Sen, the comparative reasoning of what is more or less just and the comparative merits of the different societies that emerge from certain institutions and social interactions is what is important, rather than any ideal notions of justice. Following this, community gardens themselves may not be most usefully viewed as an ideal solution to enhanced justice in the provision of green and open space, or to the notion of the 'good life'. In examining unfreedoms, they do offer, however, a valuable insight into what may be 'more' or less' just in terms of urban space provision and free and fair distribution of urban resources. Furthermore, a focus on unfreedoms may be significant in realising the potential role of the sites in enhancing not only individual and collective wellbeing but also a participative and critical capacity to reason and question the design and development of our urban environments.

References

Alkire, S. (2002): Dimensions of human development. *World Development* 30 (2): 181–205.

Alkire, S. (2003): *Valuing Freedoms: Sen's Capability Approach and Poverty Reduction.* Oxford: Oxford University Press.

Alkire, S. (Ed.) (2008): *The Capability Approach: Concepts, Measures and Applications.* Cambridge: Cambridge University Press.

Bateson, G. (1979): *Mind and Nature: A Necessary Unity.* Hampton: Hampton Press.

Campbell, A. (1976): Subjective measures of well-being. *American Psychologist* 31 (2): 117–124.

Certomà, C. and Tornaghi, C. (2015): Political gardening: transforming cities and political agency. *Local Environment* 20 (10): 1123–1131.

Clavin, A. (2011): Realising ecological sustainability in community gardens: a Capability Approach. *Local Environment* 16 (10): 945–962.

Eizenberg, E. and Fenster, T. (2015): Reframing urban controlled spaces: community gardens in Jerusalem and Tel Aviv-Jaffa. *ACME* 14 (4): 1132–1160.

Elster, V. (1983): *Sour Grapes: Studies in the Subversion of Rationality.* Cambridge: Cambridge University Press.

Finnis, J. (1980): *Natural Law and Natural Rights.* Oxford: Oxford University Press.

Frediani, A. (2010): Sen's Capability Approach as a framework to the practice of development. *Development in Practice* 20 (2): 173–187.

Griffin, J. (1996): *Value Judgement.* Oxford: Clarendon Press.

Harper, D. (2002): Talking about pictures: a case for photo-elicitation. *Visual Studies* 17: 13–26.

Harvey, D. (1990): *The Condition of Postmodernity.* Oxford: Blackwell.

Harvey, D. (2005): *A Brief History of Neoliberalism.* Oxford: Oxford University Press.

Layard, R. (2005): *Happiness: Lessons from a New Science.* London: Penguin.

Lefebvre, H. (1991) [1974]: *The Production of Space.* Oxford: Wiley-Blackwell.

Marten, G. (2001): *Human Ecology: Basic Concepts for Sustainable Development.* London: Earthscan.

Max-Neef, A. M. (1993): *Human Scale Development: Conception, Application and Further Reflections.* London: Apex Press.

Nussbaum, M. (2000): *Women and Human Development: The Capabilities Approach.* Cambridge: Cambridge University Press.

Nussbaum, M. (2007): Human rights and human capabilities. *Harvard Human Rights Journal* 21: 21–24.

Orr, D. (1992): *Ecological Literacy: Education and the Transition to a Postmodern World.* Albany: Suny Press.

Pink, S. (2007): Walking with video. *Visual Studies* 22 (3): 240–252.

Qizilbash, M. (1998): The concept of well-being. *Economics and Philosophy* 14 (1): 51–73.

Rawls, J. (1971): *A Theory of Justice.* Cambridge, MA: Harvard University Press.

Robeyns, I. (2005): Selecting capabilities for quality of life measurement. *Social Indicators Research* 74: 191–215.

Robeyns, I. (2008): Ideal theory in theory and practice. *Social Theory and Practice* 34 (3): 341–362.

Rose, G. (2007) [2nd edn]: *Visual Methodologies: An Introduction to the Interpretation of Visual Materials.* London: Sage.

Rosol, M. (2012): Community volunteering as neoliberal strategy? Green space production in Berlin. *Antipode* 44 (1): 239–257.

Samuels, J. (Ed.) (2005): *Removing Unfreedoms: Citizens as Agents of Change in Urban Development.* Rugby: Practical Action.

Schmelzkopf, K. (1995): Urban community gardens as contested spaces. *Geographical Review* 85 (3): 364–381.

Sen, A. (1983): Poor relatively speaking. *Oxford Economic Papers* 35 (2): 153–169.

Sen, A. (1999): *Development as Freedom.* Oxford: Oxford University Press.

Sen, A. (2006): What do we want from a theory of justice? *The Journal of Philosophy* 103 (5): 215–238.

Sen, A. (2010): *The Idea of Justice.* London: Penguin Books.

Smith, N. (1984): *Uneven Development.* New York: Basil Blackwell.

9

Food for all? Critically evaluating the role of the Incredible Edible movement in the UK

Michael Hardman, Mags Adams, Melissa Barker and Luke Beesley

Introduction

The practice of Urban Agriculture (UA) – the growing of food and/or rearing of livestock within the city context – is on the rise globally (Hardman and Larkham, 2014). Arguments for UA vary, ranging from its potential to contract the food supply chain by relocating production closer to urban consumers, to the potential for improved social engagement, through bringing communities together on allotments, communal gardens and other growing spaces (Gorgolewski et al., 2011; Wiskereke and Viljoen, 2012). Proponents of UA often cite Detroit (USA) and Havana (Cuba) as exemplars in which such practices have resulted in various positive impacts: regenerating space, feeding people in need and creating sustainable economies (Giorda, 2012). An emerging argument in Europe surrounds the potential for UA to create a more 'just' food system (Alkon and Agyeman, 2011). Whilst the link between food justice and UA has a nascent research base in North America, there is little exploration elsewhere, particularly in the UK (Tornaghi, 2014). There is also emerging research which focuses on the environmental benefits derived through UA, particularly its contribution to local ecosystems and usage of urban by-products as growing substrates (Chipungu et al., 2013). Conversely there are warnings sounded in recent literature about the risks associated with UA, particularly in relation to the contaminated soils and waters and materials use to compose growing substrates (Chipungu et al., 2013).

At its most basic level UA involves bringing food production into the cityscape (Caputo, 2012): from community gardens and allotments, to radical vertical cultivating systems and rooftop farms, all constitute examples of UA in practice (Gorgolewski et al., 2011). Whilst allotment gardening has been embedded within UK culture for some time, new forms of UA – such as community gardening – are only just gaining momentum. The core argument for UA is often based on the need for greater food security; with global population increasing and the rapid growth of cities, the way we cultivate crops is being reconsidered (Wiskerke and Viljoen, 2012). Fundamentally UA challenges the idea that the urban and rural are separate spaces and that the city is a place outside nature with the rural forming the productive heartland (Scott et al., 2013).

This chapter provides an interdisciplinary evaluation of the role of local food initiatives, such as Incredible Edible Todmorden (IET), in creating more just food systems. The Incredible Edible movement emanated from a small town in England; with informal roots it started in 2008 through guerrilla gardening practices before legalising and growing into a formal collective (IET, 2017). The movement now crosses the globe and is a popular model replicated in a variety of urban areas across the UK. Across Europe, and particularly in the UK, similar initiatives are becoming more popular, receiving large amounts of praise and public funds to advance their work. Despite this, to date there is little critical analysis of these popular UA schemes. Often such projects are assumed to be inherently 'good' since actions are devolved to the local scale (see Born and Purcell, 2009) and yet recent literature shows that there is more to these practices which requires further investigation, including concerns about participation and exclusion, about risk and safety and about democratic decision-making (see for instance Allen, 2014; Hardman and Larkham, 2014). Furthermore, whilst there is a distinct lack of objectivity with regards to their impact, there is also a general lack of data on crop yields and consumption as well as the safety of such practices in terms of crops becoming contaminated (Chipungu et al., 2013).

Drawing on research on the Incredible Edible movement, this chapter questions the extent to which local food initiatives can be said to be inclusive, with regards to involving the wider community, and what this means in terms of any such small-scale UA being viewed as contributing to food justice. Of particular focus is its ability to empower communities to grow, sell or eat healthy produce, the key principles underpinning the concept of food justice. A mixed methods approach is employed to critically evaluate the movement and its impact on communities, drawing on both qualitative and quantitative data to provide an in-depth exploration of its value to inner-city communities. The chapter critically evaluates a number of taken-for-granted assumptions about the role and place of such local food initiatives and suggests ways in which local food initiatives might be better structured to contribute to food sovereignty. In addition to this, the chapter presents an insight into the risks associated with the 'grow it anywhere' philosophy in terms of the lack of access to safe and fertile soils in urban centres and the subsequent adoption of UA practices on potentially contaminated land.

The rise of urban agriculture: informal to formal

Whilst allotment gardening has been popular globally, particularly in the UK, new forms of UA are on the rise: community gardens, urban farms, high-tech growing and other activities are increasing in cityscapes (Wiskerke and Viljoen, 2012). Indeed, the latter forms mostly originated from American practice and have had a strong influence on other parts of the world. The often-communal nature of the UA activity is a draw to communities who often see the spaces as a mechanism for cohesion and beautification (Tornaghi, 2014). Many of these spaces started through informal activity, in which guerrilla gardeners adopted land without permission, often due to oversubscription of allotment plots (Hardman and Larkham, 2014).

There is very little academic exploration of those who practise UA informally, despite the fact that many of the most visible, community engaged and productive growing projects around the globe started through such action (Crane et al., 2012; Reynolds, 2008). The term 'guerrilla gardener' is often attached to those who pursue such an agenda; an umbrella term for a form of growing activity which does not have the necessary permission such as planning consent or landowner agreement (Johnson, 2011; McKay, 2011; Tornaghi, 2014). Although guerrilla gardening is often viewed as a small-scale activity and is often undertaken for thrills or for urban beautification rather than food production, the activity may also involve large-scale cultivation, with unpermitted community gardens and urban farms falling under the umbrella term (Hardman and Larkham, 2014).

The informal movement

Guerrilla gardening is practised worldwide. From the 'trendy' and relatively 'soft' intransigent political movements in North America and Europe, to those pursuing it for survival in Africa and other global South nations, the activity is very broad (Adams et al., 2014; Reynolds, 2008). In the case of Africa, most of the UA practised across the continent could be viewed as guerrilla gardening, as city authorities and national governments often discourage the practice of UA (Chipungu et al., 2013). In a similar manner, residents of Havana, Cuba – one of the most frequently cited exemplars of UA – faced barriers from authorities and originally practised guerrilla gardening (Hardman and Larkham, 2014). Once the positive aspects of UA were realised, municipal authorities encouraged the activity and provided support, along with guidance, for those interested in growing across Havana (Viljoen, 2005).

Despite these examples, it is usually the subversive, illegal aspects of guerrilla gardening, with participants colonising land under the cover of darkness, which more often attracts media interest (Lewis, 2012). The modern movement began with the Green Guerillas (*sic*) who beautified neglected spaces across

New York City in the 1970s. The creation of the website guerrillagardening. org, by Richard Reynolds in 2004, brought the guerrilla gardening movement up to date, widening its profile and enabling participants to connect through the internet and social media before carrying out any action (Reynolds, 2008). The movement has grown rapidly, with social media enabling guerrillas to share and plan action on a scale never seen before; but even so the guerrilla focus on edible productivity is small, in common with many guerrilla projects in general (see Hardman and Larkham, 2014).

Although there may be a media-led stereotypical image of a guerrilla gardener being a young hipster who plants flowers to beautify an area, research about those involved reveals that a wide variety of individuals including businessmen, professionals and retired people take part in the action (Adams and Hardman, 2014). The action is increasingly involving the planting of edibles, with schemes such as IET providing evidence that guerrilla gardening can facilitate UA on a large scale. In this case, residents of Todmorden – a small town in West Yorkshire – adopted sites across the locality to plant a variety of produce (IET, 2017). The scheme was so successful that a large international network evolved, with other towns and cities replicating the Incredible Edible concept.

This, and evidence from several academic studies, suggests that guerrilla gardening has acted as a mechanism for much larger green movements (see for instance Crane, 2011; McKay, 2011; Zanetti, 2007). It has enabled people to have greater access to food and started many more formal movements; an example of such impact can be seen in the many case studies exhibited in *On Guerrilla Gardening*, a textbook on how to go about guerrilla gardening by Richard Reynolds (2008). Reynolds shows how guerrilla gardening has enabled people to have greater access to greenspace and how it has significantly changed a wide range of urban sites; from inside prisons to underground areas and on the street corner, every space can potentially be colonised and made useful.

Whilst guerrilla gardening practices generate many positive impacts, from the ability to engage people in innovative ways to beautifying spaces or growing food for those who require it (Reynolds, 2008), there are also problematic aspects to the activity. For instance, Allen (2014) argues that guerrilla gardening is a reactionary activity and that the activity is not a solution to the oppressive force of powerful elites who control elements of urban space stewardship. He also draws attention to how the guerrillas perform their activities without obtaining the permission of the local authority or landowner, and for failing to consult with local communities and 'guardians' active in the area (Allen, 2014). This view is substantiated through research conducted by Hardman and Larkham (2014), who demonstrate how guerrilla gardening can have negative impacts ranging from the lack of maintenance of colonised spaces, to the guerrilla activity designedly excluding those who surround the areas.

Incredible Edible Todmorden (IET)

IET started through guerrilla gardening and is perhaps the most successful project of its kind originating from the informal route. Frustrated with a lack of authority support, community members started planting across the town, using leftover space to create havens of production (IET, 2017). After raising awareness of their cause and demonstrating the potential of UA, the group legitimised and found the Incredible Edible movement. Following success in Todmorden the concept spread elsewhere, first in the UK and then globally. There are now over 100 movements who fall under the umbrella of the recently created Incredible Edible Network. The Incredible Edible model differs somewhat to other UA movement in that the focus is to grow everywhere; using train platforms, emergency service stations and even graveyards. This 'out of the box' thinking has made the movement popular and the creation of an easy to use toolkit by the Todmorden element has enabled others to follow their model, obtaining funding and using similar organisational structures to coordinate activities.

This chapter focuses explicitly on the Todmorden case of this global movement, the reason being that this was the catalyst and focal point for the concept's growth. We adopted a qualitative approach to exploring the town and movement, using observational and semi-structured interviews with an array of actors. These actors involved members of the IET committee alongside community members, not all of which were involved in the UA activities. Observations focused on the use of the sites and the project's development, providing an extra dimension to the interview material.

The focus of the interviews was with community members, although some IET members were interviewed too, notably Mary Clear (Chairperson) and volunteers. Community interviewees were sought from across Todmorden, particularly from those not previously involved in the project. A wide selection of the community was interviewed, all ranging in terms of gender, age and social status. Confidentiality was paramount in this study, due to the small size of the site in question and closeness of the community.

Results: engaging the community

Incredible Edible Todmorden is putting the unremarkable Todmorden on the map.
(Paull, 2011: 29)

Starting in 2008 with small community plots and herb gardens the focus was to get the town talking about food. Mary Clear, the Chair of Incredible Edible Todmorden, gave a brief description of their ethos in an interview: 'we are volunteers from Todmorden who spend a little or a lot of time in this Incredible group, we grow food for sharing around the town in all sorts of places and are very passionate people working together to create a better world for ourselves and the planet, food is a unifying theme; if you eat you're in!' Linking to the guerrilla gardening theme earlier, a volunteer adds to Mary's quote by showing how the movement started through informal activity, 'we had permission for the most part but sometimes you just have to dive straight in, no one was using the derelict land outside the Abraham Ormerod Centre so we thought this would be a perfect place to start growing some vegetables'.

One could argue that IET is perhaps one of the most successful guerrilla projects globally due to its sustainability and impact on other towns/cities. This is almost unheard of in terms of guerrilla gardening, with perhaps only the New York 'Green Guerillas' (with one 'r') as one other example. This is mainly due to the often sporadic and unordered nature of guerrilla gardening, in which the 'thrill' element is often the drive, perhaps alongside a passion for the community and to create more aesthetically pleasing spaces (McKay, 2011). Todmorden turns this on its head and shows the potential of guerrilla gardening; it is not merely small-scale in nature but can spring into large, successful and sustainable initiatives.

In Todmorden alone several interviewees quote that one third of residents are involved in the project, this equates to some 5,200 citizens according to the latest census of the town. The sheer volume of growing locations and the innovative branding certainly appears to have galvanised interest among residents. Nevertheless, as Figure 9.1 demonstrates, IET is much more than merely growing; the scheme also promotes the wider concept of urban sustainability, through embedding beehives and other features throughout the town.

Much like the guerrilla gardening movement, to date there has been no critical exploration of the IET scheme. Rather, mainstream press and academic articles provide a positive overview of the project and its impact, with little critique. Although we do not wish to purposely critique IET in this chapter, we do follow the principles of Born and Purcell's (2009) 'local trap' which urges academics to critically question the common assumption that local is good. In this sense we aimed to engage with local residents and to understand the real role of local food in the Todmorden context.

Figure 9.1 A beehive in the middle of a busy Todmorden town centre car park

Over twenty semi-structured interviews took place, in which local residents of Todmorden were asked a series of open-ended questions about Incredible Edible and their opinions about the programme's work; Grounded Theory's point of saturation was used to influence sample size (Glaser and Strauss, 1967). These interviews largely took place in 2015/16 and were conducted by researcher Barker, a resident of the town herself. They ranged from more informal conversations of 20–30 minutes to an hour apiece. Thematic analysis was used to review the data collected, with participants anonymised to protect identities.

One of the first questions asked during the semi-structured interviews was 'what does the expression Incredible Edible mean to you?' This was in order to gain a basic understanding of local perceptions towards the overarching concept. One Todmorden resident answered: 'IE is an organisation run by local people growing food around the town which is very community based and they try to involve as many people as possible.' The resident has a clear view of work IET undertakes and is similar to the definitions within the literature. In contrast, another resident argued that IET is 'not much really, nothing even. It is not all that incredible in my eyes'. This starts to show that not all views on IET are positive, indeed many residents held critical views on the group's practices. We now proceed to delve deeper into the scheme and review its wider impacts, in terms of creating a more just food system and the hindrances of the model.

Creating a just food system

The core focus of this chapter is around IET as a potential tool for enabling a more just food system: was it able to enable residents to grow their own and create a thriving local food system? Or were there hidden barriers and issues lurking beneath the overwhelmingly positive media coverage of the scheme? The vast majority of the residents that were interviewed had positive impressions of IET, indeed all interviewees mentioned positive attributes of the scheme. In response to a question based upon first impressions of IE and how these impressions have changed over time, the residents felt it was a good concept based on a clever idea. One resident replied to the question saying 'definitely, its food everybody is entitled to pick what they want, herbs especially, I have known of people going and picking a few leaves and taking them with them'. This appears to be another common theme, as other residents often explained how the growing of food is a positive activity and acts as a good source for extra food and vegetables. It is a scheme that appears to benefit the town, and according to one resident it is 'better than going to the supermarkets if locally produced food can be gathered for free instead'. Indeed, this connects well with the idea of food justice, in which a more resilient local food system is at the heart of the concept; in this case it appears that IET is making this a realisation.

A second positive theme derived from the interviews surrounded social cohesion, with an elderly resident explaining that 'there is this community togetherness surrounding it which is good and it makes the town look better I think, also environmentally speaking it is definitely a good thing growing your own food and not relying on supermarkets'. This connected well with an argument by Breitbach (2007) that the social element is an important factor in a more just food system, enabling communities to share practice, form relationships and work together on wider goals. Adding to this another community member argues that the aesthetic value is also a huge positive alongside the community benefits: 'it also makes the town look better, brightens up the place, it is nice to see vegetables springing up in different areas of Todmorden'.

The economic impact was also mentioned by numerous interviewees, particularly the tourism value of IET. One such resident argued: 'I think it benefits the town not only by growing food but in recent years by bringing tourism to the area, it is attracting so much attention from people all round the world, and they now come for tours around Todmorden.' Indeed, observations during this study showed tourists from as far as Japan and the United States making stops in Todmorden to witness IET first-hand. The popularity has even drawn in royalty, as a proud resident described: 'it is probably the most well-known thing about the town at the moment, Prince Charles came to visit it a few years ago which was good, it brought a lot of positivity and the town really came together'.

The tourism factor generates revenue through formal talks organised by IET members. The tours charge a generous price per head and involve a two-hour exploration of the various growing schemes, enabling visitors to experience IET's impressive (and ever-expanding) sites; the space, depicted in Figure 9.2, demonstrates the open nature of the food-growing sites across the town. The tourists are often obliged to stay in the Yorkshire town and thus contribute to the local economy in a more direct way. It still remains that the key focus of this economic element is to support the burgeoning local food-growing initiatives, enabling funds to be recycled back into projects, provide tools/training for community members and anything else which is required.

A final theme surrounded the involvement of schools and how IET has engaged children and adults who had little knowledge about growing food. Education is essential with regards to UA; engaging the younger generation can often ensure buy-in, less vandalism and a generation open to such radical ideas (Reynolds, 2008). In this context, Todmorden High School is largely associated with IET as it is home to the Incredible Aqua Garden which combines state-of-the-art aquaponics and hydroponics. This creates a unique learning environment and provides more local food for the community and school. As a nearby resident discussed, the Aqua Garden is great for local students: 'the Aqua Farm seems like a great idea, I didn't really get to see it when I was in sixth form but I have heard it is all state of the art which is great for the students and the school'.

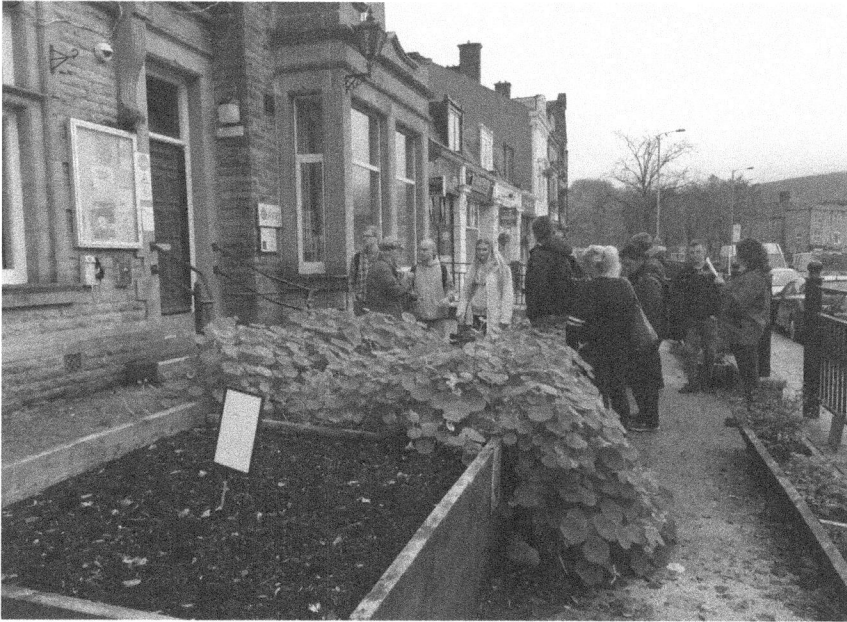

Figure 9.2   Raised beds at Todmorden train station

Hindrances of the IET approach

As mentioned previously, the literature surrounding IET is overwhelmingly posi-tive and does not take into account the local residents' opinions of the project. In this section we now proceed to challenge the basic notion that IET creates a more just food system and that there are still some obstacles to overcome to achieve this ambitious aim. Due to the small nature of Todmorden, interviewees were made anonymous as per the rest of this chapter to ensure confidentiality. This allowed residents to speak openly about the project to researcher Barker whilst she was in the field collecting data.

The first theme that was discovered was the lack of understanding with regards to IET's purpose. It quickly became apparent that residents did not always under-stand the concept and the group's goals. When asked about the IET's activities and what they aim to achieve, one resident replied 'not particularly no, I know they plant vegetables but I don't know why, it all seems a bit pointless'. This resident was not alone in their confusion and lack of understanding. It appears that many residents felt left out of the scheme and did not know how to get involved with IET. One resident even argues that the food for everyone philosophy does not work: 'I thought it was pretty useless because nobody even picks the vegetables or uses it, I don't think it's worth it just for a few leaves, I'd much rather it wasn't there.' They expanded on this point and appeared to believe that social norms prevented many residents picking the free produce; they would be seen as poor and unable to afford produce from mainstream supermarkets. In many ways such a fear is not new and has been witnessed in other UA projects (see for instance St. Clair et al., 2017).

A second theme that came about during the interviews was the untidiness of the planters. A number of residents complained that the raised beds were not taken care of and started to look like 'jungles at the side of the road'. It is clear that some of the residents believe IET is not maintaining the beds well enough all year round. As another Todmorden resident argued, 'I'm not a great lover of it, I mean some of these things that they have about just look like jungles; that Pollination Street on the market looks like a mess it doesn't enhance the town it makes it look worse'. Ironically, Pollination Street (Figure 9.3) is consciously planned in such a way to ensure it is appropriate for the bees.

Another theme surrounded maintenance and how some areas looked scruffy in nature. For example, whilst walking around Todmorden it was clear that some raised beds were poorly maintained. Figure 9.3 shows some beds outside of a nursing home in the town centre which are in a state of disrepair. The images in this figure were taking during the growing season and not at a point one would expect the raised beds to be without vegetation. This issue has been witnessed with other UA projects, particularly guerrilla gardening, in which regular maintenance has been an issue (Hardman and Larkham, 2014).

A third negative perception reported surrounded the placement of raised beds on busy pavements (see Figure 9.4). Some residents believe that the raised beds on public footpaths are an obstruction and should not be there. A Todmorden resident gave their views about the raised bed along pavements:

Figure 9.3   Neglected raised beds in Todmorden

Figure 9.4   Raised beds on a pavement next to a busy road

> Some [raised beds] I don't think should be there, like on public foot paths where they are obstructions and obstacles on the footpath, like outside the Hippodrome [Theatre] they take up quite a bit of room and are obstacles for people with disabilities or with prams … the planters need to be tended to more to keep them looking nice and some of these on the pavement could do with removing, I don't agree with them at all, pavements are for walking on not for growing things.

Finally, residents complained that IET was not appropriate for such an urbanised environment, due to vandalism and its exposure to environmental hazards. For example, a resident explained how IET's work could portray her town in a negative light: 'I don't think it gives off the best impression really some of them have been vandalised and there is litter just thrown in them.' The risk factor was also documented by a fellow resident who argued that 'I wouldn't pick any, I don't want to pick something that's been vandalised or had litter chucked on it, dogs might have even had a wee on it you just don't know!' In both cases, the lack of security resulted in negative perceptions by the residents of the UA projects. In one case, the proximity to roads, car parks and the town as a whole was a barrier to being involved. In a similar manner to most points here this has been raised with other UA projects, including guerrilla gardening (Reynolds, 2008).

Reviewing the potential of the IET model

Our data collection presents the first critical analysis of IET and demonstrates the need to look beyond the veil. It must be noted that the critical remarks from the community are similar to that of other UA schemes: risk, security, maintenance and participation. Although these themes have appeared before, this is the first time they have been raised in the Todmorden context. In this sense the results demonstrate that IET, although perhaps more successful than most UA projects, still faces similar issues. Perhaps the largest obstacle is to make IET appealing to the population who feel disenfranchised. Whilst some 5,000 residents are involved, this still leaves around 10,000 without any direct involvement with IET, a concept which has revolutionised their town. There is a disconnection at present between IET members/volunteers and residents not involved or aware fully of the concept.

It could be said that IET may fall under Born and Purcell's (2006; 2009) idea of the local trap. Born and Purcell (2006; 2009) argue that food systems have become increasing established within the urban environment, however they believe that local food systems are no more likely to be sustainable than systems on other scales. Born and Purcell (2006: 195) argue that 'the local trap is not an argument against the local scale per se, rather the local trap is the assumption that local is inherently good'. In the case of IET the literature often focuses on how successful the scheme has been for the town and how it is good for the local residents. However, using the example of the local trap, the benefits of IET can be exaggerated and romanticised which is in keeping with the discourse of the local equalling better. Again, as academics there is an urgent need to employ a critical lens in order to avoid the trap. Although IET's contribution to the food system has not been explored in this chapter, its function and connection to the community has been covered, revealing some results not previously seen.

Despite the critique of IET, it must be noted that the group has made remarkable progress since its inception in 2008. IET now ranks amongst the largest and well-known UA movements and proves that guerrilla gardening can lead to success. With the latter, this is an important point and should demonstrate to key decision-makers the power and potential of the informal movement. With local authorities beginning to embrace guerrilla activity, we could see more IET movements appearing in the near future. In terms of creating a more just food system, IET has been a tool for making great strides through creating new growing spaces, upskilling the community and providing support for growing activities.

IET actively labels itself as a group that aims to tackle social injustices and enable a food-for-all philosophy (*Guardian*, 2012). With this in mind, our study shows that IET is making great strides to realising this ambitious aim and, whilst there are negative comments, most of these surround a lack of understanding rather than genuine concerns. The overwhelming majority of interviewees provided a positive review of IET's actions, arguing that the group bring social, environmental and even economic benefits. With the latter, tourism has increased and Todmorden is now known globally, with tours regularly operated around the town.

Concluding remarks

This study sought to critically explore IET through engaging with local residents in Todmorden. Our key findings reveal the community's overly positive experiences of the project and provide a basis through which to improve practice and that of the wider network; although there were some critiques of the scheme, these were somewhat minor in comparison. On a wider note, we also demonstrate how the majority of the public engage well with the idea of UA and could potentially warm to the notion of upscaling. With more local authorities investing in high-tech and large-scale UA, projects like IET provide a mechanism for the community to understand the basic concept before more radical options, such as high-tech and large-scale, are introduced.

Ultimately, IET has been able to generate interest in UA across a wide array of other towns and cities. In the UK alone there are over a hundred active groups following the model and using IET's online tools. Each of these groups aims to achieve IET's success through replicating activities and learning lessons from the original. Through doing so, the groups are able to operate in a more sustainable manner as they form part of this wider network. IET has been the catalyst for spreading UA in the UK and has engaged tens of thousands of people through its wider model.

As we have argued throughout this chapter, IET has made huge contributions to the food justice movement. Although our focus has been on the local context, its origins in Todmorden, it must be noted that the wider network has put into practice the original model and this has resulted in significant impacts globally; ultimately, IET has helped to advance the food justice movement in a wide range of countries. On a basic level this has been through the creation of more UA spaces, but the education programme and other elements have also been replicated through organisations using the Incredible Network's online tools. This in turn has allowed countless communities to exercise their right to more local, healthy produce to cook and sell as they see fit (Justfood.org, n.d.).

Further research is required on this wider network and internationally to understand the models used in more detail. A critical lens should be adopted in all instances to view practice and those affected by the various projects. More work is also needed on the potential to upscale activities and evaluate options for expanding the IET model to make a real impact on health and wellbeing, urban economies and social cohesion.

References

Adams, D. and Hardman, M. (2014): Observing guerrillas in the wild: reinterpreting practices of informal gardening. *Urban Studies* 51 (6): 1103–1119.

Adams, D., Hardman, M. and Scott, A. (2014): Guerrilla warfare in the planning system: revolutionary progress towards sustainability? *Geografriska Annaler Series B: Human Geography* 95 (4): 375–387.

Alkon, A. H. and Agyeman, J. (2011): *Cultivating Food Justice*. Boston: MIT Press.

Allen, M. (2014): Guerrilla gardening in the UK is a sign of failure. www.theguardian.com/lifeandstyle/gardening-blog/2014/oct/22/guerrilla-gardening-uk-failure (accessed 13 July 2017).

Born, B. and Purcell, M. (2006). Avoiding the local trap: scale and food systems in planning research. *Journal of Planning Education and Research* 26 (2): 195–207.

Born, B. and Purcell, M. (2009): Food systems and the local trap. In: Inglis, D. and Gimlin, D. (Eds): *The Globalization of Food*. Oxford: Berg, 117–139.

Breitbach, C. (2007): The geographies of a more just food system: building landscapes for social reproduction. *Landscape Research* 32 (5): 533–557.

Caputo, S. (2012): The purpose of urban food production in developed countries. In: Viljoen, A. and Wiskerke, J. S. C. (Eds.): *Sustainable Food Planning: Evolving Theory and Practice*. Wageningen: Wageningen Academic Publishers, 259–270.

Chipungu, L., Magidimisha, H., Hardman, M. and Beesley, L. (2013): The importance of soil quality in the safe practice of urban agriculture: an exploration of the practice in Harare, Nairobi and Johannesburg. In: Thomas, A. and Brearley, F. (Eds): *Land-Use Change Impacts on Soil Processes in Tropical and Savannah Ecosystems*. Surrey: CABI, 72–84.

Crane, A. (2011): Intervening with agriculture: a participatory action case study of guerrilla gardening in Kingston, Ontario. Unpublished Master's dissertation. Queen's University, Canada.

Crane, A., Viswanathan, L. and Whitelaw, G. (2012): Sustainability through intervention: a case study of guerrilla gardening in Kingston, Ontario. *Local Environment: The International Journal of Justice and Sustainability* 18: 71–90.

Giorda, E. (2012): Farming in Mowtown: competing narratives for urban development and urban agriculture in Detroit. In: Viljoen, A. and Wiskerke J. S. C. (Eds): *Sustainable Food Planning: Evolving Theory and Practice*. Wageningen: Wageningen Academic Publishers, 271–282.

Glaser, B. C. and Strauss, A. L. (1967): *The Discovery of Grounded Theory: Strategies for Qualitative Research*. Chicago: Aldine Publishing Company.

Gorgolewski, M., Komisar, J. and Nasr, J. (2011): *Carrot City: Creating Places for Urban Agriculture*. New York: Monacelli Press.

Guardian (2012): Free food, caring and sharing: new spirit of community in Yorkshire. www.theguardian.com/society/2012/may/06/lifestyle-communities-hebden-bridge-todmorden (accessed 1 July 2017).

Hardman, M. and Larkham, P. J. (2014): *Informal Urban Agriculture*. London: Springer.

IET (2017): What we do. www.incredible-edible-todmorden.co.uk/projects (accessed 20 March 2017).

Johnson, L. (2011): *City Farmer: Adventures in Growing Urban Food*. Vancouver: Greystone Books.

Justfood.org (n.d.) What is food justice? http://justfood.org/advocacy/what-is-food-justice (accessed 7 October 2017).

Lewis, T. (2012): 'There grows the neighbourhood': green citizenship, creativity and life politics on eco-TV. *International Journal of Cultural Studies* 15 (3): 315–326.

McKay, G. (2011): *Radical Gardening: Politics, Idealism and Rebellion in the Garden*. London: Frances, Lincoln.

Paull, J. (2011): Incredible Edible Todmorden: eating the street. *Farming Matters* 27 (3): 28–29.

Reynolds, R. (2008): *On Guerrilla Gardening: A Handbook for Gardening without Permission*. London: Bloomsbury.

Scott, A. J., Carter, C. E., Larkham, P., Reed, M., Morton, N., Waters, R., Adams, D., Collier, D., Crean, C., Curzon, R., Forster, R., Gibbs, P., Grayson, N., Hardman, M., Hearle, A.,

Jarvis, D., Kennet, M., Leach, K., Middleton, M., Schiessel, N., Stonyer, B. and Coles, R. (2013). Disintegrated development at the rural urban fringe: re-connecting spatial planning theory and practice. *Progress in Planning* 83: 1–52.

St. Clair, R., Hardman, M., Armitage, R. P. and Sheriff, G. S. (2017): The trouble with temporary: impacts and pitfalls of a meanwhile community garden in Wythenshawe, South Manchester. doi: 10.1017/S1742170517000291

Tornaghi, C. (2014): Critical geography of urban agriculture. *Progress in Human Geography* 38 (4): 551–567. doi: 10.1177/0309132513512542

Viljoen, A. (Ed.) (2005): *CPULs: Continuous Productive Urban Landscapes*. Oxford: Architectural Press.

Wiskerke J. S. C. and Viljoen, A. (2012): Sustainable urban food provisioning: challenges for scientists, policymakers, planners and designers. In: Viljoen, A. and Wiskerke J. S. C. (Eds): *Sustainable Food Planning: Evolving Theory and Practice*. Wageningen: Wageningen Academic Publishers, 19–36.

Zanetti, O. (2007): Guerrilla gardening – geographers and gardeners, actors and networks: reconsidering urban public space. Unpublished MA dissertation. Queen Mary, University of London.

10

The foreseen future of urban gardening

Efrat Eizenberg

Nature is abundant, and its positive impact on human beings is solidly established in research that covers a wide range of implications. Our health, psychological wellbeing, recovery capacities, cognitive processes, such as attention, and affectional capacities, which function to generate a sense of belonging and a sense of care and attachment, are all associated with nature (just to mention a couple of seminal works: see Hartig, 1993; Kaplan, 1995). Interestingly, most of this research relates these various benefits to even the mere exposure to nature (in a picture, through a window or by sitting in a park), i.e. a passive consumption of nature, if you will.

The 'practice' of nature or deep involvement with it (as defined by Kaplan) through hiking, protecting, gardening and so on, produces an additional set of advantages. Advantages of 'practising nature' include exercise, community life, political development and place-identity. This list presents only a few of the ways people experience nature, but we will get back to this topic later.

Despite these advantages and cures, with increasing urbanisation, nature becomes highly scarce, so much so that some scholars claim to the extinction of experience of nature (based on Pyle, 1993). That is, with urbanisation, nature is disappearing from the hearts and minds of people, and their capacity to experience it is deteriorating. However, different forms of urban horticulture have been part and parcel of the physical environment and planning of many European and American cities for a very long time. Along with city- and neighbourhood-level parks, these forms of green space seem to support an ongoing experience of nature within the urbanised landscape.

The more than a century-long tradition of urban allotment gardens continues to be practised in many European cities (Keshavarz and Bell, 2016), though not without challenges (Eizenberg et al., 2016). At the same time, the urban allotment garden has almost completely disappeared from US cities since the middle of the twentieth century (Bassett, 1979). Nevertheless, another more contemporary form of urban gardening appeared in North American cities sometime in the 1970s, a time of economic crisis and massive urban restructuring. As Fox-Kämper describes in the foreword to this volume, at that historical time, urban gardening evolved as an act of survival and as a response to crisis by those urban residents who had nothing to lose and had to take care of themselves. They needed a fresh tomato and a piece of green to look at in their devastated neighbourhoods. They needed to create for themselves a safer and more secured daily experience and found a marvellous way for some salvation in the form of urban gardening. Urban community gardens provided a personal salvation that was achieved by means of collaboration with others and for the benefit of many others more (Eizenberg, 2012a; Schmelzkopf, 1995).

Since then, the idea has crossed oceans. The impressive bundle of benefits to human physical and psychological health, as well as to urban community life, might explain the surge of different forms of communal urban gardening during the last few decades on all five continents, including Asia and Africa. In some parts of the world, an old tradition was revived in the contemporary context and adjusted to the urbanised landscape. In other parts, the idea was imported by local residents, the authorities, or by supporting NGOs (see, for example, Alon-Mozes and Eizenberg, 2018 for their review of Mediterranean Basin forms of urban agriculture). The impressive spread of the phenomenon brought about a similarly intensive surge in research examining it, producing since the wake of the millennium a plethora of articles, books, research groups and guidelines.

Hopes, promises, potentials and their negations

The literature on contemporary forms of urban gardening, namely, community gardens, urban farms, guerrilla gardening, etc. tends to present the generation of such spatial forms as acts of necessity. People need to take care of themselves and are trying to improve urban living. However, from the onset, these acts were also associated with a bigger project – a social-spatial project. These urban forms were understood as instances of the social production of space (see Lefebvre), which are rare in the modern, neoliberal city. They, in fact, contest the current state of affairs; the privatisation of space, displacement of the less privileged from public space, and urban alienation, among other issues. Urban gardens oppose this state of affairs by representing a demand for spatial justice; for the right to the city; and for open space, community cohesion, diversity and more (e.g. Eizenberg, 2016; Okvat and Zautra, 2011; Schmelzkopf, 1995; Staeheli et al., 2002 for the United States; Ioannou et al., 2016; Müller, 2007 for Europe; and Barron, 2017).

The 'big project' associated with the seemingly naive practices of seeding and harvesting herbs and vegetables, as well as organising festive community events, needed a careful and critical examination. These hardly tangible arenas of justice, wellbeing, freedom and empowerment, along with the unique urban constellations that enabled urban gardening despite its oblivious contradiction with the neoliberal production of space, were extensively and maybe also enthusiastically examined, and research yielded various concepts and frameworks.

In the last two decades, this interplay was vastly analysed based on case studies from different parts of the world, and urban gardening was framed by and through grand notions, presented here only through a few examples, such as urban commons and the practice of communing (Eizenberg, 2012a; Follmann and Viehoff, 2015), spatial politics (Calvet-Mir and March, 2017; Schmelzkopf, 2002), citizenship (Baker, 2004; Ghose and Pettygrove, 2014), food security and justice (Horst et al., 2017; Tornaghi, 2017), the making of community and community space (Eizenberg, 2012b; Firth et al., 2011), social ecology and resilience (Chan et al., 2015; Ferris et al., 2001; Schwarz et al., 2016), and maybe most notably, the right to the city (Certomà and Notteboom, 2017; Crossan et al., 2016). In addition, these research arenas are still highly prolific.

However, the literature on contemporary forms of urban gardening did not remain enthusiastic, enchanted and hopeful, united around the benevolence and progressive promises it identified in this phenomenon. More recent scholarship critically examines the downsides and unexpected consequences of urban gardening. This scholarship brought to the surface a more complex understanding of urban gardening forms and practices and of the social relations it produces. Cynicism, manipulation, exploitation and control are now also attached to the understanding of urban gardening.

At times, in complete opposition to the previous understanding of it, this body of research comprehends urban gardening as a tool at the hand of urban authority for controlling people and subjectivities (Ernwein, 2017; Pudup, 2008), for controlling community space from alternative, grassroots ideas and practices (Celata and Coletti, 2017; Eizenberg and Fenster, 2015), for gaining a cost-free landscaping workforce (Rosol, 2012), or merely as a privileged fashionable expression of identity and needs (Zukin, 2009). Thus, the understanding of contemporary urban gardening has shifted from necessity practices to new social, political and even economic promises, to urban structural requirements, and to the dominant forces taking control in order to reproduce existing social relations.

This book progresses this polemic discourse a step forward by deconstructing and delineating both well-accepted and new concepts and ideas on contemporary urban gardening in order to negotiate between and make sense of its different parts. As thoughtfully framed in the introduction to the book, justice, as well as injustice, have many forms and manifestations and the overarching question should be 'whether and how urban gardening practices are able and suitable to address social and spatial (in)justice in the urban context' (Certomà et al., this volume). The different chapters of the book critically tackle this question while embracing what I would consider as the four main spheres in which contemporary urban gardening are commonly understood: human experience; politics; urban economy; and the physical space. These spheres obviously overlap, but there are benefits to discussing the promises and possible demise of urban gardening in each separately. In this concluding chapter (based on Eizenberg, 2018), I demarcate the four spheres as follow:

Human experience: how people think and perceive urban gardening, how they feel towards the specific space of the garden or the farm and how they extrapolate from there to experiencing the neighbourhood or the city as a whole. What is important for people in the practice of gardening or the space of the garden? What are the personal and communal benefits they gain or perceive to be gaining out of urban gardens and gardening? Well-researched concepts such as freedom, wellbeing, personal and community empowerment, and subjectivities and identities, etc. are attached to this sphere.

Politics: the relations between the practice and the space of urban gardening and the power structure at different scales. What is the interplay of urban gardening as a spatial practice and issues of rights and rights' distribution and redistribution? How does the practice or the space of urban gardens engender new forms of political practice and understanding, and how do these contribute to local struggles or key social struggles of the time? Well-researched concepts such as community/city democracy, the right to the city and spatial and food justice are attached to this sphere.

Urban economy: the forms of economic practices and notions that are related to urban gardening may be new and alternative ideas and practices that counter the hegemonic neoliberal logic or may be in concert with neoliberal principles of conduct and reasoning. Moreover, urban gardens are a material as well as social product, and they play multiple roles in the complex system of fiscal considerations.[1] Well-researched concepts such as the urban commons and communing, share- and community economies, reuse practices, no consumption, and self-production of food are attached to this sphere.

The physical environment: the physical environment of the city in general and of the gardens in particular obviously encompass the three previous spheres, but urban gardening is first and foremost a spatialised phenomenon. Thus, the physical environment is also a sphere of its own, encapsulating both ecological issues, such as urban climate (which is very briefly mentioned in this chapter), and planning issues, such as urban densification and open space. Well-researched concepts such as DIY urbanism, informal planning and urban biodiversity are attached to this sphere.

---

[1] For example, urban gardens may contribute to value appreciation of the real estate surrounding them, as was found in a study on New York City community gardens (Voicu and Been, 2008). At the same time, urban gardens are the main victim of land price appreciation and increase in development feasibility.

These four arenas are discussed in the literature on urban gardening both separately and connectedly. Indeed, the conceptual relations that they maintain are very tight. Yet, looking at the different accounts presented in this book under these four arenas is productive not only in showing the scope of the book but also in making some new associations between the different parts. There is no doubt that urban gardening is a unique socio-spatial phenomenon in which so many aspects of urban life intersect in major chords. In the following, I bring together major conceptions that are related to each with new approaches and insights that are offered in the different contributions to this volume.

Coming to terms with a complex reality

Human experience

The structure of contemporary urban gardens – being located within (usually dense) neighbourhoods, established on relatively small plots and characterised by many shared (rather than individual) gardening spaces (in comparison to the allotment gardens) – makes urban community gardens a fertile ground for the development of community relations and community growth.

The issue of 'community' in community gardens is central in the study of the phenomenon. Residents of dense, mostly socially alienated urban neighbourhoods establish a place-based platform for generating social interaction and shared practices, and through these practices they grow communities. Moreover, there are different examples for urban gardens that became a community asset much beyond gardening. The Rincon Criollo (i.e. Creole Corner) Cultural Centre in the South Bronx, New York grew from a community garden and became a cultural centre for the revival of traditional Puerto Rican music and dances (Eizenberg, 2010), and the Nature Museum Garden in Jerusalem, Israel, became an educational centre for home and urban agriculture (Eizenberg and Fenster, 2015). Beyond the making of a community, one of the most interesting aspects of urban gardening is the opportunity to co-determine space. Research associated this action with potencies for personal empowerment and political development (Eizenberg, 2016). On the other hand, as mentioned earlier in this chapter, gardens were also understood as a place for creating makeshift communities in order to gain greater control over maladjusted citizens (Pudup, 2008).

Working within these tensions, Pitt (chapter 7) inquired into the nature of inclusivity that characterised collective urban gardening. By examining how community evolves through the practices of gardening, collaboration with other gardeners, and connection to space, Pitt actually portrays how urban gardening falls short of true inclusivity and the aspiration to generate a broader impact beyond the garden towards sociability and collaboration. Moreover, Pitt understands this intrinsic exclusionary tendency as an obstacle to the sustainability of gardens and urges the promotion of non-exclusionary practices by, as a first step, disenchanting the perception of 'community' in urban gardens as benevolent and inclusive in character. In addition to that, an aspiration to induce wider social impacts should include awareness of the dangers of exclusion as well as inclination to manage tensions and differences.

Clavin (chapter 8) continues this analysis and asks whether the collective practice of urban gardening generates personal wellbeing and freedoms. Addressing the above tensions with critical use of the Capability Approach offered by Sen, Clavin's analysis brings to the fore both freedoms and unfreedoms that are afforded or limited by the gardens. Moreover, by utilising the Capability Approach and examining the freedoms and unfreedoms garden users experience, Clavin transcends the usual divide to inner and outer wellbeing and uses the platform of the urban garden to entangle them together and offer a hybrid perception. In this way Clavin offers a new approach to understanding the contribution of urban gardens to wellbeing.

Politics

Something is growing in urban gardens besides tomatoes and cucumbers. From the opportunity to establish neighbourly relations through co-determination of space, some collective ideas evolve and stretch beyond the perimeters of the site (Eizenberg, 2016). On one hand, urban gardens are envisioned as a real social movement struggling for democracy and against neoliberal principles, and on the other hand, they are used as a tool at the hand of the neoliberal city to control space and groups and as a fuel for neoliberal progress.

Whereas some recent literature suggests that urban gardening should be understood as both a major challenge to the system and an active player in its maintenance (McClintock, 2014), this book offers some other resolutions. In a way, it offers to get at the roots of the different concepts and perceptions related to urban gardening and to re-examine from there. Wright and Fraser (chapter 2) offer an in-depth review of the process of becoming political from growing vegetables together as a community. The *process*, which they posit at the centre of analysis, is 'iterative; with gardeners mobilising to tackle localised injustice(s), to (re)negotiating and catalysing awareness of broader systemic societal injustice(s)' (p. 43). Their conceptualisation refines what I suggested several years ago as the politicisation process happening to ordinary residents through the practice of gardening together in New York City community gardens. I described a spiral process in which gardeners move from resilience and survival to the reworking of specific problems and to oppositional awareness and resistance (Eizenberg, 2016). By bringing the process of political gardening to the fore, Wright and Fraser emphasise the DNA of the gardens rather than marking its trajectory as a movement or full-fledged resistance.

'The right to the city is like a cry and a demand' (Lefebvre, 1996 [1967], cited in Marcuse, 2009) of those who usually lack most other rights, such as property rights and citizenship. While most 'ordinary' residents of the city have very little opportunity to be involved in the production of the space of the city, the under-privileged are usually excluded from basic services and rights to use space. Urban gardens, and specifically community gardens, were understood as a struggle for the appropriation of urban space for the realisation of the right to the city, often by underprivileged groups (Germany – Follmann and Viehoff, 2015; New York City – Eizenberg, 2016; Staeheli et al., 2002; Lisbon – Cabannes and Raposo, 2013, among many other examples). At the same time, urban gardens around the world are being used by municipalities as a social tool to empower under-privileged populations, such as the poor and elderly in Melbourne, Australia, and Jerusalem, Israel (Agustina and Beilin, 2012; Eizenberg and Fenster, 2015), and for immigrants and minorities in many cities in North America and Europe (Shan and Walter, 2015; Twiss et al., 2011).

Roys' research (chapter 6) navigates between these two ways of understanding the phenomenon by revealing those that still are denied different rights by the same policies empowering immigrants in Copenhagen, namely, the homeless. Roy concludes that the policy of using community gardens to empower minor-ities in Copenhagen represents the intersection of 'traditional welfare driven pri-orities ... with emerging neoliberal policy trends' (p. 118). As such, this policy suffers from the many blind spots of its planners as to the effects of the general context of neoliberal urbanisation on disadvantaged groups, including minorities that are excluded from empowerment processes and lack rights.

Urban economy

In comparison with the above two spheres, much less has been written on the relation of urban gardens to various aspects of urban economies, and in some of the research devoted to this sphere, economic aspects are not the central factors of the analysis. In a special issue (2018), Coles and Costa propose to approach urban food growing as a productive landscape and reconsider it also as part of urban economic development. Along with this new effort, there are several crit-ical accounts of the practice of gardening and neoliberal urbanism in general (e.g. Eizenberg et al., 2016; McClintock, 2014) and more specific accounts of how gardens are used to increase the economic gains of private (e.g. Quastel, 2009 in Vancouver, Canada) or municipal stakeholders (e.g. Rosol, 2012 in Berlin, Germany; Eizenberg and Fenster, 2015 in Tel Aviv, Israel).

Aliperti and Sarti (chapter 5) examine urban gardening as an urban area regeneration strategy. More specifically, urban gardening was examined as part of a municipal policy to increase the attractiveness of the historic centre of the city of Perugia (Italy) for visitors as well as to support businesses (namely, retail) in the area. While the policy was oriented towards a participatory conduct and included various stakeholders in its preparation, Aliperti and Sarti point to a certain contraction in the policy's goals that became explicit only in the resulting regeneration. The policy was successful in attracting visitors and tourists to the area and in increasing retail revenues as a result, but at the same time, the urban gardens that were introduced as part of the plan were construed as public spaces in the eyes of the local community who were supposed to maintain them, and thus the policy failed to attract the local residents into the gardens. The imminent threat is in the deterioration of the gardens and the potential resulting effect on the recently achieved attractiveness of the area.

Urban environment

Urban space in general, and its development specifically, can be conceived in many different ways. Gawryszewska et al. (chapter 3) show how wastelands, usually treated as a stock of land for future development of highly regimented space, can actually yield benefits for many human and non-human urban groups while also contributing to more diversified and interesting urban spaces. Their work, which is connected also to spatial urban justice, reverses the idea of transforming 'wastelands' not only from unused to highly and diversely used space but also to a productive space, producing vernacular, rather than unified and rigid, forms of development of neglected urban areas.

Vis-à-vis the spontaneous production of wastelands in Warsaw, two studies cover two additional approaches. Nikolaidou's study (chapter 4) examines municipally produced urban gardens, and Hardman et al.'s study (chapter 9) examines the work of the widely growing Incredible Edible movement that produced urban agriculture sites for food consumption for free. Nikolaidou's research shows how municipalities in both Greece and Switzerland utilise urban gardening as a new multifunctional way of managing and reactivating abandoned and misused vacant open spaces while at the same time affording their citizens the right to use these open spaces. As aforementioned, urban gardens that are produced from the top down received a lot of criticism for their incapacity to really engage the community and create place-attachment. Research has shown that in New York City, top-down produced gardens failed to concur with the interests and even with the aesthetic needs of the community; these gardens were produced as showcase gardens in neighbourhoods where residents really wanted to grow fresh produce (Eizenberg, 2012b). In Jerusalem, NGOs and the municipality took the lead in managing, outreaching and orchestrating events in community gardens in poor neighbourhoods, but by doing so, deactivated the development of leadership and the sense of belonging among community residents (Eizenberg and Fenster, 2015). In other cases, top-down gardens were understood as 'organised gardens projects' and were criticised for manipulating and patronising participants, with the purpose of producing them as conformist, well-adjusted subjects (Pudup, 2008). Nikolaidou's study offers an integrative approach; it suggests that top-down gardens that are planned through the combination of municipal needs and visions, and the interests and needs of the community become a viable and valuable urban space for both the city and the community. The chapter shows how the municipal search for economic resilience in Athens, Greece, and a new densification policy in Geneva, Switzerland, facilitated municipal support for urban gardens and their integration in strategic plans. This effort was in concert with the needs of the community and in reply to its demand for 'access to fresh, qualitative, healthy and affordable food and more sustainable land use' (Nikolaidou, chapter 4) in both cities. Alongside their success, Nikolaidou also notes that urban gardens as a strategic use of vacant lots in both Athens and Geneva are only at the very initial stages of integration to spatial planning and long-term productive green spaces in the dense city.

Hardman et al. investigate the reception and perception of the Incredible Edible movement by the community in Todmorden, UK. They found that while many people are aware of the work performed by Incredible Edible in town, many people do not understand its cause and purposes and, more importantly, there are negative perceptions associated with its work. Hence, despite the expansion of the movement to many towns in the UK and beyond, and despite its vision of providing fresh foods to all, communicating its causes and how to use the plots, as well as various planning considerations on locating and maintaining plots and beds, remains a challenge.

A possible future

This book offers complex and dialectical accounts of key concepts and issues associated with the phenomenon of urban gardening today. Its contributions assume the idea that, as a product of this time, urban gardening contains neoliberal practices and ideas as well as their negation. As promised, it truly unveils the myriad effects, conflicts and opportunities offered by contemporary practice of urban gardening (Certomà et al., chapter 1). Therefore, the analyses presented here do not approach urban gardening as either alternative and revolutionary or confirmative and reactionary. Rather, they each offer a critical way to better understand the substantive, procedural and spatial dimensions of justice with their various tensions, gaps and negations that are intrinsic to urban gardening.

Castells once suggested that any alternative should take the form of the dominant power in order to prevail (1996), and De Angelis (2007) and Harvey (2012) suggested that the alternative modes are under threat of being consumed by the dominant power or sometimes even turned into a generative force of the dominant power. Urban gardens are an amazing site to understand these dynamics. They are sites on which to examine questions concerning the social-spatial relations of our time and contemporary forms of injustice next to new alternatives and their co-existence.

Like their physical manifestations, the future of urban gardens is highly diverse and multiple. These gardens depend on many economic and political circumstances and on planning and policy trends and fashions. Nevertheless, there is one significant characteristic that can assure the long duration of the gardens – their extensive diversity.

References

Agustina, I. and Beilin, R. (2012): Community gardens: space for interactions and adaptations. *Procedia-Social and Behavioral Sciences* 36: 439–448.

Alon-Mozes, T. and Eizenberg, E. (2018): Mediterranean urban agriculture. In: Zeunert, J. and Waterman, T. (Eds): *Routledge Handbook of Landscape and Food*. New York: Routledge, 183–194.

Baker, L. E. (2004): Tending cultural landscapes and food citizenship in Toronto's community gardens. *Geographical Review* 94 (3): 305–325.

Barron, J. (2017): Community gardening: cultivating subjectivities, space, and justice. *Local Environment* 22 (9): 1142–1158.

Bassett, T. (1979): Vacant lot cultivation: community gardening in America, 1893–1978. Unpublished Master's thesis. Department of Geography, University of California, Berkeley.

Cabannes, Y. and Raposo, I. (2013): Peri-urban agriculture, social inclusion of migrant population and Right to the City: practices in Lisbon and London. *City* 17 (2): 235–250.

Calvet-Mir, L. and March, H. (2017): Crisis and post-crisis urban gardening initiatives from a Southern European perspective: the case of Barcelona. *European Urban and Regional Studies*. https://doi.org/10.1177/0969776417736098

Castells, M. (1996): *The Rise of the Network Society: Economy, Society, and Culture*. Oxford: Blackwell.

Celata, F. and Coletti, R. (2017): The policing of community gardening in Rome. *Environmental Innovation and Societal Transitions* (in press). doi: 10.1016/j.eist.2017.09.002

Certomà, C. and Notteboom, B. (2017): Informal planning in a transactive governmentality: re-reading planning practices through Ghent's community gardens. *Planning Theory* 16 (1): 51–73.

Chan, J., DuBois, B. and Tidball, K. G. (2015): Refuges of local resilience: community gardens in post-Sandy New York City. *Urban Forestry & Urban Greening* 14 (3): 625–635.

Coles, R. and Costa, S. (2018): Food growing in the city: exploring the productive urban landscape as a new paradigm for inclusive approaches to the design and planning of future urban open spaces. *Landscape and Urban Planning* 170: 1–5.

Crossan, J., Cumbers, A., McMaster, R. and Shaw, D. (2016): Contesting neoliberal urbanism in Glasgow's community gardens: the practice of DIY citizenship. *Antipode* 48 (4): 937–955.

De Angelis, M. (2007): *The Beginning of History: Value Struggles and Global Capital*. London: Pluto Press.

Eizenberg, E. (2010): Remembering forgotten landscapes: community gardens in New York City and the reconstruction of cultural diversity. In: Fenster, T. and Yacobi, Y. (Eds): *Remembering, Forgetting and City Builders*. London: Ashgate, 7–26.

Eizenberg, E. (2012a): Actually existing commons: three moments of space of community gardens in New York City. *Antipode* 44 (3): 764–782.

Eizenberg, E. (2012b): The changing meaning of community space: two models of NGO management of community gardens in New York City. *International Journal of Urban and Regional Research* 36 (1): 106–120.

Eizenberg, E. (2016): *From the Ground Up: Community Gardens in New York City and the Politics of Spatial Transformation.* New York: Routledge.

Eizenberg, E. (2018): One Landscape, Multiple Meanings: Revisiting Contemporary Discourses on Urban Community Gardens. *Built Environment* 44 (3): 326–338.

Eizenberg, E. and Fenster, T. (2015): Reframing urban controlled spaces: community gardens in Jerusalem and Tel Aviv-Jaffa. *ACME: An International Journal for Critical Geographies* 14 (4): 1132–1160.

Eizenberg, E., Tappert, S., Thomas, N. and Zilans, A. (2016): Political-economic urban restructuring: urban allotment gardens in the entrepreneurial city. In: Bell, S., Fox-Kämper, R., Keshavarz, N., Benson, M., Caputo, S., Noori, S. and Voigt, A. (Eds): *Urban Allotment Gardens in Europe.* London: Routledge, 94–116.

Ernwein, M. (2017): Urban agriculture and the neoliberalization of what? *ACME: An International Journal for Critical Geographies* 16 (2): 249–275.

Ferris, J., Norman, C. and Sempik, J. (2001): People, land and sustainability: community gardens and the social dimension of sustainable development. *Social Policy & Administration* 35 (5): 559–568.

Firth, C., Maye, D. and Pearson, D. (2011): Developing 'community' in community gardens. *Local Environment* 16 (6): 555–568.

Follmann, A. and Viehoff, V. (2015): A green garden on red clay: creating a new urban common as a form of political gardening in Cologne, Germany. *Local Environment* 20 (10): 1148–1174.

Ghose, R. and Pettygrove, M. (2014): Urban community gardens as spaces of citizenship. *Antipode* 46 (4): 1092–1112.

Hartig, T. (1993): Nature experience in transactional perspective. *Landscape and Urban Planning* 25 (1–2): 17–36.

Harvey, D. (2012): *Rebel Cities: From the Rights to the City to Urban Revolution.* London and New York: Verso.

Horst, M., McClintock, N. and Hoey, L. (2017): The intersection of planning, urban agriculture, and food justice: a review of the literature. *Journal of the American Planning Association* 83 (3): 277–295.

Ioannou, B., Morán, N., Sondermann, M., Certomà, C. and Hardman, M. (2016): Grassroots gardening movements: towards cooperative forms of green urban development? In: Bell, S., Fox-Kämper, R., Keshavarz, N., Benson, M., Caputo, S., Noori, S. and Voigt, A. (Eds): *Urban Allotment Gardens in Europe.* London: Routledge, 62–90.

Kaplan, S. (1995): The restorative benefits of nature: towards an integrative framework. *Journal of Environmental Psychology* 15: 169–182.

Keshavarz, N. and Bell, S. (2016): A history of urban gardens in Europe. In: Bell, S., Fox-Kämper, R., Keshavarz, N., Benson, M., Caputo, S., Noori, S. and Voigt, A. (Eds): *Urban Allotment Gardens in Europe.* London: Routledge, 8–32.

Lefebvre, H. (1996 [1967]): The right to the city. In: Kofman, E. and Lebas, E. (Eds): *Writings on Cities.* London: Blackwell, 63–184.

Marcuse, P. (2009): From critical urban theory to the right to the city. *City* 13 (2–3): 185–197.

McClintock, N. (2014): Radical, reformist, and garden-variety neoliberal: coming to terms with urban agriculture's contradictions. *Local Environment* 19 (2): 147–171.

Müller, C. (2007): Intercultural gardens: urban places for subsistence production and diversity. *German Journal of Urban Studies* 46 (1): 1–6.

Okvat, H. A. and Zautra, A. J. (2011): Community gardening: a parsimonious path to individual, community, and environmental resilience. *American Journal of Community Psychology* 47 (3–4): 374–387.

Pudup, M. B. (2008): It takes a garden: cultivating citizen-subjects in organized garden projects. *Geoforum* 39 (3): 1228–1240.

Pyle, R. M. (1993): *The Thunder Tree: Lessons from an Urban Wildland.* New York: Houghton Mifflin Company.

Quastel, N. (2009): Political ecology of gentrification. *Urban Geography* 30 (7): 694–725.

Rosol, M. (2012): Community volunteering as neoliberal strategy? Green space production in Berlin. *Antipode* 44 (1): 239–257.

Schmelzkopf, K. (1995): Urban community gardens as a contested space. *Geographical Review* 85 (3): 364–381.

Schmelzkopf, K. (2002): Incommensurability, land use, and the right to space: community gardens in New York City. *Urban Geography* 23 (4): 323–343.

Schwarz, K., Cutts, B. B., London, J. K. and Cadenasso, M. L. (2016): Growing gardens in shrinking cities: a solution to the soil lead problem? *Sustainability* 8 (2): 141.

Shan, H. and Walter, P. (2015): Growing everyday multiculturalism: practice-based learning of Chinese immigrants through community gardens in Canada. *Adult Education Quarterly* 65 (1): 19–34.

Staeheli, L. A., Mitchell, D. and Gibson, K. (2002): Conflicting rights to the city in New York's community gardens. *GeoJournal* 58: 197–205.

Tornaghi, C. (2017): Urban agriculture in the food-disabling city: (re)defining urban food justice, reimagining a politics of empowerment. *Antipode* 49 (3): 781–801.

Twiss, J., Dickinson, J., Duma, S., Kleinman, T., Paulsen, H. and Rilveria, L. (2011): Community gardens: lessons learned from California healthy cities and communities. *American Journal of Public Health* 93 (9): 1435–1438.

Voicu, I. and Been, V. (2008): The effect of community gardens on neighboring property values. *Real Estate Economics* 36 (2): 241–283.

Zukin, S. (2009): *Naked City: The Death and Life of Authentic Urban Places.* Oxford: Oxford University Press.

Index

EU authorised representative for GPSR:
Easy Access System Europe, Mustamäe tee 50,
10621 Tallinn, Estonia
gpsr.requests@easproject.com

www.ingramcontent.com/pod-product-compliance
Lightning Source LLC
Chambersburg PA
CBHW052008270326
41929CB00015B/2833